Communication and Human Rights

This book is inspired by Hannah Arendt's belief that the human faculty of action interrupts the course of daily life towards ruin and destruction. As she argues, this faculty is rooted in the fact of natality and thus I dedicate *Communication and Human Rights* to all the children on this planet.

Communication and Human Rights

Towards Communicative Justice

CEES J. HAMELINK

polity

Copyright © Cees J. Hamelink 2023

The right of Cees J. Hamelink to be identified as Author of this Work has been asserted in accordance with the UK Copyright, Designs and Patents Act 1988.

First published in 2023 by Polity Press

Polity Press
65 Bridge Street
Cambridge CB2 1UR, UK

Polity Press
111 River Street
Hoboken, NJ 07030, USA

All rights reserved. Except for the quotation of short passages for the purpose of criticism and review, no part of this publication may be reproduced, stored in a retrieval system or transmitted, in any form or by any means, electronic, mechanical, photocopying, recording or otherwise, without the prior permission of the publisher.

ISBN-13: 978-0-7456-4983-2
ISBN-13: 978-0-7456-4984-9 (pb)

A catalogue record for this book is available from the British Library.

Library of Congress Control Number: 2022949656

Typeset in .11 on 13pt Adobe Garamond Pro
by Cheshire Typesetting Ltd, Cuddington, Cheshire
Printed and bound in Great Britain by CPI Group (UK) Ltd, Croydon

The publisher has used its best endeavours to ensure that the URLs for external websites referred to in this book are correct and active at the time of going to press. However, the publisher has no responsibility for the websites and can make no guarantee that a site will remain live or that the content is or will remain appropriate.

Every effort has been made to trace all copyright holders, but if any have been overlooked the publisher will be pleased to include any necessary credits in any subsequent reprint or edition.

For further information on Polity, visit our website:
politybooks.com

Contents

Preface vi

1 Human Rights Before Human Rights 1
2 Human Rights and Communication 26
3 Communication Rights 50
4 Challenges and Communication Rights 71
5 The Trouble with Human Rights 93
6 Communicative Justice 122
7 The Practice of Communicative Justice 150

Notes 163
References 167
Index 176

Preface

> It will be the dominated and excluded themselves who will be in charge of constructing a new symmetry; it will be a new real, historical, critical, consensual community of communication.
>
> Enrique Dussel

The question that inspired me to write this book is, how should we communicate with each other in order to live and flourish together? At the heart of this question I found the permanent challenge presented by the two types of power that are intrinsic to human life: destructive and constructive power. Power can be conceived of not only in the adversarial and competitive sense but can also, in the spirit of mutuality and solidarity, be seen as a reciprocal process of empowerment (Freire, 1970, 69). Hannah Arendt saw power as 'the human ability not just to act but to act in concert' (1968, 44). Power can both destroy and build human togetherness. The abuse of power ruins compassion, whereas the other face of power strengthens it. To be effective, both types of power need communication. The international human rights regime that developed after the Second World War focused primarily on the protection of all against the abuse of power by governments, governmental agencies, judiciary institutions, corporate entities and powerful individuals. Such protective provisions encompass recognition of the inherent dignity and the equal and inalienable rights of all members of the human family, the right to life, liberty and security of the person, the right not to be subjected to torture or to cruel, inhuman or degrading treatment or punishment, and the right not to be subjected to arbitrary arrest, detention or exile. Human rights also defend constructive power and self-empowerment through provisions on the freedom of movement, the right to marry and to found a family, the freedom of thought, conscience and religion, the freedom of opinion and expression, and the right to take part in the government of one's country. In *Media and Conflict* (Hamelink, 2011) I focused on the destructive power of communication in processes of escalating evil. In *Communication and Peace* (Hamelink, 2019) I discussed the constructive power of communication to create 'sheer human togetherness' (Hannah Arendt) through 'deep dialogue'. What remained on my agenda was the question of how to develop a mode of communication that would do justice to the human capacity for compassion. Since compassion is central to human rights, I want to explore whether the international human rights regime can guide us to a practice of communicative justice.

The opportunity offered by Polity Press to explore the significance of the relationship between communication and human rights posed a peculiar challenge because I had already written so much on the topic. Drawing on material I had developed over the past years I would have to extend that writing and thinking into a new perspective on the connection between communication and human rights. I wanted to find out why so little of what was on paper – often in abstract moral language – found its way into concrete communicative behaviour. Why could we not manage to translate the guidance inherent to the principles in the international human rights regime into a human rights-based communication practice?

Accordingly, I first set out to examine the values that had guided communication before human rights were encoded in international law after the Second World War. From there I followed developments until the United Nations World Summit on the Information Society in the early twenty-first century and dusted off the debates on the controversial issue of a right to communicate. I began to see what had gone wrong. In most work on communication and human rights we had ignored Article 28 of the Universal Declaration of Human Rights, which provides that 'Everyone is entitled to a social and international order in which the rights and freedoms set forth in this Declaration can be fully realized.' Human rights hold the promise of a fairer and more just future. Human communication holds the promise of mutual understanding as the basis of a world in which we can flourish together. These promises confront the reality of today's social and international order in which justice and understanding often seem part of a distant future. The war that erupted in Eastern Europe in early 2022 is a depressing reminder of how human rights claims clash with destructive power. Human rights are on a collision course with a world of extractive, exploitative and inegalitarian economics and politics, with colonial practices that continue unhindered and with impunity, and with racism that keeps haunting black lives. Human rights provide protection of free speech. But however crucial this may be, in the prevailing social order and its political and economic interests this protection is symbolic only. It barks but it does not bite. Such protection will be discretional and usually to the advantage of the winners. In societies that exclude and degrade people, human rights are the eternal losers.

In 2022, we live in a world in which the human rights claims remain wishful thinking. They can only be realized if we position them in a social and international order that fundamentally differs from the prevailing inegalitarian, abusive and predatory order. The connection between communication and human rights implies that there should be symmetry in the communicative actions between humans. This can only be realized when we liberate ourselves from exploitative, oppressive human relations and transform them into a convivial and caring order. The transformation to a human rights friendly social order demands that we reflect on the question of whether the societal arrangement that prevails in our life measures up to the standards that human rights set out for living together.

Human rights and human communication are mutually interdependent. Human rights need communication in the form of education and consciousness-raising, reporting and exposing violations and violators – particularly the institutional and structural perpetrators – and offering platforms for dialogue about a new social order. Communication needs human rights as standards for free speech, privacy, cultural participation, protection against incitements to violence, and the promotion of non-humiliating communicative behaviour.

The human rights articulated in the international human rights regime embody a set of moral principles that are seen by people around the globe as protective standards of humaneness and as conditions for living together, but also as political justification for intervention in sovereign countries in attempts to change their current regimes. Their codification in hard or soft law instruments is part of a process of moral evolution in which humans have developed a distinction between acts they consider right and those they label as wrong. Human rights are also the result of a long history of reflection on the question why we should do what is right. Important guidance in this respect was provided by the recognition of the inherent dignity of all people. This principle was recognized in human history as essential to cooperation, which itself is a central feature of human life. Dignity and cooperation are principles that require, for their implementation, institutional support. They need functioning moral institutions. The moral institution that was created in the wake of the Second World War, and that became the guardian of human rights, was the United Nations.

This institutional embedding did not mean that human rights would proceed uncontested however. They are part of a continuing political debate in which adversaries have very different interpretations of what a human rights culture could mean. What one person may see as protection of the dignity of all people, the other may see as undesirable leniency for the evil bastards. Neoliberals will have a perspective on human rights that differs from the human rights expectations that socialists will entertain. Where some will applaud human rights as instruments of self-empowerment, others will reject them as tools of neo-colonialism. Human rights provide currently the only universally available set of standards and institutional practices to protect the dignity of all human beings. It is in the interest of all people that they be respected. The defence of human rights is accepted virtually everywhere. But as Lukes observes, the principle of the defence of human rights 'is also violated virtually everywhere' (1993, 20).

The human species does not distinguish itself by a historical record that radiates benignity. For most of its history, the human being occupied himself (and to a more limited extent: herself) with an impressive variety of humiliating acts against fellow human beings. Against this gross indecency of human history more enlightened individuals have committed themselves to the articulation and codification of basic moral standards that are intended to restrain human aggression, arbitrariness and negligence. Most of such moral prescriptions had a limited scope in terms of the agents they addressed and/or the geographies they covered. This changed dramatically in 1945, when in response to the assaults against human dignity during the Second World War, the United Nations began to develop a universal framework of moral standards.

The novelty of this international human rights regime was the articulation of the age-old struggle for the recognition of human dignity into a catalogue of legal rights. Moreover, the political discourse shifted from the 'rights of man' to the more comprehensive 'human rights'. The defence of fundamental rights was no longer the exclusive monopoly of national governments but became an essential part of world politics. More importantly yet, the enjoyment of human rights was no longer restricted to privileged individuals and social elites. The revolutionary core of the process that began in San Francisco in June 1945 was that 'all people matter'. Basic rights were to apply to everyone and to exclude no one. The new regime that transcended all earlier moral codes, since it incorporated 'everyone', claimed universal validity. If at the core of the international human rights system and practice stand the protection and promotion of the dignity of all people, then in connecting human rights with communicative action it needs to be assessed how – and if at all – human communicative behaviour could contribute to this standard.

The human rights–communication axis can best be illustrated by the essence of human communication: its narrative structure. We are 'storytellers' and all the flows of ideas, opinions, observations, knowledge, information, data, sounds and images that make up human communication can be brought under the umbrella concept of storytelling. We perceive the world through the stories that we are told. The Greek philosopher Plato held that 'Those who tell stories rule the world.' And as Alexa Robertson writes, 'Through the agency of storytelling, our situation in the political and cultural landscape, and that of everyone else, is set out, maintained, negotiated

Preface

and adapted to new circumstances' (Robertson, 2010, 2). Kenneth Boulding helps us to understand this even better by saying, 'It is what we think the world is like, not what it is really, that determines our behaviour' (Boulding, 1959, 120). The international political arena is largely dependent upon stories that nations and their representatives tell each other for diplomatic, propagandistic, public relations or war-mongering purposes. Human rights are among those stories. They invite us to imagine a decent, inclusive, convivial and compassionate world. At the same time, around the globe people tell each other stories that fundamentally threaten human dignity. Deceptive, abusive, secretive, ambiguous, hostile and fear-mongering stories abound. The most existential challenge for the 'speaking animal' (Plato) may be how to speak in prosocial, cooperative and caring ways. Are the normative standards that promote and protect the freedom and the equality of human communication sufficiently robust to protect the fragility of human dignity against humiliating communicative action and to protect cooperative communicative action against anti-social interventions that are inimical to communicative freedom?

Overview of the chapters

In the first chapter of this book the precursors of today's communication rights are introduced. In the second chapter the focus is on the source of most classical communication rights: the Universal Declaration of Human Rights. The third chapter looks at specific communication rights. The fourth chapter raises questions about the significance of these rights in the context of challenges from developments in information and communication technology and from ecological degradation. The fifth chapter then looks at the different factors that stand in the way of a full-blown implementation of communication rights. This is followed up in the sixth chapter in which the features of a social and international order in which human rights can be fully realized are explored. The concluding chapter discusses a communication practice that is inspired by communicative justice and is based upon an ethics of human togetherness.

* * *

The composing and writing of most books need a supportive community. I am both honoured and grateful that this book, my twentieth academic monograph, received encouragement and constructive critique, and some gentle reminders, from the wonderful editors at Polity Press, Mary Savigar and Stephanie Homer, from the extraordinarily perceptive anonymous peer reviewers, from the angel who watches over me, Gabriela Barrios, from my comrades-in-intellectual-arms, Bob and Claire van Buren, Wichert Claassen, Loek Dullaart, Maria Hagan, Huib Kraaijeveld, Flavio Pasquino and Glenn Sankatsing, and the numerous students who, without realizing it, were crucial contributors to my proposals and explorations. Thanks are also due to the wonderful copy-editing of Jane Fricker, and special mention should also be made of my academic family, the International Association for Media and Communication Research, whose members never failed to provide the inspiration for yet another book!

Cees J. Hamelink, Amsterdam and Mexico City, 25 June 2022

1 Human Rights Before Human Rights

Introduction

In the history of human societies normative principles have evolved to enable human beings to live and flourish together. As then UN Secretary General Kofi Annan stated in a speech in 1997, these principles 'are deeply rooted in the history of humankind' (Annan, 1997). There is a historical continuity in the values that human communities have considered essential for their survival. There is also a historical discontinuity, as the human rights articulated in the Universal Declaration of Human Rights (UDHR) no longer focus solely on members of communities but on everyone. The humanistic universalism of the UDHR shares some of the sentiments of earlier references to the 'one family of humankind', but it is a discontinuity from a politics of ordering relationships at home, within the community, to a politics of solidarity with strangers abroad. Therefore, we may find inspirational thoughts, ideals and experiences with regard to basic human values throughout history, but these are not necessarily precursors of human rights in a continuous historical flow. The novelty of the international human rights regime that emerged in the 1940s was the formulation of these values as universal moral standards that were new for all parties in the international community. The emergence of human rights confronted not only non-Western cultures with a historically new situation: they were a new and difficult challenge for all cultures. No culture, religion or moral system had known a set of rights and duties such as those developed in the Universal Declaration of Human Rights. In the Declaration, in contrast to most cultural and religious traditions, the recognition of human dignity is formulated as a claim to be enforced by law. Moreover, this claim recognizes that the individual is entitled to rights not only through membership of a community, but in his or her own individual capacity as a human being.

Before human rights

In order to understand contemporary human rights, we must embark on a brief historical journey from the ancient Middle East, to Hellenist and Roman thinkers, and through native people's civilizations to African and Asian cultures and the philosophers of the European Middle Ages, the Renaissance, the Reformation and Enlightenment. The purpose of this journey is to see that the normative standards that became the constituents of twentieth-century communication rights have evolved over a long history of different schools of religious and philosophical thought.

There were human rights declarations way before 1945, such as the Magna Carta of 1215, the English Bill of Rights of 1689, the Bill of Rights of the State of Virginia in 1776, the American Declaration of Independence in 1776 and the French Déclaration des droits de l'homme et du citoyen (Declaration of the Rights of Man and of the Citizen) of 1789. Characteristic of all these documents was that they laid out basic rights exclusively for some social actors and excluded others. For example, the American Declaration of Independence stated that individuals have inalienable rights, but slaves and women were excluded from these rights. The 1789 Declaration of the Rights of Man and of the Citizen was a fundamental document of the French Revolution. It provided that the rights of man are universal: valid at all times and in every place, pertaining to human nature itself. The French Declaration excluded women – although there were strong demands for the equal rights of women at the time. Among those voices protesting was Olympe de Gouge, who issued in 1791 the Declaration of the Rights of Woman and the Female Citizen.[1] The French National Assembly of 1792 rejected this declaration and Olympe de Gouge was executed by guillotine. Vincent Oge pleaded for rights for mulattos and their inclusion in the National Assembly at Paris. He too was executed.

The ancient Middle East

King Urukagina reigned between 2380 and 2360 BC in Mesopotamia. He is best known for his efforts to combat corruption and the abuse of power. Although the actual text of his code has not yet been discovered, much of its content could be constructed from references that have been found. As some historians like Jack Finegan (2019, 46) suggest, Urukagina's code represents probably the first time in recorded history that the standard of freedom was mentioned. That freedom – most likely – did not extend to women as they were heavily punished in cases of polyandry, and from text fragments it may be concluded that female freedom of expression was strictly discouraged. Marilyn French (2008, 100) refers to it as 'the first written evidence of the degradation of women'.

Africa[2]

It is contestable whether the term 'rights' is applicable to pre-colonial Africa. Human rights scholar Jack Donnelly suggests that 'traditional African societies had concepts and practices of social justice that simply did not involve human rights' (in Lakatos, 2022, 192). His position has been criticized by African scholars who argued that using the liberal European notion of human rights as the only standard undermined the universality of human rights (ibid., 192). According to these scholars, pre-colonial African societies 'considered the individual to be a valuable being that possessed certain basic rights, including the rights to choose their rulers' (ibid., 192). Lakatos concludes that human rights were present in pre-colonial Africa, but 'they were certainly not codified or formally articulated in a European manner but rather existed at the concept level' (ibid., 193). Traditional African societies affirmed rights to life, freedom of expression, association and religious liberty. These rights, however, were contested by slave traders and colonial administrators.

African scholar Claude E. Welch Jr concurs that 'protection of human rights certainly existed in the pre-colonial period'. He identifies six major sets of rights in traditional society: 'the right to life, the right to education, the right to freedom of movement, the right to receive justice, the right to work, and the rights to participate in the benefits and decision-making of the community' (in Traer, 1991, 148). These rights were embedded in the lives of communities that had a strong sense of collective interest and in which procedures of conciliation, arbitration and mediation for the implementation and protection of these rights were crucial. As Yougindra Khushalani (formerly with the UN Centre for Human Rights) explains, 'traditional African society recognized the rights of individuals and groups and through consensual procedures provided an almost sacred protection of fundamental human rights' (ibid., 148). In *Human Rights in African Cultural Traditions* (1983) Senegalese historian Iba Der Thiam argued that the pre-colonial Wolof societies recognized 'the freedoms of assembly, of association, and of expression as well as the rights to own property and to work, to education and to one culture, to privacy, to collective solidarity, and to go to law' (ibid., 149).

Asia

It can be argued that throughout the traditional societies of Asia, human rights have been present. The forms within which these rights were articulated may have differed between the different cultural contexts of Asia. As the Asian region is enormously diverse, in terms of religions and languages, the Chinese, the Indian and the Filipino may have found different conceptions of human rights more adequate to their respective societies, but across Asian civilizations human rights were seen as inherent to social life as they protected communal responsibility and solidarity. Sanek Chamarik, Professor of Political Science in Bangkok, has argued that in spite of the different forms human rights may take in Asian versus Western political realities, the aspiration to respect human dignity is universal as it is rooted in human nature (Traer, 1991, 158). When Mahatma Gandhi sought justification for human rights, he turned to the sacred texts of the Bhagavad Gita, which express principles that precede their formulation in modern human rights. In the Hindu tradition rights stem from duties. In the Buddhist tradition, the human person is always in relation to others as equals, which affirms the person's rights while affirming the rights of others. In Japan, the clearest signs of predecessors to current human rights come from the writings of eighteenth-century thinker Ando Shoeki, who taught about the equality of all *men* as they were all entitled to the same dignity. He defended a position of egalitarianism based upon his philosophy of nature and human cultivation of the Earth against Confucian notions of social distinctions. As long as men practise the way of direct cultivation, 'there is no room for domination of man over man' (Inagaki, 1986, 189).

Traer concludes that in Asia human rights reflect old traditions 'that affirm human dignity' (1991, 165). It could be argued, as Joseph Chan does, that the Confucian tradition *is* compatible with human rights because of its central elements: the ideal of community, the respect for seniority, the preference for harmony rather than litigation, and its respect of freedom of expression, although not on grounds of personal autonomy but rather 'as a means for society to correct wrong ethical beliefs, to ensure rulers would not indulge in wrongdoing, and to promote valuable arts and cultures in the long run' (Chan, 1999, 237).

Latin America and the Caribbean[3]

In the colonial period the notion of human rights first appeared in the region in 1512. In the Law of Burgos, it was provided that 'the Indians should be treated a free people; one clearly entitled to hold property' (Lakatos, 2022, 143). Other sixteenth-century laws, issued by the King of Spain, confirmed that 'natives were to be considered free' and no free labour or services could be demanded from them (ibid., 143). Throughout colonial history, however, the region has been rich in artistic strategies like storytelling (such as Fray Bartolomé de las Casas, *Brevísima relación de la destrucción de las Indias*) to relate the abuses of power and indigenous rights.

In the eighteenth century human rights came to be seen as civil and political rights that were 'equal and individual entitlements'. In the nineteenth century national independence movements emerged that established constitutional regimes that – largely influenced by the US Constitution of 1787 and French Declaration of the Rights of Man and of the Citizen (1789) – aimed at the protection of the rights of citizens. In the same century the Pan-American conferences dealt with issues like slavery, citizenship, extradition and asylum (Lakatos, 2022, 145). In 1938 at the inter-American conference in Lima, Peru, a declaration in defence of human rights was adopted. The conference acclaimed resolutions on the rights of women, on the freedom of association for workers, and in condemnation of racial and religious persecution. At the conference in Mexico City in 1945 the participants proposed the inclusion of a transnational declaration on human rights in the UN Charter.

Judaism

In Jewish teachings human rights are embodied in nature and its laws because of the special place in nature assigned to man (though not women). As Kaplan formulates it, 'The Jewish teaching is that the rights of man belong to the way of the world as God meant it to be; to deny these rights is to depart from God's way' (Kaplan, 1980, 55). Because of the divine image of the human being, 'Man is to be treated, therefore, with something of the love and respect, not to say awe, which would be evoked by God Himself' (ibid., 55). The core of Martin Buber's concept 'Thou' (Buber, 1970) is that man should never be treated as a means, 'I am not to use the other . . . but to realize him and thereby actualize myself' (ibid., 56).

The Judaic ideal is of the human being (expressed in the Yiddish tradition as 'mensch') 'having compassion, sympathy, and consideration for the other' (ibid., 57). In the Old Testament Israel's prophets stood up against the violation of human dignity by kings such as David and Ahab. In the Jewish tradition, the right to political liberty is celebrated when the exodus from

Egypt is memorialized; the Book of Esther confirms the rights of minorities; the Torah demands the protection of the rights of the stranger; Chanukah celebrates the freedom of religion; and Yom Kippur confirms the absolute freedom of conscience (Traer, 1991, 100). The Torah demands that individuals be treated as equals regardless of their position. Here we find support for civil and political rights that limit the interference of government in the lives of equal citizens (ibid., 102). The Talmud recognizes a series of rights, including judicial review, civil disobedience and the right to dissent. Israeli lawyer Haim Cohn wrote in his commentary on the Universal Declaration of Human Rights that Jewish law addresses individual rights just like the UN Declaration proclaims rights, but does not provide social mechanisms for their enforcement. Jewish law includes the right to life, the right to liberty and security of the person, the right to privacy, rights to freedom of thought, speech and conscience and the right to education and participation in cultural life. Cohn also asserts that 'biblical law stands out among the legal systems of all times as a model of nondiscrimination against strangers' (ibid., 105).

Islam

In a 1980 seminar of the International Commission of Jurists on Human Rights in Islam, the participants agreed that 'Islam was the first to recognize human rights and almost fourteen centuries ago set up safeguards for personal rights' (1982, 9). Crucial in Islamic thought is the belief in human dignity. The value of the human person is recognized in the Quran 5:32, 'whoso slays a soul not to retaliate for a soul slain, nor for corruption done in the land, shall be as if he slain mankind altogether'. This means that the value of the human person is absolute because the individual represents humanity as a whole. The Quran places 'the unconditional duty to save human life above all else; for to save one is to save all' (Sinaceur, 1986, 215).

In his inaugural address in 1980 the Emir of Kuwait noted 'the Prophet and his followers took refuge in Medina and set up a community where the exercise of human rights, previously a mere aspiration and hope, became a reality' (Traer, 1991, 112). The Emir also asserted that 'to preserve the dignity of man, it is necessary that society guarantees him food, drink, lodging, clothing, education and employment as well as his right to express his opinion, particularly in the political life of his country and to be assured of his own security and that of his kin' (ibid., 113). The most basic value in Islam is 'justice in order to preserve human dignity accorded to man by

God' (ibid., 113). Whatever later positions there are in Islamic practice with regard to discrimination on grounds of religious beliefs, the basic statement in the Quran is that there shall be no compulsion in religion. However, as Traer writes, 'it must also be granted that the practice within Islamic cultures has often denied freedom of religion and conscience' (ibid., 118).

Christianity

In the history of the Christian churches (Roman Catholic and Protestant) one finds many references to principles that in the twentieth century would become hallmarks of the international human rights regime. An example is the notion of human dignity, which figures prominently in the early collection of prayers in the Christmas Oration that begins, 'God, who has wondrously created the dignity of human existence . . .'. The defence of rights as communal values goes back to the apostle Paul, who saw individual rights as subordinate to the welfare of the community. Building blocks for human rights are found in the stories about Jesus and his commitment to the forgotten people in the world, thus reaffirming their worth and dignity. Also the early church fathers used a human rights idiom 'avant la lettre' when it was claimed, as did Basil of Caesarea in the fourth century, that the wealth of the rich in fact belonged to the poor. Or when Gregory of Nyssa criticized slavery, stating, 'Who can buy a man, who can sell him, when he is made in the likeness of God?'

In the Middle Ages voices like those of the theologian Doctor Venerandus Godfrey of Fontaines (1250–1306 or 1309) claimed that if a beggar stole a loaf of bread from his rich neighbour, he couldn't be charged for theft since he had a natural right to that bread in order to survive. As everyone is bound by the law of nature to sustain their life, 'therefore also by the law of nature each has dominion and a certain right in the common exterior goods of this world which right cannot be renounced' (De Wulf, 1904, 18). In the so-called Dark Middle Ages Godfrey also defended the right of the poor to the necessities of life, the right of self-preservation, rights to property, the right to a fair trial and the right of self-defence. In the sixteenth century European Reformation thinkers developed the idea of individual freedom. However, what freedom concretely referred to remains largely unclear and we need to ask what its significance might have been in the historical context of societal environments that were not egalitarian and very hierarchical and in which freedom and dignity were only secured for a privileged few.

European Enlightenment

It is one of the inspirational legacies of the Enlightenment thinkers that the human being has an inherent dignity. This legacy inspired their successors to link this quality of being human to inviolable human rights. The notion of respect for the dignity of persons as the very essence of morality and the foundation of all other moral duties and obligations owes much to the eighteenth-century German philosopher Immanuel Kant, who argued that respect for persons, including oneself as a person, should be at the very centre of moral theory. He insisted that persons are ends in themselves with an absolute dignity that must always be respected. In his *Metaphysics of Morals* (1785/1957), Kant developed the implications of his view of persons as ends in themselves. In his doctrine of justice he argued that persons, by virtue of their rational nature, are bearers of fundamental rights, including the innate right to freedom, which must be respected by other persons and by social institutions. This duty of respect owed to others requires that we show no contempt for them, do not treat them arrogantly, do not defame them by publicly exposing their faults, ridicule or mock them.

Central to Kant's moral philosophy is the respect for human autonomous agency. The capacity of others to act in autonomous ways should not be impaired and people should not be coerced or deceived. In Kant's thinking we respect the dignity of one another when we hold each other mutually accountable as free and rational agents. Respect for human dignity became a leading normative principle in humanistic liberalism. However, it often applied only to human beings like 'us'. This philosopher of dignity did not think that black and native people were deserving of dignity. Therefore the Kantian conception of human dignity would have to be re-thought in non-racist terms. Moreover, in recent years it has been stressed in moral philosophy that the respect that was reserved for the human being as superior to other animals should also be awarded to other sentient beings and to nature. Here, however, I would like to be careful about connecting names of particular individuals to debates on important social issues. What they proposed was most likely already being debated in coffee houses, salons and taverns among educated people. We should also be aware of the suggestion that in its civilizational arrogance Europe suggested it had invented the Enlightenment ideals. However, they were more likely borrowed from experiences with indigenous cultures and their ways of arranging societies.

The indigenous societies that the sixteenth-century European invaders encountered 'were the product of centuries of political conflict and self-conscious debate ... societies in which the ability to engage in self-conscious political debate was itself considered one of the biggest human values' (Graeber and Wengrow, 2021, 452). The European colonizers found social relations that were not defined in terms of equality or inequality. They encountered social, political and scientific ideas that were totally new to them and that ultimately resulted in what we now know as the Enlightenment. Graeber and Wengrow (2021) write that indigenous communities in the Americas had a low opinion of their invaders. The Mi'kmaq in seventeenth-century Nova Scotia considered themselves better than their French colonizers, who were described as quarrelling, greedy, lacking in generosity and in freedom. The seventeenth-century indigenous critique exposed the social pathology of societal arrangements in Europe. 'Americans were equal insofar as they were equally free to obey or disobey orders as they saw fit' (ibid., 45). The logical consequence of not allowing compulsion was that social cohesion had to be created 'through reasoned debate, persuasive arguments and the establishment of social consensus' (ibid., 45).

A short history of normative principles for human communication

Since human life is impossible without communication, over the course of the history of moral ideas normative principles for human communicative behaviour were developed also. Before twentieth-century human rights law, essential normative principles for communicative behaviour were: respect for human dignity (which includes respect for the truth and respect for privacy), protection of confidentiality in communication, and freedom (which includes freedom of thought and free speech). In order to probe the relationship between human rights and human communication, I want to look at these three principles in the development of standards for human communicative behaviour.

The principle of respect for human dignity[4]

Among the first normative rules for communicative behaviour were the instructions that Vizier Ptahhotep in the fifth Egyptian Dynasty (3580–3536 BC) gave to his wise men to convey to their sons. Several of these rules have normative implications for how people should speak to each other. The Vizier proposed that a general norm for human speech was that it should be fair. This means people should refrain from speaking in an unpleasant way, they should not use vile words, should be humble in speaking and listening to one another, and not be angry when a debater does not agree with them. They should beware of creating enmity through their words and perverting the truth. They should not engage in gossip or exaggerated speech, they should realize that silence is more profitable than an abundance of speech and they should speak as true friends.

As early as the Bronze Age (the third millennium BC), the rulers that were intent on civilizations living together and not destroying each other engaged in cultural diplomacy. Their emissaries who conveyed messages and brought learning back were instructed by their kings that their communicative behaviour should be guided by modest and respectful speech. Among the predecessors to respectful speech are also notions found among indigenous communities from the times before the encounter with the Europeans.

The communication ethics of the Shuswap community[5] (probably numbering more than 15,000 in eighteenth-century British Columbia, Canada) mandated that one spoke to everyone, especially elders, with great respect (Cooper, 1998, 79). Shuswap communication rules included: do not interrupt other people's dialogue, be careful and respectful with words, welcome silence, respect other people's privacy (meaning particularly not interrupting silence with endless chatter or collective babble) *and* exercise extreme care in communicating with the white man as he may use it against you, censor it, sell it or steal it from you (ibid., 132). The children of the Ubangi of the Congo River basin were taught never to shout without explanation. They were taught 'a communication ethic of compassion and respect' (ibid., 80). In native communication, respect for one's listener or audience, for the speaker or artist, or for one's partner in dialogue is an essential norm (ibid., 187). In *The Sacred Tree* Lane et al. (1984/2020) present the teachings that are universal to all native tribes, such as 'not walking between conversing partners, . . . not interrupting, speaking softly, genuinely listening . . . honoring the religions of others, and never speak unkindly of others' (ibid., 74). As respect would be the first value central to a communication code for the natives, 'a primary means for such respect to be communicated is through silence, stillness, and inner listening' (Cooper, 1998, 94). Hesitancy to immediately answer a question was considered a sign of respect (ibid., 94). The communication ethics of the Navajo Indians advised to 'communicate with respect for the other individual'. Even a five-year-old's decision is worthy of respectful consideration. One should 'communicate so as to cooperate with all nature, maintain even-tempered emotions, aim to bring about unanimous decisions, communicate to all as if they were your relatives, be polite and open, when in doubt remain silent' (ibid., 150).

Truth as a sign of respect for human dignity

Speaking the truth is an ancient form of civilized behaviour. Truth-telling is a universal principle for all native peoples. Among the Shuswap people, the rule was 'Always tell the truth'. There were evidently double standards: 'tribe members might elect to speak truthfully to their families and friends but less openly to members of other bands. . . . Telling the truth to the enemy might lead to the capture or massacre of his family' (Cooper, 1998, 136). Frequently the following adage was followed: 'First we learned to lie from the white man. Then we learned to lie to the white man.' For the Navajo tribe lying was the white man's form of communication (ibid., 155). Many creation stories of native peoples talk about the times before the first lie. For natives, lying might mean insanity – 'one who did not speak truth surely must not know what it is and therefore must have lost touch with reality' (ibid., 104). Also for the ancient Egyptians in the Pharaonic laws truth was essential and lying was forbidden. In the world religions, truth is a basic understanding.

The Old and New Testaments are clear in their rejection of the lie. The standard of truth in communication is found in the Ten Commandments that were given through Moses to the Hebrew people. One of these commandments (Exodus 20.16) provides that one shall bear no false witness. Although it is contested whether this contains a general prohibition to lie, it would seem to refer to an admonition to speak the truth at least in legal matters. In Exodus 23:1 we find, 'Thou shalt not raise a false report: put not thine hand with the wicked to be an unrighteous witness.' Psalm 5:6 says: 'Thou shall extinguish liars; the LORD considers the man of flesh and blood and of deception an abomination.' In the Book of Leviticus (19:11), God told Moses: 'Thou shalt not steal, lie or deceive.' Deuteronomy (5:20) says, 'Neither shalt thou bear false witness against thy neighbour.' And in the New Testament (in John 8:44) it is written of Satan, 'You belong to your father, the devil, and you want to carry out your father's desires. He was a murderer from the beginning, not holding to the truth, for there is no truth in him. When he lies, he speaks his native language, for he is a liar and the father of lies.' According to the Gospel of John, 'Satan is the father of the lie.' Elsewhere in the New Testament, in his First Letter to Timothy Paul places liars in the same category as father killers, mother killers, harlots and abductors.

Alongside this strict moral requirement to tell the truth, the stories of the Old and New Testaments confront the reader with a long series of liars. Stories of deception and ruses are told from the start. In the second chapter of the Bible, the serpent in Paradise lies to Eve, telling her that she will be equal to God if she eats the forbidden fruit. When Eve is seduced by this lie, it results in some nasty consequences. After Adam and Eve are driven out of Paradise, they have two sons: Cain and Abel. Because Cain is jealous of his brother, he beats him to death and when God asks where Abel is, Cain lies: 'I don't know.' The wife of patriarch Abraham, Sarah, lies, just as Jacob does, and who, in turn, is also deceived. And then there are liars such as King David, the whore Rahab, the traitor Judas and the disciple Peter. The high standard was seemingly not lived up to by many of the main characters of the holy writ.

Also in other religions, like Islam, we find a strong moral preference for speaking the truth. In the Quran we read, 'Woe that day unto those who cry lies.' Islam forbids the lie in respect for Allah and the Prophet Muhammad. However, in the tradition of Islamic teachings we do see that lies and deception are permitted under certain circumstances. The famous and respected Muslim theologian Imam Abu Hammid Ghazali says the following about truth and lies: 'Speaking is a means to achieve objectives. If a praiseworthy aim is attainable through both telling the truth and lying, it is unlawful to accomplish it through lying because there is no need for it. When it is possible to achieve such an aim by lying but not by telling the truth, it is permissible to lie if attaining the goal is permissible' (Ahmad ibn Naqib al-Misri, 1997, 745). Although speaking the truth is preferred, lying is permitted in certain situations.

Classic Indian literature considers honesty and trust to be important standards. At the same time, we see that in the Ramayana Epos even the noblest characters lie and cheat. They speak 'white lies', for which the justification is that someone needed protecting, or that feelings must be taken into consideration.

This double standard is understandable since much human interaction is characterized by deception (Hamelink, 2006). Lies are important tools in human communication. Throughout history, across cultures, irrespective of social class or education, people lie in relations between parents and children, employers and employees and between lovers. Deceptive communication occurs in politics, business and science. The modern mass media are also often associated with false, prejudicial and distorted communications about the world's events. Against this reality, various legal and professional instruments have provided the normative guidance that communication should be true. This is often justified by the relation between truth and respect for human dignity. In deceptive behaviour 'the others', those being lied to, are not taken seriously as autonomous agents and are treated not as an end in themselves but as instrumental means. However, the norm of speaking the truth is not so easy, since 'We human beings are torn by a fundamental conflict – our deeply ingrained propensity to lie to ourselves and to others, and the desire to think of ourselves as good and honest people. So we justify our dishonesty by telling ourselves stories about why our actions are acceptable and sometimes even admirable' (Ariely, 2012, 166).

Ariely gives an economic and a psychological motivation for lying. He writes, 'We want to benefit from cheating . . . we want to be able to view ourselves as wonderful human beings' (ibid., 237). We manage to do both by 'our capacity for flexible reasoning and rationalization' (ibid., 237). This works as long as we cheat only a little bit. And 'all of us are perfectly capable of cheating a little bit' (ibid., 238). Although it must be acknowledged that we often let opportunities to cheat pass by, Ariely concludes that the experiments he conducted 'are indicative of dishonesty in society at large' (ibid., 239). Good individuals, companies, credit card companies and banks all cheat, but just a little.[6]

On the one hand, there is utter clarity on the moral principle. On the other hand, there may be the necessity to deviate from this norm. There are good arguments for speaking the truth. The most powerful argument that is usually mentioned is the necessity of social and relational trust. In social and personal relations mutual trust is essential. The lie undermines this trust and reduces the basis of human society. Sissela Bok wrote in her study on how lying affects the basis of human society that if everyone permanently lied to everyone else social life would become unbearable (Bok, 1978). An argument against lying is that the liar uses the other person to do things that he or she would not have done without the lie. In doing so, lying damages the freedom of people. It limits the freedom of others to determine their own ideas and opinions. However, in a society where honesty prevails people may be more vulnerable targets for those who continue cheating, because they want to believe that the liars are honest. Adrienne Rich (1995) suggested that between two people there is always the possibility of telling or withholding and we should realize that between too much honesty and too much dishonesty 'we both know we are trying, all the time, to extend the possibilities of truth between us' (Rich, 1995, 193).

The principle of protection of privacy and confidentiality of communication

Privacy has a very long history and has its origins in ancient societies. Even the Bible has some passages where shame and anger followed intrusion into someone's private sphere. Adam and Eve start to cover their bodies with leaves in order to preserve their privacy. The Code of Hammurabi contains a paragraph against intruding into someone's home. The idea of privacy suggests a distinction between what is private and what is public. In Greek philosophy Aristotle proposed the distinction between two spheres of life: the public sphere of politics and political activity (the 'polis') and the private or domestic sphere of the family (the 'oikos'). This dichotomy may originate from the need of humans to distinguish between themselves and the outer world.

In early tribal life there was a widespread information grapevine about local incidents and privacy was a foreign notion. However, 'one's soul and thoughts were private, and those who inquired about or intruded into such personal matters were not to be trusted' (Cooper, 1998, 155). Among the hunter-gatherers children would often sleep with their parents, either in the same bed or in the same hut and see their parents having sex. In the Trobriand Islands, Malinowski was told that parents took no special precautions to prevent their children from watching them having sex: 'they just scolded the child and told it to cover its head with a mat' (Diamond, 2013, ch. 5).

Early Christian saints pioneered the modern concept of privacy as seclusion. The most committed followers of biblical writings decided that their evil demons could only be fought when they were away from social distractions. In the same spirit, the Great Council of Lateran in 1215 decided that confessions should be mandatory for the masses. This emphasized that morality should be a matter of the private sphere and no longer a communal matter.

In the European Middle Ages, privacy was not a societal principle. Most people lived in small communities under the permanent surveillance of other members of the community. This changed with the appearance of cities and the shift from community to society (Tönnies, 1887/2002). In nineteenth-century Europe, people began to live in crowded cities, but away from constant social control. The urban private sphere, however, was intruded upon by the advent of newspapers and photojournalism with a commercial interest in gossiping. Samuel D. Warren and Louis D. Brandeis recognized the threats to privacy caused by these technological and societal developments in a famous article in the *Harvard Law Review* ('The right to privacy', 1890). They wrote, 'For years there has been a feeling that the law must afford some remedy for the unauthorized circulation of portraits of private persons; and the evil of the invasion of privacy by the newspapers, has long been keenly felt.' Warren and Brandeis described the right to privacy as 'the right to be let alone' (ibid., 193).

Throughout history the private domain has always been contested territory and its protection always a matter of ambiguous morality. Plato recognized a dualism between the visible material body and the invisible immaterial human soul. More often than not in human history the needs and desires of the material body (for money, prestige and power) were prioritized over the invisible soul, which became a prime target for religious and secular surveillance authorities.

The confidentiality of communication

The right to privacy includes those communicative acts that take place in the private sphere where participants deem it essential that their exchanges remain confidential. This is particularly clear in encounters between medical, legal or clerical professionals and their patients/clients. The pledge to confidentiality in communication in the medical profession goes back to the Hippocratic Oath, which states, 'Whatsoever things I see or hear concerning the life of men, in my attendance on the sick or even apart there from, which ought not to be noised about, I shall keep silence thereon, counting such things to be as sacred secrets' (*c.*400 BC).

The nineteenth-century regulation of international postal and telegraphic traffic introduced among its basic norms and rules the freedom of transit and free passage of messages. In the world's first international communication conventions (the 1874 Treaty of Berne, which founded the General Postal Union, the Berne Telegraph Convention of 1858, which founded the International Telegraph Union, and the 1865 International Telegraph Convention) the confidentiality of correspondence across national borders was secured. At the same time, however, governments reserved the right to interfere with any message they considered dangerous to state security or in violation of national laws, public order or morality. This tension between the right to confidentiality and the right of states to interfere in private communications would remain an issue of political controversy, throughout the twentieth and into the twenty-first century.

The norm of confidentiality is constantly challenged by ordinary human curiosity and increasingly also by the administrative requirements of modern states (the tax bureaucracy and the law enforcement system), the commercial interest in acquiring and selling personal data and the widespread availability of surveillance technology.

The principle of freedom

Freedom of thought[7]

It can be argued that the Greeks (particularly the Ionians because 'Ionia in Asia Minor was the cradle of free speculation' (Bury, 1913, 8)) were (among) the first defenders of the freedom of thought. Among the early philosophers, Heraclitus and Democritus were not hindered 'by fantastic tales of creation, imposed by sacred authority' (ibid., 9) as they developed their rational theories about the world and the universe. They prepared the way for the Sophists, whose general spirit 'was that of free inquiry and discussion. They sought to test everything by reason' (ibid., 9). As Bury warns, however, this free thinking was limited to a minority, whereas the masses of people were superstitious believers. In the middle of the fifth century BC statesman Pericles, a free thinker, was attacked by his political enemies through accusing his friend Anaxagoras of blasphemy. Although Pericles was able to save his life, Anaxagoras was heavily fined and had to leave Athens. This story would be one often repeated in the fight for the freedom of thought. The free thinkers stood always against those who for reasons of the exercise of power defended superstition, unreasoned religious belief and irrational accounts of how the universe operated.

Free thinkers such as Socrates established the rationale for freedom of thought, for the right of the individual to the autonomy of conscience and the social significance of reflective and free discussion. Throughout history this position would continuously come under attack, usually for political reasons. In Roman times the general rule was to tolerate throughout the Empire all religions and opinions and blasphemy was not punished (ibid., 13). The Jewish religion was because of its intolerance and hostility to other beliefs looked upon with suspicion but was left alone. Among those who ruled the Empire there was always the worry nevertheless that Roman citizens could be recruited to the Jewish or the Christian religion. Roman administrators feared that imperial unity was especially at risk with the expansion of Christian thinking, which did not tolerate deviations from its holy creed and was ready to abuse its growing power for the suppression of other religions. The Christians would invoke the principle of tolerance and freedom, which as soon as the state became Christian was forgotten. From its early beginnings the church went after the 'heretics' with a bloody and lethal vengeance. The wholesale murder of the free-thinking Albigeois under Pope Innocent III and the history of the torture and killing by the Inquisition testify to this.

In European history, the church, both Catholic and Protestant, and their functionaries and theologians were the key enemy of freedom of thought and by implication of scientific reasoning. Their main instrument was persecution, which was firmly established on scriptural grounds by church father St Augustine. In the incessant campaigns against heterodoxy political figures also featured prominently, such as mediaeval French kings and King Henry VIII, under whom a heretic was boiled to death. The judgement of heresy as the worst of all crimes was also broadly supported by public opinion. Throughout the Middle Ages, the heretics claimed their right to free thought and its expression. However, the freedom to express free thoughts was always limited through censorship, arrests, book burning or propaganda, and this tended more often than not to discourage such freedom. In the late sixteenth century, Queen Elizabeth I revoked a tough censorship law, because, according to Sir Francis Bacon, she did 'not [like] to make windows into men's souls and secret thoughts' (Noel, 2020, 98). During her reign, philosopher, mathematician, astrologer and astronomer Giordano Bruno took refuge in England from the Italian Inquisition, where he published a number of his books regarding an infinite universe and topics banned by the Catholic Church. After leaving the safety of England, Bruno was eventually burned as a heretic in Rome for refusing to recant his ideas. He may be considered an early martyr for free thought.

The period of the Reformation did not establish liberty of religious thought. Both Luther and Calvin opposed all thinking that they deemed inconsistent with the Scriptures. Against this position, the Declaration of the Rights of Man and of the Citizen issued by France's National Constituent Assembly in 1789 provided in Article 10 that 'No one may be disquieted for his opinions, even religious ones, provided that their manifestation does not trouble the public order established by the law.'

The seventeenth-century philosopher Thomas Hobbes was a free thinker, although he wrote in *Leviathan* that it is the duty of subjects to conform to the religion of the sovereign. During the reign of Charles II his books were burned. When the Press Licensing Act was dropped in 1695, there emerged more space for attacks on Christianity. But the enemies of free thinking had powerful weapons, such as Ecclesiastical Courts and a Statute from 1698 that imposed serious prison terms on those who denied that Holy Scriptures were of divine origin. Many of the free-thinking writers sought refuge in a variety of guises such as satirical support for orthodox beliefs or the dramatic genre that Voltaire used. Rousseau contributed to free thinking not only by his religious scepticism but even more through his political theories. His books were publicly burned in Paris and he was persecuted.

Thomas Paine, who wrote *Rights of Man*, got into trouble for his revolutionary ideas, critique of the monarchical form of government and plea for representative democracy. He was thrown into a Parisian prison on the order of the most prominent leader of the French Revolution, Robespierre. The publisher of Paine's *The Age of Reason* was imprisoned for a year. In the nineteenth century, the freedom of thought remained a contested principle. And in 1909, the free thinker Francisco Ferrer was killed in Barcelona on the order of a military tribunal that followed the false accusation concocted against him by the ecclesiastical authorities. This marked the beginning of a century during which freedom of thought would be severely repressed under totalitarian political regimes.

Freedom of speech
Although the notion of freedom is often linked with ancient Greek society, in Athens, in particular, 'a growing number of intellectuals began to question whether popular self-government really did lead to freedom for all' (De Dijn, 2020, 43). The wealthy few contested the democratic conception of freedom. From their perspective, 'democracy did not lead to freedom but rather to another form of tyranny – by the poor' (ibid., 43). A member of the Athenian elite, usually referred to as the Old Oligarch, identified Athenian democracy as 'the rule of the poor and the uneducated. . . . They ruled in their own interest, and thus to the detriment of the rich' (ibid., 46). The Old Oligarch believed that democracy could be an oppressive regime, although he also did not believe that freedom would fare any better under the elite. For him, like for Thucydides – a general during the Peloponnesian war between Athens and Sparta – all politics was power politics and 'ideals like freedom were used to cover up the real source of strife: the self-interested pursuit of domination' (ibid., 47).

When Athenian democracy was restored in 403 BC, the Old Oligarch, Thucydides and the Sophists who had joined the choir of critics gained support from the philosopher Plato. For him the best possible regime was 'rule by the best man' (ibid., 52). For Plato the democratic city was a place full of 'freedom and frankness' (ibid., 54) in which 'a man may say and do what he likes'. Democracy meant self-government so that 'the individual is clearly able to order for himself his own life as he pleases' (ibid., 54). However, in the end, he believed that this individual independence would spill over into anarchy and lead to tyranny. 'Ordinary people could not be trusted to use their freedom wisely' (ibid., 56). Eventually, Plato argued people should be the 'willing slaves of the law'. This political slavery would be more conducive to human happiness than democratic freedom. For centuries after Plato, his argument that people should be subjected to the rule of the best and the wisest played an important role in anti-democratic politics.

Early in human history, the idea emerged that in order to maximally profit from the human communicative capacity the freedom of the word should be promoted and protected. Since the development of language there was always the idea that without the freedom to speak humans' capacity to use language, unlike animals, would be meaningless. Concern about the freedom of information is reported as early as 350 BC, when the Greek statesman and orator Demosthenes said that taking away the freedom of expression is one of the greatest calamities for human beings. Athenian political freedom in the fifth and fourth century BC extended to all citizens also included freedom of speech. As I.F. Stone (1989) wrote, Socrates could have won acquittal from the death sentence if he had reminded his judges of the great importance of free speech and free thought.

Despite a level of intolerance of free thought, such philosophical schools as the Stoics, the Epicureans and the Sceptics developed and claimed a large measure of intellectual freedom. According to Stone, the jury was reluctant to convict Socrates as the trial went against the essence of Athenian tradition, 'the trial of Socrates was a prosecution of ideas. . . . If he had conducted his defence as a free speech case, and invoked the basic tradition of his city, he might easily, I believe, have shifted the troubled jury in his favor' (ibid., 197). Stone suggests that Socrates should have referred to 'the Athenian rule until now, the pride of our city, the glory on which your orators dwell'. This rule by the people ('demos') is based on the equal right to speak freely. But for Socrates 'free speech was the privilege of the enlightened few, not of the benighted many. He would not have wanted the democracy he rejected to win a moral victory by setting him free' (ibid., 230).

Freedom of thought was a standard principle in Athens from the sixth century BC till 529 AD when Emperor Justinianus gave in to Christian intolerance and closed the philosophical schools of Athens. This right to free speech is first mentioned as 'isegoria' ('isotes' = equality) in Herodotus and its equivalent 'isologia' appears in the third century BC in the writings of historian Polybius. Herodotus attributed the victories of the Athenians in the Persian wars to their equal right to speak in the assembly. In the theatre of fifth-century Athens, free speech was very common. There are references to free speaking tongues in Aeschylus' *Suppliant Maidens*, and in Euripides' plays the freedom of speech ('parrhesia') is a favourite topic. 'Parrhesia' can be defined as outspokenness and political freedom of speech (ibid., 222). Interestingly, Euripides related the right to free speech to the duty to listen and to hear the arguments of both sides (ibid., 223).

Roman historian Tacitus (55–116 AD) praised the rule of Emperor Trajan as felicitous times when one could freely express whatever one wanted to say. Romans attached much importance to freedom in the sense of the liberty to govern themselves. As De Dijn argues, the Romans 'seemed to believe that popular self-government was necessary for individual security and personal independence' (2020, 73). However, in the popular assembly of Rome there was no debate. Only voting was possible on proposals brought forward by officials. Free speech did not exist in the Roman assemblies. As Stone wrote, 'Latin had no word for isegoria. Roman law had no use for it' (1989, 218).

Freedom of information was facilitated by the advent of the printing press that made the dissemination of ancient texts like those of Herodotus, Tacitus and Plutarch possible. This development broadened the audience for reflection on freedom, which also became a topic of interest among painters and sculptors. Cities like Florence and Siena 'decorated their cities with frescoes, statues, and paintings that glorified the ancient republics and their love of liberty' (De Dijn, 2020, 144).

Against the secular suppression of the freedom of expression, John Milton published his *Areopagitica* in 1644. In this famous speech to the Parliament of England on the liberty of unlicensed printing, Milton claimed: 'Truth needs no licensing to make her victorious' (Milton, 1644/2017). In 1695, the Regulation of Printing Act against which he spoke was revoked. Interestingly enough, Milton's plea for freedom of printing did not apply to Roman Catholics, as he felt one should not extend principles of tolerance to those who are intolerant. In 1689 the British Bill of Rights made free speech in the House of Commons possible. In Sweden an Order on the Freedom of the Printing Press was enacted in 1766 as formal law, including the rights of access to public information.

The oldest catalogue of fundamental rights (in the sense of human and civil rights that possess a higher legal force) is the Declaration of Rights preceding the constitution of the state of Virginia in 1776. Here the freedom of expression was formulated as press freedom: 'That the freedom of the Press is one of the greatest bulwarks of liberty, and never be restrained by despotic governments.' Following the Anglo-Saxon tradition, the French Declaration on the Rights of Man and of the Citizen was formulated in 1789. This declaration went beyond the Virginia declaration in stating that the unrestrained communication of thoughts or opinions is one of the most precious rights of man: every citizen may speak, write and publish freely, provided he is responsible for the abuse of this liberty, in the cases determined by law. Then, in 1791, the US Bill of Rights stated in Article I the famous provision that 'Congress shall make no law . . . abridging the freedom of speech, or of the press' (Hamelink, 1994b, 150–1).

In nineteenth-century legislation on fundamental rights, the right to freedom of information emerged in many countries and the freedom of the press, primarily in the form of the prohibition of censorship, became a central issue. This was reflected in many national constitutions. In his tract *On Liberty*, John Stuart Mill (1859) pleaded for tolerance at all costs.

'Without tolerance rational criticism, rational condemnation are destroyed' and this is tantamount to 'collective moral and intellectual suicide' (Berlin, 1969, 184). Quintessential of Mill's thinking is a quote from *On Liberty*: 'If all mankind minus one, were of one opinion, and only one person were of a contrary opinion, mankind would be no more justified in silencing that one person than he, if he had the power, be justified in silencing mankind' (ibid., 197). The subject of *On Liberty* was civil and social liberty and the leading question was about the limits of the power that can be legitimately exercised by society over the individual. Mill thought that:

> the peculiar evil of silencing the expression of an opinion is that it is robbing the human race; posterity as well as the existing generation; those who dissent from the opinion, still more than those who hold it. If the opinion is right, they are deprived of the opportunity of exchanging error for truth: if wrong, they lose, what is almost as great a benefit, the clearer perception and livelier impression of truth, produced by the collision with error. (in Robson, 1966, 23)

In chapter 2 of *On Liberty*, he wrote that 'to refuse a hearing of an opinion, because they are sure that it is false, is to assume that their certainty is the same thing as absolute certainty. All silencing of discussion is an assumption of infallibility' (ibid., 23). Mill then argued that people are not inclined to take precautions against their own fallibility. Yet this is important as 'every age having held many opinions which subsequent ages have deemed not only false but absurd; and it is certain that many opinions now general, will be rejected by future ages, as it is that many, once general, are rejected by the present' (ibid., 25). In Mill's writing the norm is that we can only know a subject 'by hearing what can be said about it by persons of every variety of opinion' (ibid., 27). Only thus can wisdom be acquired, by being 'cognizant of all that can be said against him . . . and knowing that he has sought for objections and difficulties, instead of avoiding them' (ibid., 27).

Mill strengthens his argument for listening to objections even against beliefs one holds to be certain, by pointing to the fact that the most intolerant of churches, the Roman Catholic Church, in processes of beatification would appoint a devil's advocate who is patiently listened to when he raises arguments against canonization. In summing up his argument on the freedom of opinion Mill states that freedom of opinion and the freedom to express opinions is necessary for the mental well-being of humankind (ibid., 68). The genuine conversationalists, he argues, are guided by the 'morality of public discussion', which implies 'giving merited honour to everyone, whatever opinion he may hold, [to] honestly state what his opponents and their opinions really are, exaggerating nothing to their discredit, keeping nothing back which tells in their favour' (ibid., 71).[8]

The threats to free speech

Early in human history the idea emerged that the freedom of the word should be promoted and protected. Equally, however, the discovery was made that words can be dangerous, that they can kill and that the control of verbal communication is essential to the exercise of power. Throughout history, communication through words became thus a terrain of contested ideas. Liberatory versus imperial conceptions of communication clashed, preferences for privileged access versus public access to communication collided, and conflicting ideas about transparency versus secrecy of information were forcefully defended. The most engaging struggle, however, was always the tension between the idea that communication should be free and the idea that communication should be controlled.

The essential struggle related to communication became the confrontation between freedom of thought and mind control, or the battle of the publishers versus the book burners. This was not always a meeting on a level playing field since in many societies the powers that be have been opposed to the idea of freedom of thought. The 'power elites' in various ages exercised censorship to protect their interests as they perceived free thought dangerous to their authority. A classic example is the burning of Mayan books by the Spanish priest Diego de Landa in 1562. The idea that people should be free to think and speak as they wish and should have access to whatever information and knowledge they need was (and is) seen by authoritative intellectual and political elites as undesirable. The philosopher Plato, who had a great disrespect for common people, was convinced that their free speech could only mean trouble.

As Sue Jansen (1991, 4) concludes, 'censorship is an enduring feature of all human communities'. Suppressing the freedom to communicate has been widely used as an instrument to maintain control by the powerful of all ages and societies. Censorship was known and widely used in the ancient Egyptian, Sumerian, Greek and Roman societies. In Egypt, the ruling class censored what knowledge could be made available. When in ancient Egypt the medium of communication ($c.2700/2600$ BC) shifted from stone to papyrus, the scribe became a highly honoured magistrate and member of a privileged profession. The art of writing was held in high esteem and the scribe 'was included in the upper classes of kings, priests, nobles, and generals'. He became part of the ruling class that monopolized knowledge (Innis, 1972, 16).

When Socrates stood trial, it has to be acknowledged that, in spite of Stone's arguments (1989, as iterated earlier in the chapter), 'Athenian censorship was so extensive that a hierarchy of sanctions from prohibition of public speech through denial of civil rights, exile, imprisonment, and execution was routinely invoked to suppress dangerous ideas' (Jansen, 1991, 36). There were charges of blasphemy against philosophers Anaxagoras and Protagoras. And, Plato, who, ironically, informs us about Socrates' commitment to free speech, proposed that all freedom of discussion should be banned from the ideal society and that knowledge should be centrally controlled. Aristotle went into exile, accused of blasphemy, and Euripides was prosecuted for impiety (ibid., 37).

In the Roman era, Emperor Augustus was probably the first political leader to promote a law that prohibited libellous writing. In early Christianity, the apostle Paul advised burning the books of adversaries (Acts 19:19). The early church suppressed several texts it considered a challenge to its power. Particularly the Gnostic texts were targets for suppression and burning. Yet, common Roman policy tolerated throughout the Empire all religions and blasphemy was not punished. As the Emperor Tiberius is reported to have said, 'If the gods are insulted, let them see to it themselves' (Bury, 1913, 13).

With the adoption of the Christian faith by Emperor Constantine the Great (313 AD), freedom of religious thought began to be violently suppressed. Heretical thought was punished by cruel torture and death. During the Middle Ages, the church fought a bitter battle against any form of heterodoxy. Heretics – men, women and even children – were hanged and burned. To effectively organize the ruthless suppression of heresy, Pope Gregory IX established in 1233 a special institution of persecution, the Inquisition. In 1493 the Inquisition in Venice issued the first list of books banned by the church. In 1559 the 'Index Librorum Prohibitorum' was made binding on all Roman Catholics and was administered by the Inquisition. Famous became the case of Copernicus' (1473–1543) publication, *On the Revolution of the Celestial Spheres*. The book was not published until after his death to avoid persecution by the church. In 1616 the church put the book on its index of prohibited books. Galileo Galilei (1564–1642) made his Copernican worldview public and was made to retract this under the threat of torture. Only in 1967 did the Catholic Church stop its efforts to prohibit texts by authors such as Erasmus, Descartes, Rousseau, Voltaire, Newton, Milton, Kant, Spinoza, Pascal, Comte, Freud and Sartre.

The protagonists of the Reformation, as noted earlier in the chapter, were no less interested in censorship than were their Catholic opponents. In sixteenth-century Geneva, heavy censorship was exercised by John Calvin, who was famous for his extreme intolerance. Theologian Martin Luther also had little difficulty with suppressing the freedom of thought. Luther was quite opposed to liberty of conscience and held that Anabaptists should be put to the sword. In 1525 he used censorship regulations in Saxony and

Brandenberg to suppress the 'pernicious doctrines' of the Anabaptists and Zwinglians. Subsequently Melanchton, Zwingli and Calvin 'enforced censorial controls that were far more restrictive that any instituted by Rome or by Luther' (Jansen, 1991, 53).

Secular powers followed such examples and issued forms of regulation to control free expression. Emperor Frederick II (1194–1250) issued legislation in which burning at the stake became the popular way of punishing the heresy of free thinkers. In France, King Henry II (r. 1154–89) declared printing without official permission punishable by death. The official rationale was later greatly inspired by Thomas Hobbes' reflections in his *Leviathan* (1651), where he extended state sovereignty to control the opinions and persuasions of the governed. An example of such sovereign control was the English Regulation of Printing Act mentioned earlier in the chapter. This licensing law provided for a system of censorship through licences for printing and publishing.

In nineteenth-century Europe legislation on fundamental freedom of the press became a central issue, primarily in the form of the prohibition of censorship. This was reflected in many national constitutions. Until the twentieth century the concern about freedom of information remained almost exclusively a domestic affair. Interestingly enough, when in the early twentieth century the League of Nations (predecessor to the United Nations) focused on the problems of false news and propaganda, it did not address the protection of freedom of expression.

Throughout history we find the human instinct to censor versus the human instinct to speak out (Smolla, 1992, 42). As political animals, humans will probably always be inclined to abuse the power of the conviction that they are right to ban books, cancel cultural events and stop subsidies for 'offensive' works of art.

Conclusion

The historical sweep of this chapter shows that before the codification of human rights in international law, there were essential ideas to guide human living and flourishing together. Ideas about freedom, equality and respect for human dignity did empower people to think and act in autonomous ways. However, they were also constantly threatened by religious and secular destructive powers that disempowered people to act as autonomous agents. Throughout the history of normative ideas, human togetherness was both facilitated and obstructed and compassion was both praised and feared.

The essential principles for communicative behaviour were respect for human dignity and freedom. The principle of freedom was accommodated in twentieth-century international human rights law as the right to freedom of thought, conscience and religion, and the right to freedom of opinion and expression. The principle of respect for human dignity was accommodated as the right to be protected by law against interference with one's privacy, family, home or correspondence and against attacks upon honour and reputation. It is interesting to note that truthful and fair speech as part of respect for human dignity is not taken up in the catalogue of human communication rights. Remarkable also is the observation that in spite of many references to the principle of equality in moral history, this principle was never seriously connected with communicative behaviour. In the next chapter I will turn to the classical standards for communicative behaviour as they are codified in international human rights law.

2 Human Rights and Communication

Introduction

After the Second World War an international human rights regime developed within the institutional framework of the United Nations. The Universal Declaration of Human Rights (UDHR) of 1948 stands at the core of modern thinking about human rights. The relation between communication and human rights first appeared as Article 19 of the Declaration: 'Everyone has the right to freedom of opinion and expression; this right includes freedom to hold opinions without interference and to seek, receive and impart information and ideas through any media and regardless of frontiers.' Herewith the freedom of information was recognized as a fundamental human right and as the touchstone of all the freedoms to which the United Nations is consecrated.

The history of a remarkable document

The international community wanted to have an International Bill of Rights as a building block for a peaceful world. A Commission on Human Rights was appointed and Eleanor Roosevelt, wife of President Franklin D. Roosevelt, was asked to chair the Commission in February 1946. The task was to prepare an International Bill of Rights to be presented to the General Assembly of the United Nations. The international human rights regime that emerged was formed by procedures for supra-national normative standard-setting and institutions for monitoring the implementation of these standards. Today its key institutional basis is the United Nations, which is both the author of essential human rights instruments (declarations, resolutions, treaties) and an association of states – many of which commit human rights violations such as invading the privacy of their citizens, censoring, arresting or torturing them.

The promotion of human rights is most forcefully exercised by non-governmental organizations such as the International Federation of Human Rights (established in 1922), Amnesty International, Human Rights Watch and numerous smaller organizations that defend the interests of children, women, indigenous peoples, sexual minorities, refugees and of people with disabilities. Implementation is largely left to institutions on the regional and national level, such as the European Court of Human Rights or the Inter-American Court of Human Rights. By and large the global implementation and enforcement of human rights standards is very weak. A key obstacle to the implementation and enforcement is the inherent tension between the key concept of international law, state sovereignty and universal human rights. The extent to which human rights will be implemented by national governments is often the result of political preferences. Governments that do not like dissident voices will tend to restrict the right to free speech. Chinese politics of censorship vis-à-vis the Internet is an example. Governments that choose to surveil their citizens because of national security will not fully honour the human right to privacy. US policy with regard to the operations of the National Security Agency (NSA) in the Edward Snowden case is an illustration. Snowden blew the whistle in 2013 on the global surveillance programme of the NSA.

Governments will also tend to treat human rights violations in other countries differently dependent upon whether the violators are client-states or enemies. Early on, the drafting of the Universal Declaration of Human Rights was a process of political agreements and disagreements, particularly because of the opposite positions of the Western countries and the Soviet bloc.

At the United Nations Conference on International Organization that took place in San Francisco (with delegates of fifty nations) from 25 April to 26 June 1945, the Charter of the United Nations was adopted. The Conference agreed that among the purposes of the institution should be 'promoting and encouraging respect for human rights and for fundamental freedoms for all without distinction as to race, sex, language, or religion' (United Nations, 1945a). The Conference declared that this would be crucial to achieve international cooperation in solving international problems of an economic, social, cultural or humanitarian character. During the Conference, Panama submitted a statement of essential human rights and delegates from Chile, Cuba and Mexico joined Panama in the effort to have this text incorporated into the UN Charter. Among the basic human rights were listed the freedom of opinion, the freedom of speech and the freedom from wrongful interference. The state was to provide protection for these freedoms.

Since time did not allow the proposal to be discussed, the Panama delegation submitted the draft Declaration again to the first session of the UN General Assembly on 11 December 1946. The General

Assembly recommended the Declaration be referred to the Economic and Social Council (ECOSOC) for later submission to the Commission on Human Rights. From June 1947 to December 1948 members of the Commission's Bureau (Eleanor Roosevelt, Pen-Chung Chang and Charles Malik, supported by a secretariat) worked through from the drafting of an International Bill of Rights to the drafting of the Universal Declaration of Human Rights, which was adopted by the UN General Assembly in its session on 10 December 1948.

The Declaration constituted the inauguration of a system of standards embedded in covenants, declarations and resolutions and an organizational practice of secretariats, commissions, sub-commissions, committees, councils, working groups, special rapporteurs and pressure groups. A complex system of national and international, state and non-state actors evolved with the mission to set standards, promote and protect these standards and monitor the implementation of international agreements. In this process – over the years – the number of human rights has increased and herewith supervisory bodies and procedures have proliferated.

The foundational document of the United Nations, the UN Charter (1945b), made explicit reference to human rights (in its Preamble and Articles 1, 13, 55, 56, 62 and 68) as integral to the mandate and mission of the United Nations. Its visionary drafters expressed their fundamental conviction that the respect for human rights would be basic to international peace and development. Following the UN Charter, human rights standards have been formulated in the so-called International Bill of Rights, which consists of the Universal Declaration of Human Rights and the two key human rights treaties, the International Covenant on Economic, Social and Cultural Rights (ICESCR) (adopted in 1966 and in force since 3 January 1976) and the International Covenant on Civil and Political Rights (ICCPR) (adopted in 1966 and in force since 23 March 1976). Different dimensions of human rights have also been codified in a series of international treaties, in regional instruments, such as the European Convention for the Protection of Human Rights and Fundamental Freedoms (1950), the American Convention on Human Rights (1969), the African Charter on Human and Peoples' Rights (1981) and in the Islamic Declaration of Human Rights, which was prepared by the Islamic Council in 1980 and presented to United Nations Educational, Scientific and Cultural Organization (UNESCO) in 1981.

The documents (often called instruments) in which human rights are formulated have different legal meanings. In international relations, rules and practices among states can over time be accepted as international custom and, as such, become a source of international law. Increasingly, however, such customary law is replaced by conventions or treaties that have become the essential instruments of international cooperation. Treaties impose binding obligations on the parties who ratify them, which means making them officially valid. Often treaties are preceded by international declarations, which may have a strong moral impact (which is the case with the Universal Declaration of Human Rights), but do not have a legally binding character. In addition to treaties and declarations, the international community can also recommend certain types of action through resolutions of its decision-making bodies such as the General Assembly of the United Nations.

The essential instrument in the field of human rights remains the 1948 Universal Declaration of Human Rights. The Declaration continues to be a source of inspiration for thought and action in the field of human rights. The UDHR, although not a binding treaty, carries important legal weight. Among legal scholars there is a considerable consensus that the UDHR constitutes binding law as international custom. The Declaration is certainly recognized by civilized nations as a common and binding standard of achievement. The text proclaims a fairly comprehensive set of rights (and puts civil and political rights on the same level as social, economic and cultural rights) and also proposes the implementation of these claims in a social and international order.

From 1945 onwards the defence of fundamental rights was no longer solely the preoccupation of national politics and became an essential part of world politics. The judgement of whether human rights had been violated was no longer the exclusive monopoly of national governments. Earlier concerns about what happened in foreign countries were largely dependent on whether this affected one's own political-economic interests. Such concerns may have been whether one's diplomats would be treated correctly by other countries. There were no standards to treat all human beings decently. International concerns were selective and did not imply compassion for humanity as such. Minority treaties under the League of Nations had little to do with respect for rights of minorities, but were inspired by concerns about peace among nations. The unfair treatment of minorities could lead to disturbance of the peace, for instance.

Concern for citizens of other states was hindered by strict conceptions of state sovereignty, but also by inadequate information. Moreover, how could states have intervened in other countries, whereas in most countries governments routinely violated those rights that later came to be called human rights? In the second place, the enjoyment of human rights was no longer restricted to privileged individuals and social elites. With the adoption of the UN Charter a process began that for the first time in history declared that all people matter. This meant that there are no longer non-persons and that basic rights hold for everyone and exclude no one. In the third place, the conventional view that individuals can only be objects of international law changed to the conception that the individual is a holder of rights and bearer of duties under international law. The individual can appeal to international law for the protection of his or her rights, but can also be held responsible for violations of human rights standards. The recognition of individual rights under international law was thus linked with the notion that individuals also have duties under international law. This was eloquently expressed in 1947 by Mahatma Gandhi in a letter to the director of UNESCO about the issue of human rights. Gandhi wrote, 'I learnt from my illiterate but wise mother that rights to be deserved and preserved came from duty well done' (Gandhi, 1947).

Most importantly, human rights standards proposed that the moral claims that people make vis-à-vis one another are solely based on their humanity. If rights are related to the human being as such, and not given by an authority, they cannot be taken away by whatever authority. They do not have to be deserved. They are not dependent on good conduct or divine grace. They are inherent to the human being, because he or she is human. International human rights standards are grounded in the conviction that all human beings have inalienable entitlements to the protection of their life and liberty because of their humanity and not as derivatives of a higher order. This notion of human autonomy is certainly not universally shared.

If progress is to be made in the implementation of human rights standards, we should get away from the common and convenient approach in which human rights are seen as mainly a problem for non-Western civilizations. It needs to be recognized that this denies that the West has great difficulties with the theory and practice of human rights. The human rights regime challenges fundamental ways of thinking in all cultural traditions. It reflects a mode of thought that is new to all societies, not just non-Western ones. There is widespread unwillingness to take human rights seriously in the East, West, North and South. For most communities around the world (whatever their cultural backgrounds), there are serious difficulties in grounding human rights. Human rights pose essential challenges to a Chinese Confucian culture, but equally to a Western consumer culture, to Islamic, as well as to Christian theology. The need for an internal critical discourse on human rights standards is equally strong everywhere.

The Universal Declaration of Human Rights[1]

The emergence of the UDHR has to be seen against the background of the repression, aggression and violence experienced during the Second World War. The aspiration towards a new moral and legal world order was expressed by Franklin D. Roosevelt in January 1941 in his Message to the US Congress. Basic to his vision of the New World Order were four freedoms: freedom of expression, freedom of faith, freedom from want and freedom from fear. Shortly after the establishment of the United Nations, a Commission on Human Rights began to draft an International Bill of Rights. The Commission used as resources the drafts that were prepared by states and regional institutions like the Organization of American States and various non-governmental organizations (NGOs) such as the American Federation of Labor.

Also constitutions from around the world were used by the secretariat headed by the Canadian law professor John Humphrey. The Chair of the Human Rights Commission, Eleanor Roosevelt, had to find a compromise within her own US delegation, where two factions collided: the liberal school of the Roosevelt period and a more traditional and isolationist approach. The text of the Declaration was drafted over two years: between January 1947 – when the Commission on Human Rights first met – and December 1948. The committee of eight that prepared a preliminary text found a consensus on the need to affirm fundamental human rights and freedoms and to include not only civil and political rights, but also social, economic and cultural rights. Member states replied to the draft, the committee revised the text and then submitted it to the General Assembly. The fifty-eight member states in the General Assembly studied the text very closely and voted some 1,400 times on words and sentences. There was a good deal of debate. Some Islamic states, for example, objected to the right to change religion, and Western countries were critical of the inclusion of social and economic rights. On 10 December 1948, the Declaration was adopted with eight abstentions. This date remains celebrated as the world's Human Rights Day. The fact that the UN General Assembly titled its human rights declaration universal, and not international, is a manifestation of the crucial importance it attached to the all-encompassing nature of the entitlements it provided to the world's people. All the claims the Declaration makes on the recognition and protection of rights and freedoms are 'erga omnes' – meaning they extend to all people, always and everywhere.

The Preamble of the Universal Declaration

This first part of the Declaration begins with reference to the recognition of human dignity: 'Whereas recognition of the inherent dignity and of the equal and inalienable rights of all members of the human family is the foundation of freedom, justice and peace in the world.' The notion of human dignity is not without difficulties, and its grounding is seriously contested in religion and philosophy. A special problem is that human dignity tends to be defined in terms of the substantially superior nature of the human being in comparison with all other beings in the universe. To a large extent this justifies questionable human conduct regarding nonhuman forms of life such as animals. Human dignity remains a vague notion and yet it provides the grounds for freedom, justice and peace.

The commitment

The Preamble confirms the commitment of the peoples of the United Nations to the defence of human rights and uses the following phrasing:

> Whereas the peoples of the United Nations have in the Charter reaffirmed their faith in fundamental human rights, in the dignity and worth of the human person and in the equal rights of men and women and have determined to promote social progress and better standards of life in larger freedom. Whereas Member States have pledged themselves to achieve, in co-operation with the United Nations, the promotion of universal respect for and observance of human rights and fundamental freedoms.

It is important to note that the text states that the protection by law is essential for human rights: 'Whereas it is essential, if man [*sic*] is not to be compelled to have recourse, as a last resort, to rebellion against tyranny and oppression, that human rights should be protected by the rule of law.'

The implementation

The Preamble continues with the observation that the implementation of human rights will, to a large extent, depend on the creation of a common worldwide understanding of what human rights are: 'Whereas a common understanding of these rights and freedoms is of the greatest importance for the full realization of this pledge.'

The nature of the Declaration and future action

> The General Assembly
> Proclaims this Universal Declaration of Human Rights as a common standard of achievement for all peoples and all nations, to the end that every individual and every organ of society, keeping this Declaration constantly in mind, shall strive by teaching and education to promote respect for these rights and freedoms and by progressive measures, national and international, to secure their universal and effective recognition and observance, both among the peoples of Member States themselves and among the peoples of territories under their jurisdiction.

Following the Preamble, there are thirty articles that identify a series of human rights of civil, political, socioeconomic and cultural nature. Among the concluding articles of the Declaration, Article 28 is crucial to the whole system of human rights and is unfortunately often given little attention. It reads, 'Everyone is entitled to a social and international order in which the rights and freedoms set forth in this Declaration can be fully realized.' Following this, Article 29 states that 'Everyone has duties to the community in which alone the free and full development of his [sic] personality is possible', and Article 30 warns that 'Nothing in the Declaration may be interpreted as implying for any State, group or person any right to engage in any activity or to perform any act aimed at the destruction of any of the rights and freedoms set forth in the Declaration.'

A common distinction among the rights and freedoms that form the core of international human rights standards refers to three generations of human rights. According to this division, civil and political rights (sometimes referred to as the classic human rights) are seen as the first generation. Economic, social and cultural rights make up the second generation, and a series of collective rights form the third generation. The latter include the right to development, the right to peace and the right to a clean, natural environment. As Baehr (1999, 7) rightly remarked,

> The term 'generations' is somewhat unfortunate. It suggests a succession of phenomena, whereby a new generation takes the place of the previous one. That is, however, not the case with the three 'generations' of human rights. On the contrary. The idea is rather that the three 'generations' exist and be respected simultaneously.

The third generation of rights were proposed in 1977 by international lawyer Karel Vašák – at the time Director of UNESCO's Division of Human Rights and Peace – which he dubbed solidarity rights (Vašák,

1977). He based this proposal on the historical distinction of revolutions. The French Revolution focused in particular on freedom rights. The Mexican and Russian revolutions focused on equality rights. Vašák argued that the world had now entered a third revolution of the liberation of colonized peoples, which implied global interdependence. Vašák designed a third UN Covenant to complement the ICCPR and ICESCR, with provisions on health, peace, environment and the common heritage of humanity. Vašák also counted the right to communication among this third generation of human rights.

The third-generation notion has been contested (among others by Alston (1982) and Donnelly (1990)). In this debate Dutch human rights lawyer Cees Flinterman took the position that a third generation of human rights would take up the challenge of Article 28 of the UDHR that provided: 'Everyone is entitled to a social and international order in which the rights and freedoms set forth in this Declaration can be fully realized.' This provision was not taken up in the 1966 covenants – the ICCPR and ICESCR. According to Flinterman a social and international order, as mentioned in Article 28, 'embodies the idea that a full promotion and protection of human rights in a particular state is dependent upon worldwide solidarity' (1990, 79). I would like to argue – in line with Flinterman – for there to be a third covenant, on solidarity rights. Solidarity is clearly missing from the earlier human rights instruments – and is the essential principle for the full realization of all human rights. I will get back to this in proposing the human right to communication as a solidarity right in chapter 6.

In the International Bill of Rights alone we find seventy-six different human rights. In the totality of major international and regional human rights instruments, this number is even greater. With the tendency among human rights lobbies to put more and more social problems into a human rights framework, the number of human rights is likely to further increase. But because this proliferation of rights does not necessarily strengthen the cause of the actual implementation of human rights, various attempts have been made to establish a set of core human rights that are representative for the totality. One effort concluded in the existence of twelve core rights (Jongman and Schmidt, 1994):

1. The right to life
2. The right not to be tortured
3. The right not to be arbitrarily arrested
4. The right not to be discriminated against
5. The right to food
6. The right to health care

7. The right to due process of law
8. The right to education
9. The right to political participation
10. The right to fair working conditions
11. The right to freedom of association
12. The right to freedom of expression

These rights are the legal articulation of underlying moral principles and their implied standards of human conduct. The three basic principles and their related norms are as follows.

The principle of equality implies that there is equal entitlement to the conditions of self-empowerment. Among the essential conditions of people's self-empowerment are access to and use of the resources that enable people to express themselves, to communicate these expressions to others, to exchange ideas with others, to inform themselves about events in the world, to create and control the production of knowledge and to share the world's sources of knowledge. These resources include technical infrastructures, knowledge and skills, financial means and natural systems. The right to equality of treatment is most prominently provided in the non-discrimination clauses in the human rights catalogue. The prohibition of differential treatment based on special features of people is a central normative standard in the international human rights regime. The prevention of discrimination has received in the UN Charter and the International Bill of Rights more attention than any other single category of human rights (Skogly, 1992, 57).

The principle of freedom implies the norm that interference with human self-determination is inadmissible. This principle protects the autonomy of the human being. The freedom principle is found in human rights instruments in a range of applications. There is recognition of, among others, the freedom of movement, the freedom of religion and the freedom of peaceful assembly. Various international and regional instruments provide for the right to freedom of expression, the limitations on this right, the legitimacy of these limitations, and legal recourse against violations of these provisions.

The principle of security implies the norm that people should be protected against attacks upon their physical, mental and moral integrity. The right to the protection of privacy, as provided in Article 12 of the Universal Declaration of Human Rights and in Article 17 of the International Covenant on Civil and Political Rights, protects people against arbitrary interference with their private sphere and against unlawful attacks on their honour and reputation. The security principle also stands for the protection against intentional harm to both physical and psychological integrity.

Underlying the principles of equality, freedom and security is the principle of respect for human dignity. As the Ethical Guide for the Transformation of Mexico states, 'no one must be humiliated' (López Obrador, 2021, 211). The principle of respect for human dignity implies the right to be protected against acts of humiliation. Such acts encompass degrading treatment, depersonalization, dehumanization, taking away people's agency and self-respect or contributing to their sense of insignificance and powerlessness.

Article 19 of the Universal Declaration of Human Rights: Freedom of information

Freedom of information is a fundamental human right and is the touchstone of all the freedoms to which the United Nations is consecrated. The UNESCO Constitution, adopted in 1945, was the first multilateral instrument to reflect the concern for the freedom of information. To promote the implementation of this concern, a special division of 'free flow of information' was established in the secretariat in Paris. In 1946, the delegation of the Philippines presented to the UN General Assembly a proposal for a resolution on an international conference on issues dealing with the press. This became the UN General Assembly Resolution 59(1), which was adopted unanimously in late 1946. According to the Resolution the purpose of the conference would be to address the rights, obligations and practices that should be included in the concept of freedom of information. The Resolution defined the freedom of information as 'the right to gather, transmit and publish news anywhere and everywhere without fetters'.

In 1948, the United Nations convened an international conference on the Freedom of Information. Following the conference one of the articles of the Universal Declaration of Human Rights was dedicated to the freedom of expression. This became the well-known Article 19, which states, 'Everyone has the right to freedom of opinion and expression; this right includes freedom to hold opinions without interference and to seek, receive and impart information and ideas through any media and regardless of frontiers.' Crucially, the authors of Article 19 constructed freedom of information with reference to five components. The first is the classical defence of the freedom of expression. The second is the freedom to hold opinions. This provision was formulated as protection against the forced imposition of a political conviction (brainwashing). The third is the freedom to gather information. This reflected the interests of international news agencies to secure freedom for foreign correspondents. The fourth is the freedom of reception. This has to be understood as a response to the prohibition on receiving foreign broadcasts during the war. The fifth is the right to impart information and ideas. This is a recognition of the freedom of distribution in addition to the freedom of expression.

The formulation of Article 19 offered important guidance for later international documents that articulated the concern about freedom of information. Important illustrations are the European Convention for the Protection of Human Rights and Fundamental Freedoms (1950), the International Covenant on Civil and Political Rights (1966), the American Convention on Human Rights (1969) and the African Charter on Human and Peoples' Rights (1981).

The key normative provisions on freedom of information permit freedom of expression 'without fetters', but also bind this to other human rights standards. The clear recognition of the right to freedom of information as a basic human right in the UDHR was positioned in a standard-setting instrument that also asked for the existence of an international order in which the rights of the individual can be fully realized (Article 28 of the UDHR). This implies that the right to freedom of speech is linked with the concern for a responsible use of communication. This linkage laid the basis for a controversy in which one normative position emphasized the free flow principle, whereas another normative position stressed the social responsibility principle. The UNESCO Constitution already contained the tension between the two approaches. It accepted the principle of a free exchange of ideas and knowledge, but it also stressed the need to develop and use the means of communication towards a mutual understanding among nations and to create an improved factual knowledge of one another.

The free speech norm can, like most other human rights, be subject to limitations. This obviously implies the risk of abuse by those actors (and particularly governments) who are intent on curbing free speech. Limitations could easily erode the significance of a normative standard. For this reason, standards have been developed in international law to assess the permissibility of limitations. These must be provided by law. They must serve purposes expressly stated in international agreements (such as public safety or public order); they must be shown to be necessary in a democratic society; they must be strictly time limited and conform with the principle of proportionality.

Over the years, the international community and individual national governments have repeatedly tried – not very successfully – to establish governance mechanisms (rules and institutions) to deal with the 'freedom versus responsibility' issue. Illustrations are provisions in instruments such as the ICCPR (1966) and the UNESCO Mass Media Declaration (1978). The international community has not managed to develop a satisfactory answer to these questions. Striking a balance between the standard of freedom of information and the standard of responsible speech and national sovereignty turned out to be too difficult a challenge.

All countries have regulatory instruments that restrict the editorial contents media can disseminate. Such limitations relate to the interests of the state (national security, public order, safety), important social values (racism, obscenity) and individual rights (defamation, privacy). For example, most countries enact laws that aim to protect the individual from unjustified defamation. Such laws can obstruct media independence when in the balancing of free speech provisions and anti-defamation provisions the emphasis is too strong on the latter. Defamation law and jurisprudence can have a chilling effect on media independence if the burden is primarily on the defendant, if the law offers inadequate defence and if the risks of considerable punishment (prohibitive compensatory payments) lead editors towards the caution of self-censorship. US libel law, for example, was constitutionalized in a landmark US Supreme Court decision in 1964, *The New York Times* v. *Sullivan*.

This means that the highest priority is given by courts to the constitutionally protected free speech except in clear cases of intentional harm to the targets of a publication. This also implies that courts generally accept a good faith defence on the part of journalists, especially in cases where plaintiffs are public persons. It could be argued that such constitutionalization is particularly necessary in countries where existing laws on defamation do not provide a reasonable balance between freedom of expression and the protection of individual rights. Related to regulation on defamation is legislation on hate speech: laws that prohibit group libel, harassment and incitement. Such regulation is found in criminal codes (with criminal sanctions), civil codes (providing for civil remedies), anti-discrimination acts, ratification of international agreements and professional self-regulatory instruments. Rules on hate speech can be abused to limit media independence, and the question is whether indeed the justification of banning hate speech is used to suppress speech of one side in a conflict or to silence critics of the government.

Freedom of thought

During a long history of ambiguities and paradoxes in which humans lived in egalitarian societies with forms of democratic rule and in totalitarian states under the rules of despotism, the freedom to think and believe has been a fiercely contested domain. With the emerging human rights regime this freedom found its articulation in Article 18 of the Universal Declaration of Human Rights, in Article 18 of the International Covenant on Civil and Political Rights, in Article 13 of the International Covenant on Economic, Social and Cultural Rights, and in Article 5 of the International Convention on the Elimination of All Forms of Racial Discrimination (1965). Article 18 of the UDHR provides that 'Everyone has the right to freedom of thought, conscience and religion; this right includes freedom to change his [sic] religion or belief, and freedom, either alone or in community with others and in public or private, to manifest his religion or belief in teaching, practice, worship and observance.'

In the human rights regime this freedom has been a case of little disagreement: 'States have not considered it difficult to allow their citizens the freedom to think' (Scheinin, 1992, 263). On 9 November 1948, the Third Committee rejected all the proposed amendments and adopted the Article as a whole with thirty-eight votes to three, and three abstentions. Amendments proposed during the earlier sessions of the United Nations Human Rights Commission included the provision that religious observance should be subject to domestic law limitations (Soviet Union) and deletion of the 'freedom to change his religion of belief' (Saudi Arabia). During the drafting process it was stated by several delegates that the freedom of an inner state of mind should have an absolute character.

When formulating the freedom of thought in the International Covenant on Civil and Political Rights, the phrase 'to change one's religion of belief' met again with resistance and was changed to the freedom 'to have or adopt a religion or belief of his [sic] choice'. Legal analysts such as Karel Partsch (1981) interpret the compromise phrasing of the right to have or adopt a religion or belief as including the right to change one's religion. However, it can be argued that the change is not sufficiently strong in the case of religions that oppose the idea of religious apostasy. The UDHR provides better protection for the change of religion. Article 18 of the ICCPR also added a provision to subject the freedom to manifest one's religion or belief to 'such limitations as are prescribed by law and are necessary to protect public safety, order, health, or morals or the fundamental rights and freedoms of others'.[2]

The problem with the provision of such limitations is that they have often been used against free thinkers. Conditions such as public safety, public order and morals are commonly interpreted from the dominant elite's perspective. The UDHR (in Article 29) mentions morality and public order but leaves out public safety and puts limitations in the frame of a democratic society. It remains a problem that both Articles 18 (UDHR and ICCPR) do not address the complex relation between thought and its expression. Can the freedom of thought be separated from the freedom to express thoughts or act according to these thoughts? Should not human rights be treated as a totality? As Martin Scheinin writes, 'The right to freedom of thought, conscience and religion is a human right that cannot be realized separately, but only in the general context of human rights' (1992, 273). This means that the protection of the inner state of mind is linked with its effective realization in expression, action and organization. It is unsatisfactory and even painful to the thinker if he or she is not permitted to communicate thoughts to others and the thoughts can have no significance for others. Moreover, it is extremely difficult to hide thoughts that have any power over the mind.

Other issues include questions such as can people be forced to act against their conscience? And, how to solve the tension between the freedom to have discriminatory thoughts and the prohibition of discrimination. In the light of the exponential growth of information technologies, what if one day the inner state of mind can be read? It is important to note that Article 4 of the ICCPR recognizes the possibility for States Parties to take measures derogating from their obligations under the Covenant 'in time of public emergency which threatens the life of the nation', but also provides that no derogation may be made from a number of Articles. These exceptions include Article 18.

The protection of confidentiality of communicative behaviour

Article 12 of the UDHR provides that 'No one shall be subjected to arbitrary interference with his [sic] privacy, family, home or correspondence, nor to attacks on his honour and reputation. Everyone has the right to the protection of the law against such interference or attacks.' If everyone is entitled to this protection, it follows that the media should operate carefully when people's privacy is at stake. This does not mean that the media could never interfere with the private sphere or could never attack someone's reputation. The European Court of Human Rights has established in its jurisprudence that certainly in the case of public persons the expectation of privacy protection cannot always be upheld. In past years, many national courts of law have judged that people who are in the public eye and who lead very public lives will have to accept that there is a limit to their privacy. Yet the problem is that the UDHR refers to everyone and does not say that some may be excluded from this provision.

The consequence is that one may at least expect from the media that when the editorial choice is made to interfere with someone's private life they have good reasons and accept public accountability for their decision.

Actually, in the preparatory negotiations, before the text of Article 12 was adopted, there was some discussion on how interference should be qualified. Various words were proposed, such as unreasonable and abusive. Arbitrary was eventually preferred and was interpreted as 'without justification in valid motives and contrary to established legal principles' (Rehof, 1992, 190). Much discussion also addressed the question of whether attacks against honour and reputation should be included. Some delegates considered this provision so general and the terms so vague that they feared this might cause unwarranted violations of the right to freedom of expression. In the debate, the Cuban representative, for example, stated that some reputations might be justifiably attacked. Several delegates offered arguments to delete all qualifications, such as arbitrary and unlawful, because these were adequately addressed in Article 27 of the Declaration. The final version of Article 12 was adopted by twenty-nine votes in favour, seven against and four abstentions. The protection of privacy became a binding norm in international human rights law through its codification in the ICCPR, Article 17. This article states, '1. No one shall be subjected to arbitrary or unlawful interference with his [sic] privacy, family, home or correspondence, nor to unlawful attacks on his honour and reputation. 2. Everyone has the right to the protection of the law against such interference or attacks.' This article seeks to establish that there is legal redress against violations.

The right to privacy has a positive obligation on the part of States Parties to act towards the effective protection of their citizens. It reinforces the sovereignty of the individual over a person-bound sphere of no intrusion, which is inherent to the person and therefore moves with the person to sites such as the workplace. The mention of correspondence in the ICCPR article implies that the provision also regards the right to the protection of confidential communications. The privacy standard obviously needs balancing against other norms such as the right to seek information. This is further complicated by the recognition that the protection of privacy can also imply the right not to know. This is relevant in the context of genetic information and people's right not to know that they are certain to develop some hereditary disease. Despite these complications, a robust formulation of the standard is needed in the light of a growing violation of people's privacies in public communication. It has become common in many countries to obtain imagery of people without their consent and use this for entertainment purposes. An example is the use by TV stations of video material taken from rescue or emergency services. Privacy is also massively under attack in countries where electronic surveillance of people is widespread. In several countries, governments are preparing legislation to prohibit the encryption of telecommunication and data traffic. The professional confidentiality of journalists is also frequently under attack from governments. This threatens media independence, particularly when national laws or editorial statutes do not contain special regulatory provisions that recognize the need for professional secrecy.

Prohibition of discrimination

In the UDHR, Article 2 provides, 'Everyone is entitled to all the rights and freedoms set forth in this Declaration, without distinction of any kind, such as race, colour, sex, language, religion, political or other opinion, national or social origin, property, birth or other status.' Furthermore, according to the Declaration, 'no distinction shall be made on the basis of the political, jurisdictional or international status of the country or territory to which a person belongs, whether it be independent, trust, non-self-governing, or under any other limitation of sovereignty'. The essential principle here is equality. Differential treatment of people based on the features of individuals or groups conflicts with the basic notion of human dignity. Article 2 is intended to provide a general protection against discrimination.

The equality standard entered international law for the first time with the UN Charter. The earlier Covenant of the League of Nations (1919), for example, did not provide this protection. The Preamble of the UN Charter refers to 'the equal rights of men of women and of nations small and large'. During the drafting of the UDHR, discussion focused among others on the grounds of discrimination. One of the controversies was whether political opinion should be included. Also notions such as status, property and birth were objects of dissenting opinions. The phrasing 'without distinction of any kind, such as . . .' implies that the enumeration should not be read as exhaustive. One of the most important treaties to codify the non-discrimination standard is the International Convention on the Elimination of All Forms of Racial Discrimination (1965). The most contested (and for media most pertinent) provision of this Convention is found in Article 4, which concerns the dissemination of ideas based on racial superiority. The Convention has been ratified by an overwhelming majority of UN member states. Its Article 4 makes it obligatory for states to provide penal sanctions for incitements to racial discrimination. This goes beyond the mere prohibition of such incitements. However, the Convention provides for due regard to the free speech standard of the UDHR.

The International Covenant on Civil and Political Rights provides (in Article 20) for the incorporation into domestic law of the prohibition of the dissemination of ideas based on racial superiority, the incitement to racial hatred or advocacy of national or religious hatred. The formulation is that 'Any advocacy of national, racial or religious hatred that constitutes incitement to discrimination, hostility or violence shall be prohibited by law.' This calls for the prohibition of discriminatory statements, but does not necessarily make them a criminal act. During the preparatory negotiations for the Covenant, some of the discussion (in both the Third Committee of the General Assembly and the Commission on Human Rights) dealt with the fear that a provision prohibiting advocacy of hatred could be detrimental to free speech. Among the objections raised was the argument that governments could abuse the prohibition to impose prior censorship against expressions by certain social groups. Those arguing in favour stated that governments should prohibit expressions that incite to violent acts. It was also argued that legislation provides no solution for problems of national, religious or racial hatred. Other important provisions against discrimination are found in the Convention on the Elimination of All Forms of Discrimination Against Women (1979). Article 5 of this Convention demands the elimination of stereotyped representations of roles for men and women and of prejudices based on the idea of the inferiority or superiority of either of the sexes.

The human rights standard of equality is extended to take into account the real inequalities that prevail in most societies. It is essential to recognize that the realization of basic human rights in situations of social inequality may require preferential measures for the large group of disenfranchised people. In the real world, some individuals or groups have more access to information and communication media than others, and some are capable of silencing others very effectively. It needs to be acknowledged that social inequality exists on many different levels. Beyond rights to political equality, rights to informational and cultural equality should be taken equally seriously. The unequal distribution of technical infrastructures and sources of knowledge among the world's people obstructs the equal entitlement to the conditions of self-empowerment and should be considered a violation of human rights.

The equality standard has important implications for media performance. People have the right to the protection by law against prejudicial treatment of their person in the media. This right to be treated in non-discriminatory ways implies that reporting by the media should refrain from the use of images that distort the realities and complexities of people's lives, or fuel prejudice by discriminatory descriptions.

The presumption of innocence

The UDHR states in Article 11, 'Everyone charged with a penal offence has the right to be presumed innocent until proved guilty according to law in a public trial at which he [sic] has had all the guarantees necessary for his defence.' The right to the presumption of innocence as provided in Article 11 of the UDHR and in Article 14 of the ICCPR guarantees that people accused of a criminal offence are presumed innocent until proved guilty in a public trial. Presumption of innocence is a general standard found in many different societies. It protects the accused against prejudgements about the outcome of a trial. According to the jurisprudence of the European Court of Human Rights, this standard serves to impose the burden of proof on the public prosecutor. Although this rule applies primarily to public authorities, it would seem sensible to also apply it to professional communicators. This is all the more pertinent because news media worldwide may report about people who are accused of criminal acts, particularly if their crime has a sensational dimension (homicide, rape, grand-scale swindling) in a prejudiced manner.

Of course, there are different professional traditions in reporting crime and, as a result, varying degrees to which the accused are exposed. This ranges from mere initials to complete identity descriptions inclusive of a photo. In all such cases, there is the considerable risk that the public has already judged the accused before he or she appears before a court of law, and certainly in cases where the defendant is found not guilty, a lot of damage to name and reputation has been wrought by publications. If the media were to apply this standard strictly, they would have to use a large measure of caution in relation to the criminal cases and the people about whom they report.

The prohibition of war propaganda

Article 20.2 of the ICCPR imposes an obligation on states to incorporate the prohibition of war propaganda into domestic law. The formulation is, 'Any propaganda for war shall be prohibited by law.' However, the text does not say what kind of law this should be. There must be a prohibition, but states are free to choose the legal means they find appropriate. There was a lot of discussion in the Third Committee of the General Assembly, and the final text remained controversial. It was adopted by fifty-two votes in favour and nineteen votes against. There were twelve abstentions, and Australia,

Belgium, Luxembourg, the Netherlands, New Zealand and the United Kingdom made reservations.

One problem was that war was not defined. The discussions, however, clarified that reference was made to war of aggression. Concerns were also expressed about the use of propaganda because it could be abused by governments to limit free speech. When news media become part of propaganda campaigns, there is the great risk that they violate the prohibition of propaganda for war. During the 1991 Gulf War, and more recent international conflicts, several times the international news media crossed the line between mere disinformation, incidental distortions and intentional propaganda. This happened when the language and imagery used in the news media presented the war as inevitable and morally justified. Major international news media were engaged in the effort to sell the morality of the war effort. In the language employed by news media civilian killings became 'collateral damage', and saturation bombing became 'laying down a carpet'. Such deceptive concepts made the battlefield look as innocent as a theatrical stage. Herewith the reality of the war was obscured.

The prohibition of incitement to genocide

Article 3 of the 1948 Convention on the Prevention and Punishment of the Crime of Genocide (CPPCG) declares that among the acts that shall be punishable is 'direct and public incitement to commit genocide'. Article 4 states that 'Persons committing genocide or any of the other acts enumerated in Article 3 shall be punished, whether they are constitutionally responsible rulers, public officials or private individuals.'[3] In conflict situations, we may find that news media facilitate the dissemination of messages that incite people to perpetrate the crime of genocide. One of the world's most critical problems is the alarming and worldwide increase of ethnic conflicts. What is most troublesome in the rise of these conflicts is that most are characterized by the exercise of gross violence against civil populations. Contrary to classical warfare between armies, violence now increasingly targets civilians of the fighting parties.

At the dramatic core of ethnic conflicts is the grand-scale perpetration of crimes against humanity. As the term suggests, these are criminal acts that render their perpetrators enemies of the human species. For people to commit such crimes, they need to believe that the violent acts are right. In situations where crimes against humanity are committed, one usually finds a systematic distribution of hate propaganda and disinformation preceding the actual criminal acts of violence. The purpose of this is the promotion and justification of the social and/or physical elimination of certain social groups. Members of such groups are often first targeted as socially undesirable. They are publicly ridiculed, insulted and provoked (often in the media). Eventually the harassment may be put into action and the victims are subjected to physical violence, even murdered. In the propagation of elimination beliefs, the other is dehumanized, whereas the superiority of one's own group is emphasized. The propagandists convincingly suggest to their audiences that the 'others' pose fundamental threats to the security and well-being of society and that the only effective means of evading this threat is the elimination of this great danger. The use of violence in this process is presented as inevitable and thus not only acceptable, but absolutely necessary.

The elimination beliefs that motivate people to kill each other are not part of the human genetic constitution. They are social constructs that need social institutions for their dissemination. Such institutions include religious communities, schools, families and the mass media. Because crimes against humanity are unthinkable without elimination beliefs, the institutional carriers of such beliefs should be seen as enemies of the human species. This implies that all those who propagate beliefs in support of genocide, through whatever media, have to be treated as perpetrators of crimes against humanity. For the prosecution of crimes against humanity, there is an important historical precedent in the acts of the post-Second World War International Military Tribunal (IMT) at Nuremberg. Before and during the Second World War, Nazi politics aimed at the active persecution and extermination of Jews and used propaganda for the realization of these goals. In 1946, the IMT condemned racist propaganda as a crime against humanity. In doing so, the IMT recognized the genocidal potency of this sort of propaganda.

The IMT also determined the individual liability for the dissemination of racist propaganda and sentenced to hanging Nazi propagandist Julius Streicher for spreading eliminationist ideology. Streicher – member of the Nazi Party since 1921 – had been editor and publisher of *Der Stürmer* (a fervent anti-Semitic weekly) between 1923 and 1945 and had incited his German audience for twenty-five years to eliminate Jews. Streicher preached the total extermination of Jews and described them as vermin that deserved to be eliminated. The important aspect of his death sentence was that the IMT judged incitement to genocide, not exclusively the execution thereof, as a crime against humanity.

In 1948, the UN International Law Commission was already being asked to draft a statute for a permanent international criminal court for gross violations of human rights. It was not until 1989 – largely as a result of the Cold War – that UN member states Trinidad and Tobago succeeded in reopening the debate on such a court. In 1996, the international community finally began to take this matter seriously and the UN General Assembly decided on a concrete agenda for the establishment of an international criminal court. In July 1998, an international diplomatic conference convened by the United Nations in Rome produced a treaty establishing the permanent International Criminal Court (ICC).

The ICC deals with war crimes and crimes against humanity. In accordance with existing treaties, the Court has the mandate to prosecute those who incite to genocide by propagating elimination beliefs. In 2003, the ICC was established in the Hague and began its work – although several countries, among them the United States, refused to acknowledge the authority of the Court. The crucial element in the success of the ICC will be the readiness of national governments to cooperate in the arrest and prosecution of perpetrators under their jurisdiction. A difficult question concerns which actors should be prosecuted: only the elite decision makers or also the lower level executors? The IMT of Nuremberg was confronted with lower ranking officials who claimed they had only executed orders given by their superiors. The court established this rule: 'the fact that the Defendant acted pursuant to order of his [*sic*] Government or of a superior shall not free him from responsibility' (Roht-Arriaza, 1995, 65). The Tribunal asked whether the defendant had the choice to act differently (ibid.). This raises a host of challenging questions to judge the degree of culpability and complicity in media organizations for the dissemination of elimination beliefs. One of the problems that needs to be addressed is whether the prohibition of incitement constitutes an invitation to censorship by governments. The prohibition certainly raises the question of how the right to free speech can be given its due weight.

The problem is complicated because those who propagate hate speech do not commit physical acts of violence. They disseminate information and opinions. Even if the messages they distribute contain incitement to hate, the content is speech. The incitement to genocide is speech, hate speech, and albeit offensive and unpalatable, as such it is protected by the fundamental human right to freedom of expression. Therefore, the difficulty is that if the free speech rule is accepted as fundamental, the implication is that its coverage should be broad and the prohibition of this speech needs a robust justification. To deal with this, various approaches are possible. One is to provide proof that inciting speech leads to actual harm. The decisive criterion here is whether violent acts can be directly linked to the incitement. In a different approach, the question is whether there is the systematic and intentional dissemination of ideas and opinions that propagate the belief that a group deserves to be eliminated from social life. In this approach, it is not relevant whether incitement does indeed lead to acts of elimination because it can be argued that the historical record demonstrates beyond reasonable doubt that once people believe that the others deserve to die, the torturing and killing of them will soon follow.

Elimination beliefs constitute a grave and imminent danger in a society. In yet another approach, courts of law have reasoned that hate speech fundamentally undermines the rationales for the protection of free speech. These rationales are the search for truth, support for democracy and fostering of individual autonomy. However good this sounds, the hate propagandist could argue that it is precisely hate speech that is necessary to uphold these values. A more promising approach would take as a starting point the observation that human rights claim universal validity. Everyone can claim the right to freedom of expression. At the same time, everyone needs to recognize that everyone else also has this right. To incite to acts that undermine or nullify this right is unacceptable. The propagandist who incites through elimination beliefs to silence others – often in the extreme sense – denies them their right to freedom of expression. Herewith the propagandist loses the claim to this right.

One can only demand the right to freedom of expression as long as one recognizes and respects that others have the same right. The basic ground to claim a right is the recognition of similar claims made by others. This reciprocity is basic to human rights because these rights are always exercised in relation to others. When this reciprocity is denied, human rights can legitimately be restricted. This is an important argument because claims to freedom of expression cannot be restricted on the basis of the contents of expressions. Free speech implies that expressions may have undesirable, objectionable or immoral contents. Finally, it needs to be observed that hate speech is usually not propagated in a climate of freedom of expression. It is not correct to assume that hate speech is made possible because a society permits free speech. Incitement to hate and violence tends to occur in situations where media employees are under a great deal of pressure from governing elites and cannot freely express their opinions. In those cases, media professionals often operate under far-reaching and systematic state censorship. Although it appears logical to fight hate speech with the restriction of freedom of expression, it would be better to expand the freedom and independence of media workers.

The public exposure of prisoners of war

International humanitarian law can be described as human rights for times of armed conflict. An important instrument in humanitarian law is the

Third Geneva Convention relative to the treatment of prisoners of war (12 August 1949). In this Convention, we find the prohibition to expose prisoners of war to public curiosity. News media violate human rights when they publish pictures of captured prisoners of war and thus expose them to the public gaze. This standard has been violated by most of the world's news media, in various armed conflicts. Well-known examples of such violations were the pictures of the Al Qaeda suspects in Guantanamo Bay, and in Afghanistan, TV station Al Jazeera showing British soldiers taken captive, and the video fragments of Iraqi military taken as prisoners of war that were broadcast around the world by Western media.

Conclusion

The 1948 Universal Declaration of Human Rights is at the core of the international human rights regime. Through its key principles (dignity, equality, freedom and security) and the related norms (no humiliation, no discrimination, no interference with autonomous decision-making and no arbitrary intrusion into people's private lives) the Declaration provides normative guidance for human communicative behaviour. The UDHR is an important inspirational source for contemporary thinking on communication and human rights. It laid the ground for normative guidance to that central feature of living and flourishing together: communication. It provided the basis for what later would be called communication rights. In the spirit of the UDHR these rights are universal, inclusive of all people, and supranational. In the next chapter I want to explore what these communication rights mean for different actors such as women, children, migrants and indigenous peoples.

3   Communication Rights

Introduction

In this chapter I will look at what communication rights mean or could mean for women, children, indigenous peoples and migrants. In the section on indigenous peoples special attention will be given to the cultural rights – and especially the right to knowledge – that are articulated in international law instruments. This raises issues such as cultural identity and its protection. Following this I will discuss the controversial issue of a right to communicate and in this context also focus on the United Nations World Summit on the Information Society that took place in 2003 and 2005.

On the communication rights of women

In 1979, the UN General Assembly adopted the Convention on the Elimination of All Forms of Discrimination Against Women (UNGA Res. 34/180), which entered into force in 1981. Article 5 of the Convention provides that 'States Parties shall take all appropriate measures to modify the social and cultural patterns of conduct of men and women, with a view to achieving the elimination of prejudices and customary and all other practices which are based on the idea of the inferiority or the superiority of either of the sexes or on stereotyped roles for men and women.'[1] In Article 10, which addresses education, there is a strong plea for the elimination of any stereotyped content of the roles of men and women at all levels and in all forms of education.

The implementation body for the 1979 Convention is the Committee on the Elimination of Discrimination Against Women (CEDAW). Although the Committee was initially not authorized to receive individual complaints, this changed when it was decided at the UN World Conference on Human Rights in 1993 that the CEDAW 'should quickly examine the possibility of introducing the right of petition through the preparation of an optional protocol to the Convention'. This protocol was subsequently prepared, debated and accepted and enables the Committee (CEDAW) to process individual complaints about violations of the Convention. It entered into force in December 2000. In a formal sense, women are gaining more rights through the Convention and the Optional Protocol. However, this does not mean that in actual daily practice the quality of their lives is improving accordingly.

On an international level, it was noticeable during the 1990s that women's groups played a significant role in a series of world conferences, such as the 1995 UN Social Summit and more particularly in the same year's Fourth World Conference on Women in Beijing. Yet lofty ideas about the need for less gender-biased media content and for more prominent decision-making positions for female communicators are not easily translated into operational effects. Few women have attained decision-making positions in the media industry, and gender-based stereotyped representations still abound in the media around the world. This is strikingly clear in entertainment and advertising. Women's struggle for human rights in the media is made complicated because they often find themselves being accused of supporting pro-censorship positions. This makes it often difficult to explain to media practitioners 'that feminist advocacy and monitoring have nothing to do with censorship, but everything to do with freedom' (Gallagher, 2001, 19). As Gallagher continues,

> One of the biggest challenges for media advocates is to make clear what lies behind the concept of fair and diverse media portrayal, to explain that it is not just a matter of substituting a 'positive' image for a 'negative' one, however these might be defined. Media people have to grasp the complex problems and limitations in typical media representations of gender, to understand these are deeply embedded social practices and interpretations, and the part they themselves play in constructing those representations. (ibid., 20)

The Fourth World Conference on Women in Beijing (4–15 September 1995) gave in its Declaration and Program of Action special attention to the issue of images in the media, stating:

> Images in the media of violence against women, in particular those that depict rape or sexual slavery as well as the use of women and girls as sex objects, including pornography, are factors contributing to the continued prevalence of such violence, adversely influencing the community at large, in particular children and young people.[2]

The proposals for action address the need to increase the participation and access of women to expression and decision-making in and through the media and new technologies of communication, as well as the promotion of a balanced and non-stereotyped portrayal of women in the media.

On the European regional level, the Committee of Ministers of the Council of Europe adopted, on 25 September 1984, a Recommendation on Equality between Women and Men in the Media. Among the measures proposed are: encouraging adoption by the media organizations of positive action programmes to improve the situation of women, particularly at decision-making levels and in technical services; developing channels of education and training facilities for women in the new media technology; ensuring application of the principle of equal treatment; and encouraging the presence of women in an equitable proportion in media supervisory and management bodies.

On the communication rights of children

As observed earlier in this book, the core element of the international human rights regime is that fundamental rights and freedoms are considered universally valid for everyone. In short, the human rights regime that emerged after the Second World War represents the moral standard that 'all people matter'. This inclusive conception of human rights is a novelty in the history of international law because until 1945 there were always social groups excluded from the protection of the dignity and worth of the human person. However significant this change was, for some time in the early stages of the new regime there remained a category that was not included in 'all people', children. This changed on 20 November 1989, when the UN General Assembly unanimously adopted the Convention on the Rights of the Child (UNCRC).

With this Convention, children also became subjects of international law in their own right. Article 2 of the Convention recognizes that 'States Parties shall respect the rights set forth in the present Convention to each child within their jurisdiction without any discrimination of any kind'.[3] The Convention concluded a process that began with the preparations for the International Year of the Child in 1979. Although there had been declarations on the rights of children by the League of Nations in 1924 and by the United Nations in 1959, it was felt by some member states that these rights should be brought under the authority of binding international law. It is important to observe that the Convention today is ratified by the majority of the member states of the United Nations. The five basic principles of the Convention are non-discrimination, the best interests of the child, the right to life, survival and development, and the views of the child. The last mentioned principle is evidently essential to the field of information and communication because it expresses the notion that children have the basic

Communication Rights

right to be listened to and to have their views taken seriously. In line with this principle, the Convention has the following important provisions in the field of information and communication (taken from the child-friendly version that was produced by UNICEF, Canada).[4]

Article 12: 'You have the right to give your opinion and for adults to listen and take it seriously.'

Article 13: 'You have the right to find out things and share what you think with others, by talking, drawing, writing or in any other way unless it harms or offends other people.'

Article 14: 'You have the right to choose your own religion and beliefs. Your parents should help you decide what is right and wrong, and what is best for you.'

Article 16: 'You have the right to privacy.'

Article 17: 'You have the right to get information that is important to your well-being, from radio, newspaper, books, computers and other sources; Adults should make sure that the information you are getting is not harmful, and help you find and understand the information you need.'

Article 28: 'You have the right to a good quality education. You should be encouraged to go to school to the highest level you can.'

Article 30: 'You have the right to practice your own culture, language and religion – or any you choose. Minority and indigenous groups need special protection of this right.'

Article 42: 'You have the right to know your rights! Adults should know about these rights and help you learn about them, too.'

All these provisions mean that children's communication rights are today codified as legal standards for the international community. On the tenth anniversary of the Convention, in 1999, the Norwegian government and United Nations Children Fund, UNICEF, organized a meeting at which children, young people, media professionals and child rights experts discussed the development of children's rights in relation to media. From this meeting emerged the Oslo Challenge. The text of the Oslo Challenge is a call to action for governments, media professionals, media owners, children and parents to contribute to the realization of the rights as laid down in the Convention.

At the 2021 conference of the International Association for Media and Communication Research (in Nairobi and online) a project was presented that invited children from different parts of the world to speak about the future they want. The project was largely inspired by the observation that much has been said about communication rights for children without ever asking children themselves. This would seem to conflict with one of the basic principles of the Convention: the views of the child. How many children were consulted in the process of drafting the Convention on the Rights of the Child? Most of the thinking about children's rights had come from adults. Even child-friendly versions of relevant texts had been produced by adults. In all these well-intentioned efforts adults shaped the children's world in order to serve adult interests. The crucial challenge that the Convention on the Rights of the Child posed was for adults to listen to children, to consult them and to make them active partners in shaping humanity's common future. Living together on one common planet, we need to decide together what future this common place will have. This can only be done by interacting with one another and including all in this encounter. Especially the children, as they will inherit the planet.

On the communication rights of indigenous peoples

Indigenous peoples are commonly the descendants of people in territories that were conquered by colonial imperialist forces. Among them are Mayans, Aztecs, Māori, Australian aboriginals and the native peoples of North America such as the Inuit. Their great civilizations were often destroyed and the first owners of their lands became workers and slaves for distant kingdoms. They share a deep respect for their natural environment, for Mother Gaia. In spite of the efforts of the colonizers to extinguish, domesticate or convert them, they still form some 4 to 5 per cent of the world population and have often managed to preserve their language, religion, music, customs and rituals. The future of indigenous peoples will depend upon the recognition by the international community of their right to culture, which implies – beyond the participation in cultural life – the protection of cultural identity, and the need to conserve, develop and diffuse their cultures.

Communication rights are important tools for indigenous communities to express their concerns, to draw international attention to their exploitation by extractive economies, to contribute to the international community with their knowledge and wisdom, to say what others may not want to hear and to be listened to. They should have the right to acquire information and the skills necessary to participate fully in public deliberation and communication. They are also entitled to be treated with respect, according to the basic human rights standards of dignity, integrity, identity and non-discrimination. In cases of wilfully disseminated inaccurate or misleading and damaging information, recourse belongs to the right to fair representation. They should have the right to demand that media avoid violations like stereotypical images that distort the realities and complexities of people's lives. Indigenous people should have the right of access to communication channels independent of governmental or commercial control. To exercise their communication rights, they should have fair and equitable access to local and global resources and facilities for conventional and advanced channels of communication and to receive opinions, information and ideas in a language they normally use and understand. They should have the right to universal access to and equitable use of cyberspace. Their rights to free and open communities in cyberspace, their freedom of electronic expression, and their freedom from electronic surveillance and intrusion should be protected. On behalf of indigenous communities, Doreen Spence from Saddle Lake Cree Nation in Alberta, Canada, wrote:

> We have Elders, storytellers, knowledge keepers, healers, historians, leadership, and advocates. These voices have been silenced for hundreds of years, now is the time to listen and learn from them. We are stronger as a society when we learn and include everyone. Everyone must be treated respectfully and valued for their knowledge and contributions. Communication rights have not been respected for Indigenous Peoples. In most cases, the media have not advocated for First Peoples. We hardly ever see, hear, or read anything in the media about ourselves in a positive manner. (in WACC *Media Development*, 18 May 2022)

Cultural rights

Essential to the communication rights of indigenous peoples is the international discussion on the need to respect fundamental cultural rights. The International Bill of Rights (UDHR, ICESCR, ICCPR) proposed to articulate entitlements in the area of culture as basic human rights. The Universal Declaration of Human Rights (1948) formulated the right to culture in the sense of participation in cultural life. Article 27 provides that 'Everyone has the right freely to participate in the cultural life of the community.' Article 22 of the UDHR states that everyone is entitled to realization through national effort and international cooperation of 'the economic, social and cultural rights indispensable for his [*sic*] dignity and the free development of his personality'.[5] Participation in cultural life raises difficult questions about the definition of communities, the position of subcultures, the protection of participation rights of minorities, the provision of physical resources of access and the links between cultural access and socioeconomic conditions. Underlying some of these difficulties was the tension between the concept of culture as public good or as private property. These positions can be mutually exclusive, when, for example, historical works of art disappear in the vaults of private collections.

The inclusive nature of human rights ('everyone') implied a shift away from an elite conception of culture to a view of culture as 'common heritage'. Actually, the UNESCO Declaration on Race and Racial Prejudice (1978) founded the right to culture on the notion of culture as 'common heritage of mankind', which implies that all people 'should respect the right of all groups to their own cultural identity and the development of their distinctive cultural life within the national and international context' (Article 5).[6] In 1968 in Paris a UNESCO conference of experts considered the question of cultural rights as human rights. The participants concluded, 'The rights to culture include the possibility for each man [sic] to obtain the means of developing his personality, through his direct participation in the creation of human values and of becoming, in this way, responsible for his situation, whether local or on a world scale.'[7]

The Intergovernmental Conference on the Institutional, Administrative and Financial Aspects of Cultural Policies (convened by UNESCO in 1970) decided that the right to participate in the cultural life of the community implies the duty for governments to provide the effective means for this participation. The Recommendation aimed to 'guarantee as human rights those rights bearing on access to and participation in cultural life' and questioned the concentration of control over the means of producing and distributing culture.[8] Regarding the mass media, the text stated that they should not threaten the authenticity of cultures and 'they ought not to act as instruments of cultural domination'. The preamble proposed that measures are taken against the harmful effect of 'commercial mass culture' and recommended that governments 'should make sure that the criterion of profit-making does not exert a decisive influence on cultural activities'. There was strong Western opposition to various elements of the Recommendation, such as the mention of commercial mass culture in a negative sense, and the use of the term 'people at large'.

Several factors explain the emergence of cultural rights in the post-Second World War era. There was the rise of post-colonial states who searched their identity in the light of both imposed colonial standards and their own traditional values. The issue of cultural identity came up particularly strongly in the process of decolonization. The newly independent states saw the affirmation of their cultural identity as an instrument in the struggle against foreign domination.

Protection of cultural identity

The protection of cultural identity became an especially hot issue during the 1970s debates on cultural imperialism. In 1973, the Non-Aligned Summit in Algiers stated that 'it is an established fact that the activity of imperialism is not limited to political and economic domains, but that it encompasses social and cultural areas as well, imposing thereby a foreign ideological domination on the peoples of the developing world' (Press release, Non-Aligned Summit, 1973[9]). Cultural domination and the threat to cultural identity was also approached by the MacBride Commission. The Commission saw cultural identity 'endangered by the overpowering influence on and assimilation of some national cultures though these nations may well be the heirs to more ancient and richer cultures. Since diversity is the most precious quality of culture, the whole world is poorer' (MacBride Commission, 1980, 31).

In its recommendations the Commission offered very little prospect for a multilateral approach to the issue of cultural domination. Its main recommendation was for the establishment of national policies 'which should foster cultural identity. Such policies should also contain guidelines for safeguarding national cultural development while promoting knowledge of other cultures' (ibid., 259). No recommendation was proposed on what measures the world community might collectively take. The Commission proposed the strengthening of cultural identity and promoted conditions for its preservation, but left this to be implemented on the national level. The notion of cultural identity was used in a somewhat cavalier fashion without much critical reflection on its possible flaws. The report proposed the move from principles to substantive action assuming there was clarity on the principles. However, there never was clarity on the principle of cultural identity as it was based upon 'untenable assumptions about the possibility of isolating an identifiable set of features that would refer to "what a culture is" and the convergence of a series of characteristics into the recognizable identity of a collective subject' (ibid., 87).

It could be argued that identity is a typical modern phenomenon and the question whether the global spread of modernity threatens local cultural identities presumes evidently that there were stable, solid cultural identities before modern times. But did people ever possess this clearly defined individual and collective identity? From the historical record it would seem that in pre-modern times identity was not such a central concern. Local personal and communal definitions of identity are increasingly affected by events that take place at a distance and this may have caused increased cultural vulnerability. It could be that the global spread of modernity weakens identities, but also leads to the emergence of stronger but different local identities.

The cultural rights discussion took place against the background of the experience – particularly in the global South – with forms of cultural imperialism that often emanated from the global North. The phrase 'cultural imperialism' refers to the historical fact that in imperial expansion cultural forces have always played a significant role. Illustrations are Christian missionary activities, the introduction of Western-style school systems, forms of colonial administration, modern conceptions of professionalism and the use of European languages in overseas colonies.

The essence of 'cultural imperialism' is that in achieving the domination of one nation over other nations, cultural sources of power and influence are of key importance. The combination of culture and imperialism achieved common currency in academic and political debates on North–South relations in the late 1960s and continued to be a recurrent topic on academic and political agendas throughout the 1970s and 1980s, particularly in Latin America. The reference to 'cultural imperialism' played a central activist role in the 1970s debates at UNESCO on the creation of a New International Information Order, later to be renamed a New World Communication and Information Order. Towards the late 1980s cultural imperialism lost its evocative attraction and the academic and political discourse shifted to such notions as 'soft power', 'post-colonialism' and 'globalization'. The issue of production, distribution and accessibility of knowledge became a leading cultural theme.

Knowledge

An essential component of communication rights of indigenous peoples is the recognition of a basic human right to knowledge for all. Although there are several references in human rights instruments to the right to education and the right to share in scientific advancement, it is debatable whether they benefit the protection of the knowledge of indigenous peoples. One finds a frequent expression of concern in the literature about the global distribution of knowledge and, indeed, using a variety of indicators (such as enrolment in educational institutions or ownership of patents), it can be documented that the current global distribution is skewed. Research and development (R&D) is shifting further away from the global South as northern countries hold most of all patents worldwide. Even many patents granted in southern countries belong to residents of the countries of the north.

As Vandana Shiva has argued, 'Western intellectual property rights (IPR) regimes have emerged as major instruments of North–South inequality. Not only do they block technology transfer, they facilitate piracy of the indigenous knowledge and biodiversity of Third World countries' (2000, 501). The global IPR regime is upheld by an effective enforcement mechanism that has robust rules and enforcement procedures such as cross-retaliatory trade measures. The World Trade Organization (WTO) rules for the protection of intellectual property rights have a crucial bearing on the accessibility, distribution and innovation of knowledge. There is growing evidence that the legal provisions of the Trade-Related Intellectual Property Rights (TRIPS) Agreement (initiated in 1995) hamper the independent generation of knowledge in developing societies and facilitate the plunder of knowledge resources (e.g. biogenetic materials) from these societies. They make northern countries into the monopoly owners of knowledge. This includes knowledge that has evolved in indigenous cultures that depend on biodiversity for their survival: 'the hijack of their resources and knowledge through IPRs is the hijack of their lives and livelihoods' (ibid., 501).

The new regime pays little attention to the knowledge of indigenous peoples, making it vulnerable to claims by outsiders. As a result, in many impoverished countries local knowledge is used for the manufacture of very profitable drugs without the informed consent of the local people. At the heart of knowledge generation lies innovation. The WTO intellectual property rights regime creates serious obstacles to the process of innovation. It fences off new ideas, merely protecting the stacking of patents. Moreover, in recent years there has been no documentary evidence of increased trade in knowledge-goods or expanded foreign direct investment in high-tech areas as a result of the protection of intellectual property rights (IPRs). On the contrary, it can be argued that the IPRs impede the access of poor countries to knowledge, as they render technology transfer more expensive.

In this context it should be remembered that there is a hierarchy in types of knowledge, and in the present order of R&D investments, knowledge about slow-ripening tomatoes is more important than knowledge about new vaccines against malaria. This leads to the question: what knowledge should be targeted by the international human rights regime? In some ways, human societies have always been knowledge societies. Even so-called primitive traditional societies always had access to a large volume of detailed and pertinent local knowledge about their environment and its resources. Knowledge about specific properties of plants and animals and the functioning of ecosystems was, and still is, crucial to their survival. This knowledge is under threat across the globe as a result of developments in advanced biotechnology and as a consequence of legal systems for the protection of proprietary knowledge. If the international community were to formulate an international human right to knowledge, the following provisions would have to be part of it:

> *Everyone has the right to knowledge. This right includes the entitlement to access to knowledge. No one shall be arbitrarily deprived of sources of knowledge. The right to knowledge shall imply due recognition and respect for the rights and freedoms of others. All peoples and all nations have the duty to share their knowledge with one another. Knowledge is an essential human resource. For its development and application, it is vital that a proper balance be established between the ownership interests of knowledge producers and the public-good interests of knowledge users.*

The international community should come to the realization that the right to knowledge is far too important to be left to commercial forces only. The much-heralded knowledge societies will amount to little more than paper tigers if their governance is delegated to the marketplace. The market will produce and distribute knowledge according to people's purchasing capacities. A human rights-inspired system of governance will favour the availability of knowledge according to people's needs and aspirations. To quote Doreen Spence (whose sacred name is Bald Eagle Women Who Leads) again, 'We know what is best for our communities and we are rightfully positioned to assert ourselves, including many well-educated lawyers and advocates. Our voices will no longer be silenced but must be heard and supported' (WACC *Media Development*, 18 May 2022).

On the communication rights of migrants[10]

Although there are several instruments in international law that refer to migrants – albeit mainly to migrant workers – these instruments make no provisions for communication and information. Nowhere in international human rights law is the importance of communication rights for migrants recognized. Yet it can be argued that the international human rights regime should make provisions for communication rights as human rights for migrants. The ability to recognize oneself or one's place in society is essential, and is closely tied to the ability to enjoy the right to freedom of expression. A key example of this is the representation in education curricula. Article 26 of the Universal Declaration of Human Rights states that 'Education shall be directed to the full development of the human personality and to the strengthening of respect for human rights and fundamental freedoms. It shall promote understanding, tolerance and friendship among all nations, racial or religious groups.'

This presents noble ideals which could be strengthened through the imperative of representing the migrant as an inherent part of society through schooling – as a given rather than as a particularity. Recognition is essential for the migrant, whose identity is in flux and undergoing constant renegotiation. If migrants see themselves portrayed in the host culture, it may reassure them if they are 'viewed as part of a community [that] has a right to a past and is presumed to have a future' (Waters and Leblanc, 2005, 136). As a result of legitimation, this identity is more likely to be reconcilable with the culture and identity of the host country, and facilitate the migrant's ability to enjoy freedom of expression and communicate about her or himself. A primary role of schooling is shaping modern citizens and workers who are able to imagine themselves as members of a common political and economic community (ibid., 129), creating a sense of belonging and a propensity for cooperation with state authorities and institutions (Preston, 1991, 61). Establishing this sense of belonging is in the interest of both the state and the individual, yielding a sentiment of mutual recognition and connection, and facilitating the newcomer's appreciation and acknowledgement of her or his rights and responsibilities (Waters and Leblanc, 2005, 136).

Communication rights should be central to negotiations and debates on the protection of fundamental rights for migrants. Communication rights stand for empowerment, recognition of agency, respect for dignity and communicative freedom. Most importantly, they acknowledge the necessity of a two-way conversation, the importance of being able to demand accountability and the requirement that human rights commitments be met. As Fox explains, accountability mechanisms are crucial for ensuring 'the capacity or the right to demand answers and the capacity to sanction' (2007, 665). Migrants are often excluded from formal accountability mechanisms in their host state, and their ability to reach out to civil society organizations, independent media or political parties to denounce breaches of their basic rights should be facilitated.

Communication enables exposure and the ability to shame perpetrators for human rights breaches and demand that such ills be rectified (Fox, 2007; Hamelink, 2001). This, however, demands efforts to facilitate interactions in the language of the migrant when necessary, and a will to listen and to converse on the receiving end. The implementation of communication rights implies reciprocity and thus intercultural dialogue. Gruson argues that intercultural dialogue implies the transformation of host societies as well as migrant populations as an outcome of interaction (2017, 177). If the host society's imaginary is littered with stereotypes of the migrant, then the establishment of a unified society is difficult to achieve. Culture therefore is an essential means of facilitating communication and the undoing of such stereotypes.

The migrant issue

The sensitivity of many societies to the 'migrant issue' makes balanced discussion even more crucial, especially at a time when populism is on the rise in the West (Gruson, 2017, 178). Over the past two centuries, histories of migration have come to play a more and more significant role, meaning that a failure to recognize this history and communicate with migrants becomes mutually problematic for the national self-image and for the self-image of the migrant. Research by Bennett et al. suggests that migrants tend to be a 'topic' of discussion in the news rather than a prominent and legitimate voice in society. This also largely depends on the political agenda of the news media in question, diversity in the media workplace and journalists' specialization in migration issues (2013, 249). While acknowledging differences according to country, Bennett et al.'s study on news media reporting on migrants in six European countries from 2000 to 2013 identified three key tendencies: negative group labelling and vague group designations; negative or victimizing representations of migrants; and an under-representation of migrants' voices in quotes (ibid., 250). These create a 'positive in-group versus negative out-group dichotomy' (ibid., 250) and frame migrants as passive and voiceless. As Sayad (2004) states, the immigrant is someone who is spoken about at length in the public sphere, without her or his own voice necessarily being heard or sought out.

Most troubling in the representation of migrants is the idea that they pose a cultural, physical and security menace to the host country. This is particularly threatening to the communication rights of the migrant, who is reduced in the public imagination to a scary, barbaric figure with whom one does not negotiate – let alone converse. As Nail remarks, once the link has been made, discourses of migration and terrorism feed off and reinforce each other through the perpetuation of language and imagery of invasion, violence and danger (Nail, 2016, 165). Most notably, the 'migrant crisis' has been dehumanized by portraying those suffering it as a 'flood', a 'swarm' or even a 'tsunami' – threatening metaphors that provoke sentiments of invasion and fear.

For Nail, the convergence of the figures of the migrant and the terrorist has come about in contemporary politics because 'they expose a double crisis of the nation-state' (ibid., 165). First, an increasing population of migrants facing serious rights restrictions exposes a failure of liberal democracies to stay true to the noble ideas of equality and freedom that underpin them. Second, it reveals a failure to nurture social conditions favouring universal human rights, which consequently prove selective according to territorial, political, legal and economic borders (ibid., 159). In Nail's view, 'the international nation-state system (UN) and regional and national state system have failed to adapt to the cosmopolitan requirements of the migrant' (ibid., 162). Article 27 (1) of the Universal Declaration of Human Rights states that 'Everyone has the right freely to participate in the cultural life of the community.' However, when considered in relation to the migrant, this suggests a right to consume the culture of the host community as opposed to the right to communicate one's own. Gruson (2017) observes that migrants are often treated as though they have no culture of their own and should acquire that of the host society. The desire to enjoy the right to participate in the cultural life of the community is no doubt tied to the recognition of oneself in it, and the possibility of communicating oneself within that space.

Identity and language

The right to protect cultural identity includes the respect for people's pursuit of their cultural development and the right to free expression in the language(s) of their choice. Language can be considered the linchpin of participation in public and political life. Migrants have the right to a diversity of languages. This includes the right to express themselves and have access to information in their own language, and the right to use their own languages in educational institutions funded by the state. Pradip Thomas states that 'if we were to peel off the layers of meaning, unpack communication rights, the first layer is that of language, the right to language – the right to use, maintain, preserve, impart, protect language' (2011, 70).

Language is inherently linked to culture and identity. Therefore, both the acquisition of the host language and the preservation of the home language become central to the debate. This discussion is at the heart of European debates on how best to integrate migrant youth (Grande et al., 2012). While in most Western European countries such as the Netherlands it is preferred – and considered the best means for integration – to exclusively teach migrants the host language, in Southern European countries more of an intercultural dialogue tends to be pursued; for example, in Italy Standard Arabic is offered as a second language in some schools (ibid., 7). An inability to communicate linguistically hinders the ability to participate at all. As Thomas warns, 'language is ironically also the means used to silence the other and by doing so make people less than human' (2011, 70). Although Article 21 (1) of the UDHR declares that 'Everyone has the right to take part in the government of his country, directly or through freely chosen representatives', this is hard to fulfil if you don't speak the language.

The right to communicate

Discussing the communication rights of different social actors it becomes clear that basic to all of them is a fundamental right to communicate. This needs to be discussed here as it is a much contested issue. After earlier debates in the late 1960s and early 1970s the proposal for a 'right to communicate' resurfaced during the preparations for the United Nations World Summit on the Information Society (WSIS) in 2003 and 2005. In 1969, Jean d'Arcy published an article titled 'Direct broadcast satellites and the right to communicate' in which he criticized the conventional focus on the content of communication rather than on the communication process. He argued that the future of global electronic communication would need a new regulatory regime based upon the recognition of a new human right. He argued for a right that would entail existing communication rights, but would go beyond them in order to offer a level of protection appropriate to the new forms of communication made possible by technological innovation. He wrote, 'the time will come when the Universal Declaration of Human Rights will have to encompass a more extensive right than the right to information. . . . This is the right of men [sic] to communicate' (ibid., 14).

Driving this new approach was the observation that the provisions in human rights law such as Article 19 of the UDHR do not adequately deal with communication as an interactive process. Article 19 addresses one-way processes of seeking, receiving and disseminating information and ideas. It deals with communication in the sense of 'transfer of messages'. This reflects an interpretation of communication that has become rather common since Shannon and Weaver (1949) introduced their mathematical theory of communication. The theory described communication as a linear, one-way process. This is, however, a very limited and somewhat misleading conception of communication, which ignores that in essence 'to communicate' refers to a process of mutuality, making common or creating a community. The word 'communication' connotes the dissemination of messages (for example by the mass media), the consultation of information sources (for example in libraries or on the World Wide Web), the registration of information (for example in databases) and the conversations that people participate in. In international human rights law the conversational mode has received only limited attention. Proponents of a right to communicate argued that communication in the interactive sense (as in conversations) needs special protective and enabling provisions.

Human rights law – in both Article 19 of the UDHR and Article 19 of the International Covenant on Civil and Political Rights (ICCPR) – covers the fundamental right to freedom of opinion and expression. These articles are undoubtedly an essential basis for forms of public communication but they do not directly pertain to interactive processes. They protect the freedom of the orator in Hyde Park's Speakers' Corner to whom no one has to listen and who does not necessarily engage in interaction with anyone in his or her audience. These articles also refer to the freedom to hold opinions. This pertains to opinions inside your head that may serve communication with yourself but does not bear any necessary relation to communication with others. The articles mention the right to seek information and ideas. This provides among others for the freedom to gather news. This is highly important but does not provide for processes of exchange. The articles also contain the right to receive information and ideas: this is in principle also a one-way process. The fact that people can receive whatever information and ideas they want does not imply they are involved in an interactive process. Finally, there is the right to impart information and ideas. This refers to a form of dissemination that goes beyond the mere freedom of expression, but, again, it does not pertain to interactive processes. In sum, all the provisions in the 'freedom of information' articles in international human rights law address one-way processes of transport, reception, consultation and allocution, and do not pertain to the two-way interactive process of conversation. Even if the news and entertainment media had maximum freedom of expression and offered the fullest possible access to information sources, this would not guarantee that people were enabled to participate in societal dialogues.

The potential for everyone to participate in an interactive process of communication beyond borders came within reach with satellite technology however. It led d'Arcy (1969) to argue that the conception of communication that underlay the formulation of the freedom of information in Article 19 was inadequate in the light of new developments. Whereas the introduction of radio had triggered Bertolt Brecht in 1932 to write his critical 'theory' on radio, in which he argued for its use to encourage listeners to become producers, for d'Arcy it was the advent of direct broadcast satellites that triggered his imagination on the potential uses of this new technology. He saw now the possibility for 'a truly democratic mode of communication free from the dominance of large public and private organizations and regulatory structures' to emerge, since it would function beyond the control of traditional economic and technological control mechanisms (McIver and Birdsall, 2002, 10).

From the early 1970s, the 'right to communicate' (in the interactive sense) was included in UNESCO's programme but over the following decades no consensus could be reached between protagonists and opponents. In the years of debate that followed, UNESCO came to be the forum of one of the great showdowns on the Cold War front, when the US and the UK quit their membership in the aftermath of the reporting by the UNESCO International Commission for the Study of Communication, better known as the MacBride Commission (1980). The right to communicate vanished from the agenda of international politics – to be mentioned mostly only sotto voce and off the record to avoid ideological conflicts breaking out again.

One of the most important initiatives that explicitly picked up the concept again was the Campaign for Communication Rights in the Information Society (CRIS), which was founded on the eve of WSIS. An alliance of NGOs had collaborated in order to use the right to communicate to enhance other human rights and to strengthen the social, economic and cultural lives of people and communities. In this respect the Information Society, it was argued, should be based on principles of transparency, diversity, participation, social and economic justice, inspired by equitable gender, cultural and regional perspectives (Lee, 2004, 9).

The World Summit on the Information Society (WSIS)

The summit hosted by the International Telecommunication Union (ITU) gave renewed impetus to the debate on the right to communicate. The preparatory conference (Prepcom II) in February 2003 in Geneva became the centre of a heated debate (Kuhlen, 2003) on communication rights. The renewed attention on the right to communicate was sparked by the emerging reality of global interactive technologies and the expansion of societal networking. These developments seemed to call even more urgently than at the time of d'Arcy's (1969) writing for a shift from the prevailing distribution paradigm to an interaction paradigm. This shift would require a form of human rights protection for the reality of communication as conversation.

In this spirit, a draft declaration on the right to communicate was proposed by representatives of civil society as a discussion document.[11] Against this draft text, representatives of the World Press Freedom Committee protested that a right to communicate would serve the purpose of muzzling the freedom of the media. This opposition was inspired by the fear that a right to communicate would revive the 1970s Third World aspirations to create a New International Information Order. Also from within the human rights community the draft declaration was so forcefully attacked that the CRIS movement decided to put the right to communicate (temporarily) on the backburner. Instead, the movement focused on the more acceptable, although also contested, notion of communication rights. During the summit in December 2003 the Draft Declaration on Communication Rights (often referred to as the Hamelink Declaration) was presented to and adopted by individuals and organizations present at the Communication Rights conference convened by CRIS. In the end, talk about relevant principles such as inclusion or participation remained limited to references to deliberately undefined standards, rendered inconsequential due to a lack of contextualization in existing governance structures concerning media and telecommunication as well as the lack of consensus on their implementation (Hamelink, 2004a).

If there is a common denominator to most of the existing work on the topic, it would be that the content and reach of communication rights would go far beyond what is addressed by the traditional freedom of expression and information. The aim of formulating such rights would be to enable individuals and communities to have their views heard. The arguments for this position mostly build on the recognition that certain minimum enabling conditions are necessary to give meaning to any freedom. Communication rights would be rights to 'inform, to be informed, to active participation in communication, equitable access to infrastructure and information, and privacy' (Richstad and Anderson, 1981, as cited in McIver et al., 2003, 8).

Despite numerous efforts to clarify the content and delineate the boundaries of the discourse on communication rights more clearly, there is an impasse that has persisted to this day when it comes to finding a 'definition embracing both universality and legalistic precision' (Birdsall, 2006, 41). Enforcement, then of course, remains the big problem, since moral declarations tend not to be a powerful tool to ensure compliance in the absence of strong implementation mechanisms (Hamelink, 2004b, 211). Still, activists who today plead for the recognition of communication rights are aware of the problems of codifying some aspects of those rights, and recognize the value of alternative standard-setting mechanisms. So, for example, the People's Communication Charter, drafted with a similar intention as the much criticized Draft Declaration on Communication Rights, states that it 'aims to bring to cultural policy-making a set of standards that represents rights and responsibilities to be observed in all democratic countries and in international law' (Fuller, 2007, 215).

As became increasingly clear – in public debate and in private conversation – part of the resistance was inspired by the realization that the right to communicate goes beyond the conventional entitlement to freedom of speech, and questions what use it is to speak if no one listens. Reflecting on this question, a further new idea emerged: there should be a 'right to be heard', in the sense of the human entitlement to be taken seriously and to have one's views listened to. Providing arguments for a right to be heard still leaves us with the question of how effective the entitlement to be listened to can be when it is encoded in the format and language of a legal claim. A legal claim implies remedial measures such as prison terms or compensatory payments and related institutional structures such as courts and lawyers. Moreover, if the legal claim is grounded in human rights law, its working must be universal and reciprocal. This means that the claim extends to all (in human rights discourse 'all people matter' and no one can be excluded) and its reciprocity means that all people have a legal obligation to listen to all other people. Is it realistic to expect that this can effectively work in society at large? Can politicians be forced by law to take the citizen seriously?

Final declaration of the WSIS

In the concluding statement the participating governments in the WSIS proclaimed that:

> We reaffirm, as an essential foundation of the Information Society, and as outlined in Article 19 of the Universal Declaration of Human Rights, that everyone has the right to freedom of opinion and expression; that this right includes freedom to hold opinions without interference and to seek, receive and impart information and ideas through any media and regardless of frontiers. Communication is a fundamental social process, a basic human need and the foundation of all social organization.[12]

And in another paragraph, participants confirmed their commitment to the provisions of Article 29 of the Universal Declaration of Human Rights that 'Everyone has duties to the community in which alone the free and full development of his [*sic*] personality is possible . . . [and that] rights and freedoms may in no case be exercised contrary to the purposes and principles of the United Nations.' The participants in the WSIS concluded that 'we shall promote an Information Society where human dignity is respected'.[13] To expect a more robust statement by the international community on communication rights is not realistic, as the issue is at present very sensitive, contested and polarized.

Crucial communication rights are currently (2020/22) in many countries under duress because of political measures during the Covid-19 pandemic, and on the Russia/Ukraine war establishment narratives have come to dominate the public discourse. Often presented in a highly polarizing way they leave little space for those who listen to the arguments of opposing sides, and bring to the fore doubts about the veracity of official information. The rapid increase of 'fact-checkers' to expose fake news – not in the mainstream media but in the alternative platforms – holds bleak prospects for freedom of speech or even freedom of thought. Moreover, the interests of big-tech companies tend to direct and censor information flows.

Communication rights as cultural rights are more effectively enforced as trading rights than human rights. The protection of intellectual property rights and privacy rights has become a rapidly growing and profitable global business, as discussed earlier. The increasing commercialization of knowledge impedes greater equality in access to and use of knowledge. Communication rights imply the preservation of public space, which today is withering away and replaced by private platforms. The rise of authoritarian governments and hierarchical administrative structures does little to encourage the realization of the right to be heard and to participate in public debate. Moreover, with increasing numbers of journalists killed worldwide and with whistleblowers such as Snowden and Assange in exile or jail, the fragility of communication rights is all too obvious.

Conclusion

The international human rights regime that developed after the Second World War provided a broad range of rights, freedoms and prohibitions in relation to communicative behaviour. These provisions are promoted and protected as a special category of rights that are distinguished from other rights as 'human rights'. This means that they are seen as fundamental to the dignity and worth of human beings and as tools for freedom, justice and peace in the world (as stated in the Preamble to the UDHR). The major implication of this is that violations of communication rights are a concrete and imminent danger to the well-being of humanity. It makes communication rights also part of a debate in which basic concepts such as freedom and equality mean different things to different people. The provisions of communication rights as human rights are for some the apex of morality and for

Table 3.1 Communication rights, provisions[14] and violations

Rights	Treaty provisions	Examples of violation
Freedom of thought	Article 18/UDHR	Mind control, propaganda
Freedom of speech	Article 19/UDHR	Censorship, threats to journalists
Privacy	Article 12/UDHR	Surveillance, data mining
Incitement to genocide	Article 3/CPPCG	Hate speech, racist propaganda
Against discrimination	Article 2/UDHR	Ethnic profiling, gender prejudice in media and social platforms
Against war propaganda	Article 20.1/ICCPR	Enemy images, one-sided reporting
Presumption of innocence	Article 11/UDHR	Judging suspects in media before trial
Cultural rights	Article 27/UDHR	Suppression of cultural expression

others, mere empty slogans. In our discussion on communication rights we have seen both the provisions in international human rights law as well as the threats to these provisions. Table 3.1 presents a summary of these.

Communication rights are important tools for the self-empowerment of – among others – women, children, indigenous peoples and migrants. They strengthen the constructive power of communication. However, when the international community had the opportunity – through the WSIS – to establish a robust framework to protect communication against destructive political and economic powers, it failed to live up to the challenge.

In the next chapter, I want to see how robust the provisions on communication rights really are as they confront new challenges and existential risks.

4 Challenges and Communication Rights

Introduction

In this chapter I want to explore the challenges that advancements in information and communication technology, and the loss of biodiversity pose for the ways in which communication and human rights relate to each other. In the light of these challenges, how do communication rights strengthen the constructive power of communication and protect communication against destructive political and economic powers?

Challenges of technology

The provisions in the international human rights system that relate to communicative behaviour were all formulated before we realized that humanoid robots might become our conversational partners. The communication rights and freedoms of the twentieth century were also established before the Internet emerged, before digital networks expanded exponentially, before the 'frightful five' (Apple, Amazon, Facebook, Google and Microsoft) came to control most of the global communication infrastructure, before the surveillance society expanded beyond Orwell's fictive vision, before cyberattacks became a daily reality and before humans became mobile-addicts fearful of being 'out of the loop'. There is undeniably an increase in digitally operated services, digital dependency and the vulnerability of societies to the abuse of digital technology by governments and organized crime. Yet, the question is whether these 'new' processes require a special set of human rights for the protection of human dignity, equality, freedom and security. Our engagement with seductive notions such as a 'new' digital age raises some red flags. The notion of 'new' should be treated with some caution.

Technology is always the further development of what was already there. So we had better be careful with ideas of new technologies and new societies. Most of what we call new was there before. There can be little doubt that digital expansion is reality for the rapidly growing global online community, although it is still unequally distributed around the world. The notion of 'new' suggests not only advances in information and communication technology, but also changes in human behaviour. This does reflect the thinking that technological developments determine societal outcomes. This crude determinism, however, finds no substance in human historical realities. The 'new' media may be free from the oligopolistic control of the barons of culture, the mogul gatekeepers of the news or the few who belong to a ruling class, an aristocratic elite or a religious priesthood. The 'new' media may have the many at the helm, but there is no historical evidence that the many will be less inclined to the escalation of evil than the few.

There is today an increasing concentration of control over the infrastructure of global communication. The five most powerful consumer technology companies are Amazon, Apple, Facebook, Alphabet (parent company of Google and YouTube) and Microsoft. They own most of the world's valuable platforms that are essential for what individuals and corporations do with the Internet. There may be very innovative start-ups but in all likelihood they will not replace the Big Five and will exist alongside them or be acquired by them, and in any case, the apps required to download their contents have to be bought from the app stores of Apple or Google. Then, in the global entertainment industry, two companies currently call the shots – Netflix and Disney. The core impediment to the realization of communication rights are the infrastructural conditions. The carriers, transporters, producers and processors that make up the global communication infrastructure are organized around profit-making, with their primary responsibility to private stakeholders. They operate large-scale economies that inevitably create oligopolies (if not monopolies) and are not driven by the collective interest of human flourishing. They trade cultural goods and services as any other commercial commodity. This infrastructure is unlikely to achieve equality, freedom and security in global communication. The 'new' media may indeed bring about more freedom to foster, express, disseminate and receive ideas, but there is no guarantee that the largely expanded and differentiated number of media producers will act more responsibly than the media moguls of the past.

In the writings of social thinkers such as Di Fiori, Lessing, Hegel, Comte, and contemporary authors on the information revolution (such as Toffler, Negroponte and Gates), history continues in progressive steps. The belief is that humanity is on the path to harmony and peace through enlightenment, rationality, and especially through science and technology. However, Auschwitz and Hiroshima showed that there is no linear progressive process. History is circular and moves around the same core: human possibility. The suggestion of moral progress is misleading.

The human species is caught in recurrent waves of grossly immoral behaviour and sophisticated moral reflection. This kind of cyclical conception is attractive. Reality is not only cyclical though, but also linear. Newscasts have been largely repetitive but there were always moments when new information added something to our worldview and lifted our views out of their fixed groove for a moment. This is the experience of our everyday life (Holl, 1985). Our lives follow a linear structure from birth to death and yet we experience cyclical patterns throughout life. In all our lives there is so much more of the same, like in the cyclical patterns of vacations, birthdays, annual Christmas dinner or feeding the ducks. Similarly, between the beginning and the end of our lives, we experience the cyclical movement of the seasons in many parts of the world. As much as the narratives of the Abrahamic religions (Judaism, Christianity and Islam) tell us about linear developments from a beginning to an end time, the Book of Ecclesiastes (1:9) warns us: 'That which is, is that which will be. And that which has been done is that which will be done. So there is nothing new under the sun.' However, if we believed that time was merely cyclical, we would exclude the possibility of human improvement. This would make such activities as promotion and protection of human rights meaningless.

Challenges of the Internet

The Internet is a good example of the mixing of cyclical and linear developments. To a large extent this communications infrastructure continues what earlier technologies did: transmitting data and information, storing information, providing access to information and offering communication channels. At the same time, there is a linear progression to a dark side of the technology. The enormous potential for digital manipulation of sound, text and images raises questions as to the authenticity of communications. Can anything digitally produced or reproduced be trusted? In cyberspace, people can communicate with each other through a 'persona' that they invented themselves. The anonymity makes lying easy and difficult to detect.

Deceptive behaviour in cyberspace is not a new issue, but it does give extra urgency to the problem of 'moral distance'. The greater the distance to potential victims, the easier it is for people to inflict harm from which they would refrain in face-to-face situations. The classical illustration is the bomber pilot who drops his lethal loads from such great distances that he never sees the consequences and may liken the experience to playing a computer game. Information and communication technologies (ICTs) tend to reinforce effects in exponential ways. Data can be copied, modified and distributed easily and quickly on a grand scale. The speed of digital communication does not create new forms of immorality but makes it possible to commit immoral acts so fast one hardly notices. Moreover, whatever one wants to communicate, it is easy to reach an almost unlimited number of recipients. The question is, do the new possibilities of the Internet such as weblogging, Facebook, Twitter, LinkedIn, YouTube, Pinterest, eBay, Yahoo, Flickr and so on pose challenges to the currently established rights and freedoms?

Since 2000, worldwide Internet access has increased by more than 500 per cent to reach a total of 2.3 billion users, leading to a rather rapid change in how we approach daily life, as well as a greater divide between those with access and those without. Nearly 70 per cent of the world's population still live without Internet access. Of those who are able to connect, the OpenNet Initiative estimates[1] that nearly half of them access a 'filtered' or censored Internet. Global network technology poses, according to Castells, an important challenge:

> The Internet networks provide global, free communication that becomes essential for everything. But the infrastructure of the networks can be owned, access to them can be controlled, and their uses can be biased, if not monopolized, by commercial, ideological, and political interests. As the Internet becomes the pervasive infrastructure of our lives, who owns and controls access to this infrastructure becomes an essential battle for freedom. (Castells, 2001, 277)

Another challenge identified by Castells is the need 'to acquire the intellectual capacity of learning to learn throughout one's whole life, retrieving information that is digitally stored, recombining it, and using it to produce knowledge for whatever purpose we want' (ibid., 278).

It is also important to note that there is a dark side to the Internet. In his book *The Net Delusion* (2011) Evgeny Morozov has demystified the Internet and argues that the freedom of the Internet is a delusion and that cybertechnology has not democratized the world. Indeed, according to Morozov, the Internet is a popular tool of repressive governments, as it can be used for surveillance, propaganda and censorship. He also names Facebook and Twitter as very helpful tools to the cause of oppressive governments.

The Internet governance challenge

Many countries have instituted advanced social media surveillance programs and a reasonable estimation would be that most Internet users are being monitored. This issue has now been debated in global meetings for some time and the main contending parties are governments that want legal control over the Internet, intergovernmental organizations that want control by international agreements, corporations that prefer market control, communities of Internet users that strive towards self-regulation, and the designers of the Internet architecture that argue for technological control over the Internet (van Dijk, 2012, 143).

A key issue in Internet governance is posed by the question of net neutrality. This fundamentally addresses the openness and security of the Internet. 'The principle of net neutrality holds that all Internet content is treated equally and moves at the same speed over the network' (ibid., 87). One complicating factor in the debate on net neutrality is that 'those in favour of net neutrality can also be advocates of more regulation to protect Internet privacy' (ibid., 142).

Another challenge relates to the question of the democratic nature of arrangements through which public choices about the governance of the Internet will be made. Democratic arrangements imply that there is the broadest possible participation of all people in processes of public decision-making. The issue of the democratization of public decision-making in the fields of information and communication has been on the civil society agenda in the recurrent debates on the Right to Communicate, in the initiative for a People's Communication Charter (in 1992) and in the non-governmental contributions to the United Nations World Summit on the Information Society (WSIS) (2003 and 2005).

A democratic arrangement has rules, procedures and institutional mechanisms to secure public accountability. The principle of accountability logically implies the possibility of remedial action by those whose rights to participation and equality may be violated. Only through effective recourse to remedial measures can fundamental standards be implemented. If those who take decisions engage in harmful acts, those affected should have access to procedures of complaint, arbitration, adjudication and compensation. The process of establishing the responsibility for decisions taken, and demanding compensation for wrongs inflicted, secures the egalitarian nature of the democratic arrangement. The accountability issue regards all Internet users. The current tendency to give up rights to free speech and privacy in exchange for either promises of security or low tariffs may have dramatic effects on the future use of cyberspace. Choices about future Internet rules and practices have to be made under the condition of uncertainty. Effects in the future of choices made today are unknown. The future is open, because we have no information about it. If we had such information, there would be no real choice. A serious human rights assessment would point to the risks of realizing choices that may not have fully foreseeable side effects and that may be irreversible once they are implemented. The possibility of error in public choice making is unavoidable. Therefore, the readiness to learn from past errors and to revise choices already made is essential to the respect for human dignity.

The surveillance challenge

Digitization renders surveillance easy and attractive. It facilitates what governments have always wanted to do: collect as much information as possible about those they govern. Because of technological limitations, this was always a difficult job. However, recent technological innovations have made grand-scale spying much easier. One consequence is that the trading of surveillance technology from rich to poor countries has become an attractive sideline for the world's arms traders. Digitization facilitates the monitoring of all communications, be it through fax machines, telephones (particularly mobile phones) or computers. It has become technically relatively easy to register all traffic that uses Global System for Mobile communication (GSM) cellular telephones. Digital bugging devices have become so small that Japanese scientists claim they can build them into cockroaches. Miniature digital cameras and microphones can be constructed in smoke detectors, alarm clocks, hearing aids, ballpoint pens and spectacles.

Digital technology also makes an unprecedented invasion into personal privacy a daily reality. In many countries, electronic surveillance is mushrooming. As Gumpert and Drucker (1998, 409) noted: 'the sanctity of privacy has been eroded by the increasing intrusion of the technology of surveillance' – through video cameras in public spaces, bugging of telephone calls, credit card firms, scanners in supermarkets, 'cookies' on the World Wide Web and international spy satellites. Most important, however, is the development of increasingly intelligent software for the registering and filtering of information. Using so-called self-learning neural networks, intelligent agents search through vast databases for the specific information that creates complete commercial and political profiles of the objects of their search. Equipment for surveillance and spying becomes cheaper all the time. Among the big buyers are employers who want to control their employees. In many countries, the permanent electronic surveillance of the workforce has become standard practice. This ranges from bugging telephone and email traffic to video cameras in toilets to keep a check on the use of drugs, tracking employees' movements through smart badges, sensors to monitor whether workers wash their hands after visiting the toilet, and monitoring the use of inappropriate websites. In many of the digitally advanced countries, the state has a strong desire to monitor civil electronic communications.

The crucial argument is that, although this violates people's privacy, it is inevitable to guarantee national security. As state institutions can compose rather precise profiles of their citizens' communications traffic, the inequality in power relations between states and citizens increases. The civil claim to the confidentiality of personal communications is violated, and the principle of information security is seriously eroded. The permanent surveillance of people hampers their free participation in communication and information traffic. When personal data about individuals are collected, processed, stored and retrieved without their consent, their information security is under threat. Information security also means that people are free to determine what information about themselves they want to share with others. The standard implies that others cannot gather information about people without their consent. In a decent society, citizens are aware of those who collect information on them, as well as how, where and for what purpose. Although there are important cultural variations in the appreciation of privacy, we can observe that, in almost all societies, people show the desire to have a small space where they can withdraw from the gaze of others. Also, most people would prefer to keep at least some of their personal secrets to themselves.

The digital trace

The protection of personal data has always been a difficult challenge, but with recent developments such as the use of algorithms on the Internet, the effort has become futile. Information about how people use the Internet is extensively collected through a variety of means (such as the so-called 'cookies'), and each act in cyberspace contains the real danger of privacy intrusion. Using electronic mail, for example, inevitably implies a considerable loss of control over one's privacy unless users are trained in the use of encryption techniques and as long as these are not prohibited by law. By engaging in cyberspace transactions, we leave a digital trace through credit cards and loyalty cards. As online transactions grow, the collection of person-related data will increase. Not only is it attractive for entrepreneurs to know the preferences of their clients, it is also lucrative to sell such data to third parties. Acquiring data about people's biogenetic profiles as well as consumer data can be of great value to, among others, insurance companies. For example, the combined information about high blood pressure and the purchase of alcoholic beverages helps the insurer to define the level of risks and therefore the costs the client will pay for the insurance policy.

With the globalization of electronic surveillance, the human rights claim to security in cyberspace is under threat. This claim clashes with forceful public and private interests in the comprehensive surveillance of people's behaviour and opinions. It is also illusory to expect that a capitalist market economy will provide robust privacy protection. In a market-dominated society, it is logical that information and especially person-related information are tradable objects. The extensive trading of data from client databases, shopping cards, mail orders and digital telephone directories is integral to the capitalist marketplace. Free markets and privacy protection are on a collision course. This is demonstrated any time there are local or international efforts at stricter data regulation. Such attempts will almost inevitably be met with strong protests from commercial interests.

As the scope of 'surveillance' in a society grows, the confidentiality of communications diminishes. After 9/11 US president George W. Bush authorized the National Security Agency (NSA) to monitor all communications of American citizens that were suspected of connections with terrorism, and this surveillance system continues to grow. Once in a while travellers get very annoyed by the inconvenience of the visible surveillance in airport screening. There is, however, no serious global citizen protest against being invisibly monitored by their governments. By and large, privacy is easily given up when people believe that this improves security against criminals and terrorists. Through one of the main instruments of global online communication, Facebook, millions of people are eager to voluntarily share details of their private lives with the spies in their governments. All the pictures on Facebook, the emails in Gmail and Yahoo are stored in the Cloud. This network of online servers, distributed around the globe, collects and stores most of our online material, offering the great comfort that this will not get lost, whatever happens to our individual PCs or tablets. The drawback is that US-based intelligence and law enforcement agencies have – on the legal basis of protection of national security – access to the Cloud data of US and non-US citizens. In the iWorld we are, as Andrejevic (2007, 218) writes, enclosed in an environment of public (governments tracking phone calls) and private (employers reading workers' email correspondence) monitoring and peer-to-peer surveillance to which people grow accustomed. The real danger lies in the 'specter of a benumbed populace' (ibid., 268): a convenient mental adjustment to practices that seriously undermine the democratic promise of the digital technologies.

The Cloud

Through the information that former NSA analyst Edward Snowden shared with the world, 'big data' became one of the hottest topics (both in politics and in publicity) of global communication in the Cloud. The Cloud is in fact the global sharing of computer utilities. The recent history of the development of shared computer resources from the early 1950s until the cloud computing of the early twenty-first century is well recorded by Vincent Mosco in his book *To the Cloud* (2014). Cloud traffic is growing, and more and bigger cloud data centres are being built around the world. Although cloud advocates often refer to the notion of 'public utility', cloud computing is largely private business controlled by only a few transnational corporations, such as Apple, Google and Microsoft. A very successful leader in cloud computing is Amazon. If you ordered this book through Amazon's service, you are in the Cloud. It is even more likely that you are on Facebook and all your virtual friendships are taken to the Cloud.

The cloud companies are expanding their market control through purchasing other companies (like Google acquiring YouTube in 2006) or through extending into hardware manufacturing and software development. The hot topic, as noted above, is 'big data'. The analysis of vast amounts of information – extracted from private and public sources and stored in data centres by cloud companies – is largely done by cloud computing. Big data analysis provides information services that can be used for political, commercial and scientific purposes alike (Mosco, 2014, 188–94). This ranges from the help Amazon Web services supplied to the Obama presidential campaign in 2012 (ibid., 177) to their referral to the books you should order next. Leading in governmental use of big data analysis is the NSA, the intelligence agency that aspires to collect data from all global communication traffic. As Vincent Mosco suggests, 'The cloud is an enormously powerful metaphor, arguably the most important development in the short history of the IT world' (ibid., 206). It is a place of no place. The Cloud is 'the home of data stored and processed everywhere and nowhere' (ibid., 207).

New rights?

The major human rights challenges related to the Internet deal with censorship (in different forms and at an increasing rate), the use of digital technology for intrusive surveillance projects, its abuse for incitement to harmful acts and issues of ownership of intellectual content. It would seem to me, however, that the current provisions on dignity, equality, freedom and security in the human rights catalogue can – in theory – address these challenges. The provision of equality can address the unequal distribution of the technological tools and distribution of communication capital. The freedom provisions can address cases of censorship on YouTube. The dignity provision should address hate speech and bullying practices, while the security provision should assist civil and political protection against erosion of the human right to privacy.

We have to take care that we are not enthralled by or anxious about the prospect of 'new' challenges that were there all along. The mushrooming of electronic surveillance diminishes the confidentiality of communication and poses urgent, but not necessarily new threats to human integrity. The argument that the violation of people's privacy is needed to guarantee public safety violates the human rights claim to confidentiality and erodes the right to informational privacy. As the engagement in cyberspace transactions increases, people leave digital traces and thus create the means of a comprehensive control of their behaviour and opinions. Governments may respond with instruments for strict data regulation, but it is likely an illusion that capitalist market economies would not circumvent privacy protection, as person-related data are tradable objects. As already noted, trading data from client databases, shopping cards and so on are integral to market-dominated societies.

However, since there is so much good literature on the digital developments, I will focus on the question of what effects the development of Artificial Intelligence (AI) may have on human communicative behaviour. Could developments in AI and particularly the advent of humanoid robotics require adaptations or novel formulations of communication rights and freedoms?

Artificial Intelligence

A special dimension of current technological developments is the design of Artificial Intelligence (AI) and its application in so-called 'expert systems'. AI research attempts to replicate human brain capacity in digital systems, and it tries to find forms of human–machine symbiosis that enlarge the problem-solving capacities of both human beings and machines. It is quite common to criticize or ridicule the pretentious forecasts of the AI community. And it is indeed true that many excited claims by AI researchers have never materialized. Critics argue that the nature of human intelligence and the limits of machine thinking render it futile to reflect on future forms of new and intelligent life. However, this criticism is based on the flawed assumption that certain developments will not occur, because we at present hold them to be unrealistic. This is not a convincing argument against the possibility that what we currently perceive as fiction could be realized in the future.

AI research raises moral issues that were not posed by other technologies. Let us assume that new types of human intelligence could be developed that would be superior to the capacities of the human species. The convergence between human beings and humanoid digital systems creates a challenge for moral philosophy. Because there are no indications that human beings will be held back by moral considerations in the search for the possibility of 'virtual people', it is only reasonable not to discard the idea of the evolution of a new humanoid species that is more intelligent than human beings. This development would imply that, for the first time in their history, human beings have to cooperate with a different species. The relations between human beings and other species have never been based on cooperation. Whatever feelings people may have for animals, they do not cooperate with them.

People have never negotiated with other species about coexistence. The humanoid robot would force humans to do so. In this confrontation, it may turn out that our moral rules are too human-centric. Many animals have suffered from this, but could not negotiate with humans about a change of the moral canon. The new species could do just this and challenge the human being to design a morality that takes all sentient beings seriously. In many societies, serious debates will take place about the morality of producing digital clones of human persons and the implied threats for human autonomy. I expect that in the end, the overriding factor is likely to be the question of whether there is a market for the intelligent cyborg.

Current developments in the application of intelligent tools have already begun to erode human autonomy. This is the case when moral choice making is 'outsourced' to applications of digital technology. Whenever digital technologies (or any other technologies for that matter) make decisions, the moral development of human beings will cease because they no longer learn from making moral mistakes. Privacy-enhancing technologies take away from the human actor the moral responsibility to protect his or her privacy. Advanced medical diagnostic systems shift moral responsibility from medical staff to computer software or at least reduce the autonomous space for moral choice by human operators. Our brains are most functional at the relatively low speed that was characteristic for life on the savannah. If the hunters could cope with the speed of a lion, they had a good chance of survival. And in those times the crucial factor was that you could run faster than your fellow-hunters who were also trying to escape being the lion's dinner. Today's ICTs develop at an exponential rate and thus exceed the limits of our bio-brains. This confronts us with a critical moment in cultural evolution. The environment is too fast and too complex for our 'stone age mind' and we can only exploit the Internet galaxy optimally if we expand our bio-brain: an otherwise impressive system but one that is too slow, operates on too few tracks simultaneously and is limited in memory and in patterning. The options are to give our bio-brain the time to catch up with technological invention, slow down the rate of technological development or expand our bio-brain with Artificial Intelligence.

According to Ray Kurzweil, the ultimate solution has to be the integration of virtual intelligence with our biological system (Kurzweil, 2005). 'Never say never' seems the best advice when intelligent technologies develop exponentially, when the capacity to turn information into digits grows in volume, velocity and variety and applications are increasingly based upon the convergence of NBIC (nano, bio, IT and cognitive science) technologies. Today humans are better at complex communication than robots. But there are remarkable advances made in language processing software, speech recognition and translation skills that will rapidly improve the robot's capacity to converse with humans. Too often one encounters in statements about future developments the term 'improbable'. It is improbable that in the coming decades fully autonomous weapons systems will be developed. But improbability, taken to mean 'there is no reason to expect', is not a solid base for decision-making.

We constantly ask the wrong questions. Like 'What tasks will the computer not be able to execute?' 'How can we avoid being replaced by robots?' There is an embarrassingly large list of wrong predictions about chess playing computers, autonomous cars, self-loading dishwashers or robots that can climb stairs. We repeatedly underestimate what computers can do and we confuse our teller and typing machines with self-learning neural networks. Another wrong question is 'What skills can a robot not acquire?' We should not underestimate what machines can do! Machines are starting to demonstrate curiosity and creativity. Through algorithms machines learn to ask questions. We now have machines that create patentable inventions. As they are not constrained by preconceptions they can think 'out of the box'.

Thinking machines

As Brynjolfsson and McAfee write, most innovators in AI 'weren't trying to unravel the mysteries of human consciousness or understand precisely how we think; they were trying to solve problems and seize opportunities' (2015, 256). For this purpose, we may not need the reverse engineering of the human brain to develop a genuinely intelligent system (ibid., 226). The emulation of the brain would require a complete understanding of how the brain functions, and we may never achieve this. We do understand remarkably little about our own functioning. Obstacles are the unpredictability, incoherence and stupidity of the human brain. For the solution of most scientific and artistic problems the common narrow form of Artificial Intelligence is sufficient. None of today's threatened jobs, like cashiers in supermarkets, requires machines to think like human beings.

At present, 'all functional artificial intelligence technology is, in fact, narrow AI' (ibid., 226). The Holy Grail in the development of AI is General Artificial Intelligence (GAI), which would lead to the arrival of thinking machines (ibid., 227–8) with an intelligence far exceeding human capacity. As GAI would equal human intelligence, 'we would soon share the planet with something entirely unprecedented: a genuinely alien – and superior – intellect' (ibid., 228). A system of GAI would 'focus its efforts on improving its own design, rewriting its software, or perhaps using evolutionary programming techniques to create, test, and optimise enhancements to its design.... With each revision, the system would become smarter and more capable' (ibid., 229). Ultimately, GAI could exceed human intelligence. Robots would learn independently and adapt their rules of conduct on the basis of their experiences. Humans would no longer understand what the machines do and what the consequences of the machine actions are. The challenge is not to build human-like intelligence but to design systems that can perform extremely complicated tasks at super-human level. Single-purpose algorithms can already take over many human tasks. As technology progresses, machines will become better at performing human-like actions such as understanding and recognizing speech, gestures and emotions. In the process we will continue to be haunted by questions such as 'Does the intelligent search engine understand what it is doing?' or 'Does the machine understand the text it translates?' We are still a long way from finding answers to such questions.

Conversations with your robot

We are already communicating with digital gadgets on a very big scale. We communicate more and more with search engines and conversational AI is becoming part of our daily lives. We talk to our intelligent household appliances, for example. The interesting question is how will developments in AI impact human communicative behaviour? Will we communicate in different ways? And as robotic conversations multiply, can we design a conversational universe with robots that respects human dignity? We are very likely to meet new conversational partners whose intelligence, understanding and feelings are unknown to us.

The great problem of any conversation is the possibility of cheating, the risk of deceptive communication. Humans are good liars and robots are probably even better at it. The smarter the communicating agents become, the better they are at deception. How to deal with the uncertainty about the veracity of the signals? How to detect that your robot is cheating on you? How to enlarge the space for honest communication? Trust is important, but blind trust can be fatal. The robot will have a near-unlimited capacity for deception so refined and undetectable that a fair conversation is no longer possible. In addition, one can probably not control what the robot does with confidential information.

Another issue is that we communicate with robots 'as if' they understand what we are saying and what the conversation is about (Turkle, 2015). But this is common to conversations between human beings. Much of the time, we pretend to understand what the other says to us. But do we understand? Does your psychiatrist really understand what your loss means to you? You may not even understand it yourself. Is authentic conversation only possible if we really understand human life? But do we? It could well be that most human communication is based upon the suggestion of understanding. Furthermore, human communication needs to be embodied. We want to look our conversational partners in their eyes! We communicate with the whole of our body. Is disembodied communication still a genuine exchange between human beings? The core characteristic of human communication is informational transformation, and a question is whether robots will change in their conversations with us. Humans are different from the great apes through the transformational process of cooperative information sharing. The bird that signals danger is tomorrow the same bird, but humans change their pheno-type. The human–robot interaction could differ substantially from the human–human interaction in the sense that in conversations we constantly make decisions (consciously and unconsciously). A very close partner will – after time – know with a degree of certainty what we will decide. The AI system knows it always and with very little error. Will this restrict our communicative freedom?

Humans relate to robots by assigning anthropomorphic features to them. As we treat robots as humans, we may treat humans as robots. Our brains register speech as human speech. 'Since human beings have for so long – say, 200,000 years – heard only human voices, it takes serious mental effort to distinguish human speech from the machine-generated kind. To our brains, speaking is something that people do' (ibid., 342).

Human rights in robotic times

Throughout its evolutionary journey, the human species has always found flexible ways to adapt to changing environments. Nor has the history of human moral evolution ended. In the twenty-first century the human species finds a new environment to adapt to: the ubiquitous robotic environment. In this environment all essential infrastructures for societal life are transformed by a convergence of technology that brings together informatics, telecommunications technology, robotics, biotechnology and AI. The exponential rate at which this technology develops leads us into an arena in which humanoid robots will become increasingly essential and could eventually take over many human tasks. This raises the most existential question of all: does the future need us?

When we began to 'automobilize' our environment, we adapted by creating rules, enforcement measures, training courses and driving licences. Without this framework the mess in traffic would have even been bigger than it is today. The digitizing of our environment is a much more encompassing project and we seem to lack guidance for the moral choices we have to make on burning issues such as net neutrality, privacy protection, big data, surveillance, free speech, security, Facebook terrorism, technology divides and Twitter intimidation. What should be the basic normative position? The human rights regime as our moral compass represents the search for a normative foundation. Human rights in robotic times address the core question of whether we can manage our societies – virtual and real – such as to make 'communicative freedom' in human conversation possible. It seems unlikely to me that we can achieve this if we leave the governance of cyberspace to the forces and interests of neoliberal politics and capitalist economies. They are too much driven by selfishness, greed, injustice, lack of compassion and the need to dominate. Human communication in the twenty-first century may require us to be intensely human by doing what we learned in our evolutionary past. We are good as social beings, we have cooperative skills, we form teams, we are empathic, we are co-creative and we are storytellers. Many applications of advanced Artificial Intelligence will lead to complex moral issues and the need for ethical reflection.

The challenge for human communication in robotic times will be that we have to make choices under conditions of uncertainty. We do not like uncertainty. A whole cottage industry of forecasters, sooth-sayers and prophets has emerged to create certainty. We find it difficult to accept that all our future plans need to be made in uncertainty. Choices have to be made under conditions of ignorance while we are obsessed with certainty and completeness. The conversation with humanoid robots will confront us with the utmost uncertainty about the veracity of the conversational contents. We have to accept and celebrate uncertainty and learn the art of improvisation. In human conversation we take risks, whereas we might prefer certainty and predictability, and we have to improvise without guidelines. The desire for certainty makes us vulnerable to deception. We need to accept uncertainty about veracity in our conversations, both with robots and with fellow human beings. Since the question whether the statements of our conversational partners are true, untrue or plausible can often not be answered, we need to rid ourselves of the almost pathological obsession with veracity and the certainty thereof.

A new set of human rights?

In many societies processes develop through which we are confronted with a rapidly increasing range of digitally operated communication services. Does this raise the need for a new set of human rights? Does this development bring new human rights challenges? I do not think that the basic challenges have really changed as the result of applying new forms of old technologies. The restrictions of freedom of information, the threats to the confidentiality of communication and to the integrity and credibility of information, the moral protection of intellectual content, are old problems that refuse to go away. Their obstinacy has little to do with technological development, but rather is due to the social structures in which they are embedded. Rather than promoting a new bill of rights for digital technology, a human rights assessment should be developed and implemented that could be part of an extended mandate for the High Commissioner for Human Rights.

It would be a significant moment if a Special UN Rapporteur on communication rights and existential risks were to be appointed. No one should have the naive expectation that this office would lead the planet into an equitable, secure and free society in the near future. But, at a minimum, it could have a consciousness-raising function. Following human rights standards, a human rights assessment of technology would have to be organized through democratic arrangements. This means that all those concerned should be enabled to participate on the basis of equality. In most conceptions of democracy, however, only a limited interpretation of people's participation is foreseen. Human rights require that the democratic process be moved beyond the political sphere and that forms of participatory democracy be designed for policy-making in the sphere of the production, development and dissemination of ICTs. This argument conflicts with the observation that there is at present a widening gap between the domains of technological development and political decision-making (Winner, 1993).

The course of technology is determined outside the political domain. Policies on technology are not made by the political system. Consequently, decisions only reach the desks of politicians and the public sphere once they have been taken (Beck, 1992, 213). Thus, the democratic control of important social domains is increasingly eroded without any major societal debate. A concrete example is the following case. In the Netherlands, in March 2018, a majority in the parliament voted for a law that would protect citizens' privacy against untargeted eavesdropping by intelligence services of communications between citizens and the sharing of intercepted information with foreign intelligence services. In 2021 it became clear that the intelligence services – with ministerial approval – had tried to tap the Internet traffic of millions of Dutch citizens, with parliamentary scrutiny only after the intrusions. The arguments used referred to national security and the threat of Russian cyberhacking. But that governments and spymasters eventually do precisely what parliaments and citizens do not want them to do, does not mean that national and international rules on the protection of privacy should be replaced with new rules. Whatever new rules were designed they would fail in a social context where the core of the prevailing political doctrine is that the innocence of citizens cannot be presumed. When governments or their agencies – such as tax offices – do not trust citizens' privacy, protection is an exercise in futility.

In the case of developments in information and communication technologies it is clear that the current international human rights regime is not sufficiently robust to deal with the disempowering use of communication through censorship and surveillance. Designing new rules or rights would be a futile exercise as the advances in technological convergence are embedded in a technological culture that is driven by the doctrine of growth. It is also highly likely that the empowering potential of communication through AI will lose out against the use of humanoid robots for purposes of control, deception and dominion. It can be argued that the challenges posed by technological developments in the fields of information and communication may not require a new set of human rights but rather a fundamental rethinking of the challenge posed by technology to the international regime of which communication rights are an intrinsic part.

This challenge concerns the artefacts and applications that result from technological development, but even more the way of thinking that can be summarized as the mindset of a 'technological culture'. This mindset suggests that the relations between human beings and technological development are defined by the syndromes of 'the technology fix' (all problems have technological solutions), 'the technology opportunity' (because technologies are available they should be used), 'Dr Frankenstein' (the refusal to accept moral responsibility for technological developments) and 'technology progress' (technological progress equates to the progress of human civilization). The technological culture leaves no space for moral considerations based upon human rights. Moreover, the technological culture may make us see ourselves as the masters of the universe, but in the end we may be exposed, as was the Wizard of Oz – a little man behind a curtain.

The challenge of declining biodiversity

When it comes to ecological issues there is worldwide discussion and disagreement on topics like CO_2 emissions, climate change, climate disruption, ecological crisis and global warming. In this section, however, I want to focus on the declining biodiversity and the sixth mass extinction.

Declining biodiversity and the technology challenge are closely intertwined since it is often suggested that technology and especially IT-steered technological applications will save us from the existential risk of extinction. Humanity finds itself now in a new phase of the planet's history, called the 'Anthropocene' by geologists. This means that humans are now, with their immense and unprecedented power, the most influential force in the evolutionary process and in the rapid extinction of other species. This 'biological extermination' (in the words of Paul Ehrlich[2]) is undermining biological diversity at such a rate that it may be only two to three decades before humanity goes from teetering on the edge of the abyss to falling into it.

People at large seem to be totally indifferent to their own extinction. They watch it as a televised spectacle taking place outside the cubicle of their daily lives. Humans may – as the most powerful species – be at the centre of the planet but we are increasingly unable to control the planet. We have to conceive of the Earth as 'an inscrutable and unpredictable entity with a violent history and volatile "mood swings"' (Hamilton, 2017, 47). It is debatable whether as Pope Francis states in *Laudation Si: On Care for our Common Home; Encyclical Vatican, 2015* that nature is our loving sister. As Clive Hamilton writes, 'Now when Mother Earth opens her arms it is not to embrace but to crush us' (ibid., 48). We no longer have to save nature, but we need to save ourselves from nature and from ourselves. The most existential threat is now in the fracture between the unprecedented human power to disrupt the Earth system and 'the uncontrollable powers of nature it [has] unleashed in the Anthropocene' (ibid., 49). This nature 'is no longer passive and fragile, suffering in silence' (ibid., 48). Therefore, we are no longer free to treat the Earth as we please. The planet is no longer a 'humans only' affair. Hamilton concludes that 'our enormous power comes with an unsettling moral responsibility that we have the power to change the course of the earth system' (ibid., 54).

This means that 'we must restrain ourselves and restrict what we do' (ibid., 54). We must understand that the forces that were expected to bring us more freedom, more equality and more civilization have also brought disruption of the Earth system, lethal arms systems, unprecedented ubiquitous surveillance and a tweeting culture that effectively erodes genuine human communication. The future of humanity is a confrontation between humans and an unpredictable Earth. This has a certain outcome if we think we can afford indifference, and an uncertain outcome – at best – if we treat an angry Mother Gaia with the care she deserves. The question is whether today's global community is capable of dealing with the existential risk of extinction.

Do we constitute a global communication community that can rescue our future? Can the procedures, bureaucracies, vested economic and political interests and the global corruption of international negotiating fora ward off impending ecological disaster? Exactly when we need political-ideological dialogues on how to survive as humanity, we appear to be entering a 'post-political' environment in which the status quo is not contested. The international and social order is no longer 'in process' but a finished project. To cope with the risk of human extinction we may not need new legal rules and political resolutions that lead to imprecision, inconsistency and no-action. We may also not need new communication rights, but rather the realization of the existing communication rights. We need more than anything else the mobilization of their core normative standards: equality, freedom, security and dignity against the doctrine of growth.

If it is indeed true that this doctrine 'serves the most powerful factions of our society' (Hickel, 2020, 126), it follows that they have no interest in an open societal dialogue about how growth damages the majority of humans, other sentient beings and nature in general. Growth means deforestation, loss of biodiversity, stealing water from agriculturalists and moving people from their lands for the super-extractive mining of resources such as silver and lithium. Here is the point where technology and ecology meet. The advanced ICTs will also be used to facilitate growth. The algorithms of Facebook are important tools to promote the growth doctrine by seducing people to more consumption. An important instrument in speeding up growth is advertising, manipulating people to consume over and beyond their needs. Advertising in 2022 was a $603 billion industry. Meanwhile, a highly oligopolized media industry offers little space for open, public conversations questioning the basic doctrines of the prevailing political and economic system.

The loss of biodiversity loss is attributed to several causes but by far the biggest culprits are habitat destruction and overexploitation of species, driven by the growth-model, exploding population numbers and unsustainable consumption patterns. Since 1970 the planet has lost some 50 per cent of wildlife populations and over the same time the human population has doubled. As more people need more space and consume more vital resources, the habitat of other living species is endangered if not destroyed. This is a communication rights issue because everyone should feel free and secure in raising questions on population growth, on de-growth, mass consumption and on the solution of environmental problems with the same methods that caused them. Ever more people demand ever more food. The resulting agricultural intensification with its focus on monocultures and pesticides contributes to more waste, more pollution and more habitat destruction. From a communication rights perspective this requires free, and uncensored exchanges of opinions and information.

These are the risks whereby humankind as a whole is imperilled. They imply major adverse consequences for the course of human civilization for all time to come. Risks in this category are a recent phenomenon. We have not yet evolved mechanisms, either biologically or culturally, for managing such risks (Bostrom, 2002). They are the result of many (often converging) factors such as carcinogenic ingredients in food supplies, organized crime, pollution by poisonous materials (acid rains, chemical products), series of natural disasters (earthquakes, volcanoes), genetic experiments, scarcity of water and energy sources, or increasing global inequalities that endanger economies and politics (Stiglitz, 2013).

In the conflict between humanity's unlimited desires and ambitions and the finitude of the Earth system, we must control the dark side of technological development. In this moral conflict we must explore whether our conventional ethical repertoire is adequate. Can we rely upon the will of

God or our love for nature? Can we trust enlightened self-interest? Can the notion of collective public duty stand up against the solid individualism of a modern capitalist society? Will the drive towards self-preservation outlive a rampant media-induced indifference?

A key challenge here is that the advanced digital technologies that make bio- and geo-engineering possible are based on a view in which people take second place. This reflects an extreme binary mode of thought that firmly separates humans from nature. Nature becomes passive material substance that can be steered and controlled. Humans that oppose the doctrine will be treated likewise. There are serious challenges to the freedom of thinking and speaking but pleading for a more robust and effective protection of communication rights is likely to be an exercise in futility. The effort may even be used as a smokescreen to distract public attention from fundamental societal transformation. As we will see in the next chapter, human rights fall prey too easily to provide a humanitarian cover for none too humanitarian geopolitical interests.

Conclusion

Living and flourishing together face in the early twenty-first century serious and complex threats. There are existential challenges coming from developments of advanced digital technologies, and from the loss of biodiversity. Communication is a critical component in this reality. Its destructive and constructive possibilities are on a collision course. This raises the question of whether the international human rights regime can protect humanity sufficiently against destructive forces and create adequate space for constructive power. I have argued that the international human rights regime is grossly inadequate as it is embedded in a technological culture and an anthropocentric societal order that is incapable of solving the problems it itself created in the first place.

The twenty-first-century challenges, risks and threats cannot adequately be met with the expansion of the existing catalogue of human rights. The existing communication rights protect – in the formal legal sense – all that is at stake: freedom, security, dignity, confidentiality and equality. The restrictions of freedom of information, the threats to the confidentiality of communication and to the integrity and credibility of information are old problems that refuse to go away. Their obstinacy is due to the societal context in which information and communication technologies and ecological degradation have evolved historically and ideologically. It is tempting to believe that adding new rights may solve old problems, but such a belief is misleading. The mantra of this societal context is that only growth can save the planet. As capitalist growth is based on the exploitation of human beings and nature (Hickel, 2020), the risk of environmental degradation cannot be solved in a growth-model. The ecological challenge is to a considerable extent caused by human non-communication with the environment. Humans refuse to communicate with other life on the planet, which would mean making community by creating an environment in which all life is involved in an ongoing dialogical project. As long as humans believe that all other forms of life are there to serve them, the planet and life, including human life, are in great danger. As Richard Louv writes in his *Last Child in the Woods*, 'our society is teaching young people to avoid direct experience in nature . . . well-meaning public-school systems, media and parents are effectively scaring children straight out of the woods and fields' (2008, 2). As I will argue later, the international human rights regime is too much a 'humans only' affair to deal with this. I would suggest that dedicating attention to movements aimed at 'healing the broken bond between children and nature' (ibid., 309) is more promising than the drafting of new rules and rights. Any rules or rights would follow organically an awareness of human dependency on nature, which will secure 'that humans never take more from their plant and animal relatives than the forest can safely provide' (Hickel, 2020, 294). Given the high stakes of the risks humanity confronts, it needs communication rights now more than ever before. However, before elaborating on this we need first to discover what – in addition to the issue of societal context – the trouble with human rights is.

5 The Trouble with Human Rights

Introduction

In July 2021 the World Association for Christian Communication (WACC) Sixth Global Media Monitoring Project (GMMP) reported:

> No country in the world meets the mark on gender equality in news content. In keeping with historical patterns, women are still most likely to appear in roles such as providers of personal experience and popular opinion in both traditional and digital news media. They are still least likely to appear in political stories, which are often the most prominent news items. (WACC, 2021)

Karen Ross, Professor of Gender and Media at Newcastle University, commented that the report shows the 'multiple discriminations, the multiple invisibilities' that exist, especially for women. 'The more that you're far from the norm of the typical news subject, which is the man – the non-disabled, likely heterosexual man – the more invisible you become. And we need to challenge that.'[1] However, for the first time in more than a decade, 'there appears to be a slight upward movement' in the proportion of stories that have women as subjects and sources, said Sarah Macharia, who coordinates the volunteer-driven GMMP. Women now represent 25 per cent of those seen, heard and read about in news stories, according to data gathered by thousands of volunteers. 'This change may only be a slight percentage point, but it is nevertheless statistically significant', noted Macharia. 'And it is the one point in the right direction, halfway to equality.'[2]

Halfway?

'Halfway to equality' is a good way to express the trouble with human rights. There is almost universal acclamation for human rights and at the same time they are only 'halfway' respected. It is easy to declare that everyone should enjoy human rights. The implementation, however, comes at the expense of political and economic costs. And, the question is, who is willing to pay the bill? Precisely because of its universal appeal, the use and abuse of the concept of human rights requires critical scrutiny. There may be few people in the world who would deny others the right to food and yet people keep massively dying of hunger. There may be global support for the right not to be tortured and yet torture practices abound around the world. The moral power of the concept is not sufficient to bring about real behavioural change. After the genocide in Rwanda, the 'responsibility to protect' doctrine was developed but it did little to protect the lives of thousands of civilians in Afghanistan, Iraq, Serbia, Darfur or Ukraine. Also, the legal power of the concept is not sufficient to bring about real behavioural change. Human rights tell us when matters turn dramatically wrong, but do little to stop the dramatic events from happening.

Because the Universal Declaration of Human Rights (UDHR) is a common standard of achievement for all peoples and all nations, we can identify within it the key aspirations of the international human rights regime. There are three prominent claims:

- a world in which human rights and fundamental freedoms are universally respected and observed.
- a world in which the inherent dignity and the equal and inalienable rights of all members of the human family are recognized.
- a world in which human beings enjoy freedom of speech and belief and freedom from fear and want.

Reality lives up to these aspirations only 'halfway'. There are certainly progressive developments, as Steven Pinker observes. In his chapter on the rights revolution (Pinker, 2011, 378–481) he reports about the decline of racial pogroms, rape and battering, infanticide, spanking, child abuse, gay-bashing, and he refers to the decriminalization of homosexuality and the decline of cruelty to animals. But 'halfway' is for basic values such as respect for human dignity, freedom, equality and security far below an acceptable standard of achievement. If there is indeed a decline of violence in contemporary history, there is – as also Pinker admits – no guarantee that this will continue. The forces guiding the early twenty-first-century history of world politics do not convincingly point towards a world as imagined in the human rights regime.

Universality

The human rights claim that underlies all the more specific aspirations towards freedom, dignity and equality is the claim to universality. The human rights regime exudes the overriding ambition to create a universal standard of achievement for one world. But only a few of the normative standards codified in the regime can be considered universally valid and accepted. And even these few will – given the fractured and polarized world we live in – always be differently interpreted in daily realities. There may be universal agreement on the principle of the right to life but not on the practice of abortion or on the issue of euthanasia. Nor even if there is agreement on the dignity of life, there is no consensus on the when and how of dignified dying. Most essential for the universal significance of human rights standards is the observation that they constitute the only global moral framework that the international community has at present. This was – after much discussion – clearly confirmed by the 1993 UN World Conference on Human Rights in Vienna. The Conference stated in its unanimously adopted declaration:

> The World Conference on Human Rights reaffirms the solemn commitment of all States to fulfil their obligations to promote universal respect for, and observance and protection of, all human rights and fundamental freedoms for all in accordance with the Charter of the United Nations, other instruments relating to human rights, and international law. The universal nature of these rights and freedoms is beyond question. (United Nations, 1993)

Although this was an important step, the recognition of universal validity did not resolve the question of the admissible variety of cultural interpretations. Universal validity does not mean that all local forms of implementation are similar. A variety of cultural interpretations remain possible. This has provoked the question to which degree local cultural interpretations can be accepted. There is increasing support for the view that culturally determined interpretations cross a borderline when they violate the core principles of human rights law. Moreover, this view holds that the admissibility of the local interpretation should be judged by the international community and not by the implementing local party. Given the world's diversity of cultures and the fact that human rights will only be taken seriously if they are seen as culturally legitimate, the reference in the 1993 UN Vienna declaration to the need for cultural interpretations makes sense. However, questions remain. What universality is left once cultural interpretations are fundamentally in conflict? For example, in the case of religions that only accept the authority of their sacred texts and authorized interpretations of such texts – if human rights texts prevail over religious texts or the other way around, there may be a non-negotiable conflict.

Another problem with the issue of cultural interpretation is posed by the flawed assumption of homogeneous cultures that totally bypasses the existing internal diversity in cultural communities. There are always in all cultures traditionalists versus modernists, for example. The West is often portrayed as a homogeneous cultural entity! But is it? Does the West exist? If so, since when? Is it a reality, or merely an ideological byproduct of the Cold War? In the early stages of the United Nations, only thirteen out of fifty-one member states perceived themselves as Western. Only six of the eighteen members on the Human Rights Commission considered themselves Western. Interestingly, the Chinese were in favour of non-discrimination and equal rights provisions in the UDHR, whereas the United States and the United Kingdom opposed these. And back in the time of the League of Nations, Japan wanted to ban racism, but lost to the United States, the United Kingdom and France.

A troublesome assumption is also the construction of totally distinct value systems between the East and West. For example, the juxtaposition of an Asian collectivism versus a Western individualism. It could be, however, that the West turns out to be less individualistic than some Asian political elites propose. There is more collective social security in the West than in many Asian countries. The common good is important in many Western countries. Indeed, taxation for the common good is standard in the West. But one often finds the accusation that Western values lead to crime and drug abuse. It would also be good to reflect on Asian values and the levels of pollution in Asian cities, and booming criminality. Moreover, it may be that so-called individual rights like the right to free speech serve collective purposes like democracy and that the right to free association represents a claim for community and social solidarity. It is often said that the human rights tradition is exclusively focused on individual rights. It is certainly true that human rights are to an important extent articulated in the language of a Western individualistic liberal tradition. However, this does not hinder the provision of collective rights, such as the rights of minorities. In the evolution of human rights, the link between individual and collective rights has become stronger. Moreover, individual rights are always tied to the rights of other members of the community and the community at large.

Non-citizens

However universal the acceptance of the UDHR may have been, this did not bring dignity for the black lives that are systematically denied dignity. Human rights did not in any significant way inspire corrective justice for the indignities inflicted by white supremacy. Moreover, the all-encompassing human rights commitments set out in the UDHR seem reserved for the citizen and not for the human. The universality of the Declaration is undermined by state legislations designed to guarantee the fundamental rights of the citizens of their countries. The access to human rights for non-citizens is challenged by the anchoring of human rights in the nation-state and citizenship, and the boundedness of human rights to the exclusionary structures of liberal democracy (Dembour and Kelly, 2011, 6–11).

Efforts have been made to reconcile the human rights of the citizen with those of the non-citizen, like the migrant. Such efforts emerged in conventions striving to reconnect human rights to being human rather than being citizen, like the 1951 Convention and Protocol Relating to the Status of Refugees adopted by the United Nations General Assembly, the 1954 Convention Relating to the Status of Stateless Persons and the 1950 European Convention for the Protection of Human Rights and Fundamental Freedoms. Moreover, further laws and conventions in defence of the non-citizen have emerged. Particularly applicable are migrant-specific legislation such as the 1990 International Convention on the Protection of the Rights of All Migrant Workers and Members of Their Families. These provisions appear to strengthen the likelihood of human rights protection for migrants, making clear the insufficiency of existing human rights for protecting the vulnerable. However, the need for the existence of such migrant-specific legislation simultaneously undermines the universality of human rights as declared in the foundational document, the UDHR. It reinforces the idea that national sovereignty trumps personhood. It reveals the disconnection between moral aspirations and the bureaucratic processes to implement them in practice. In spite of the universalist claims, there continue to be important obstacles to thinking about the inclusion of groups of non-citizens.

Freedom of speech

Applying human rights claims to communication, we face a world in which we are more than a 'halfway' distance from universal respect for principles such as freedom, dignity and equality. The reality of the freedom of speech is not by any standard universally respected. In late 1946 the UN General Assembly adopted unanimously Resolution 59(1), which stated that freedom of information is the 'touchstone of all the freedoms to which the United Nations is consecrated'. Meaning that this freedom is the standard of the freedom to life, the freedom from fear, freedom of belief, freedom to be equal in dignity, freedom from discrimination, freedom from degrading treatment, arbitrary arrest or detention, freedom from arbitrary interference with one's privacy, freedom of movement, freedom to found a family, freedom of peaceful assembly and association, freedom to choose employment, freedom of education, freedom to participate in cultural life, the freedom to enjoy the arts and share the advancement of science, and the freedom to take part in the government of one's country.

These freedoms encompass virtually the totality of individual and communitarian social life. The conclusion from this is that if the freedom of information is eroded, social life collapses. Keeping this in mind we should take a good look at present realities. Freedom of information is under serious (sometimes even irreparable) threat on the following counts.

The human rights provisions on the freedom to express opinions and the right to impart information turned out to be no hindrance for the big info-monopolists – particularly Facebook and Alphabet (owner of Google/YouTube) – to censor state-unfriendly messages on their networks. In a variety of court cases against the censors, judges found in favour of the transnational corporations, neglecting that the claim to freedom of expression implies that expressions may have undesirable, objectionable or immoral contents. Usually in these cases courts of law make a distinction between ideas and facts. On ideas, the US Supreme Court in its landmark decision on *Gertz v. Robert Welch, Inc.* (1974) ruled 'there is no such thing as a false idea. However pernicious an opinion may seem, we depend for its correction not on the conscience of judges and juries.'[3]

The censoring by platforms such as YouTube recently was commonly based upon the corporation's Covid policy to stop the distribution of incorrect information about the coronavirus. However, most of the information about the virus consisted of value judgements and opinions from different actors. And as the European Court of Human Rights concludes, 'the truth of value judgments is not susceptible to proof . . . this requirement infringes freedom of opinion' (Delimatsis, 2007, 33). Judges would often claim that they judged statements of facts. On this, the European Court has generally accepted false statements of facts as a necessary part of free debate. Indeed, under Article 10 of the European Convention on Human Rights and Fundamental Freedoms, the Court has found the legal requirement of proving the truth of publications a violation of the freedom of expression as it would hinder the societal function of journalism. In several cases, judges have referred to the property rights of corporations that would justify their restrictive measures. But property rights do not mean that owners can do anything they want with their properties. They are bound – however big they may be – like other citizens to rules of social responsibility. As corporations increasingly claim for their own operations the protection of human rights and among them the right to free speech, judges should point out to them that these rights work in reciprocity.[4]

One can only demand the right to freedom of expression as long as one recognizes and respects that others have the same right. The basic ground to claim a right is the recognition of similar claims made by others. This reciprocity is basic to human rights because these rights are always exercised in relation to others. If communication corporations claim protection against violations of their human rights, they should also respect the democratic need of citizens for access to information about 'matters of public interest'. Their censoring interventions violate this basic right. Also, in European countries, judges often ignore relevant opinions that the European Court of Human Rights has formulated on the basis of Article 10 of the European Convention on Human Rights and Fundamental Freedoms. The Court has frequently stressed the fundamental role of freedom of expression in a democratic society, in particular where, through the press, it serves to impart information and ideas of general interest, which the public is moreover entitled to receive. This can only be successfully accomplished if even unpopular, untrue or undesirable opinions receive protection – as their expression is the best way to test these opinions. The popular defence of this position is that 'the cure for bad speech is more speech'.

Dissident voices continue to be suppressed by imprisoning or killing journalists. Amid a global pandemic and widespread political upheaval, a record number of journalists were imprisoned worldwide in 2020, and the number singled out for murder in reprisal for their journalistic work more than doubled from a year earlier. The prison census 2021 of the Committee to Protect Journalists (CPJ) found a new global record of 293 journalists in jail in relation to their journalistic work, exceeding the number of 280 in 2020. At least twenty-four journalists were killed because of their coverage in 2021 and so far, in 2022, eighteen others died in circumstances too murky to determine whether they were specific targets.[5]

Exposing evil deeds of governments is a dangerous activity, as the case of Julian Assange shows. Assange is the founder of Wikileaks and in 2008 a top-secret US State Department report described in detail how the US intended to combat this new 'moral threat'. A secretly designed targeted personal smear campaign against Assange would lead to his criminal prosecution. The publisher of governmental war crimes in the war against Iraq is facing a prison sentence of 175 years if he is extradited to the United States from the United Kingdom where he (in January 2022) is in the Belmarsh maximum-security prison. If sentenced under the US Espionage Act this will send a strong deterrent signal to the defenders of free speech.

Assange stands for the freedom to collect and disseminate information, for the freedom to form and express opinions on that information and for freedom of thought. He also stands for the democratic necessity of making government policy transparent, exposing the lies of governments and demanding the 'powers that be' be held accountable for their actions. For this, he has been deprived of his freedom and dignity since 2012. There have been worldwide protests against this, but not in a massive way. In particular, the large international news media that used his revelations failed to realize that they should have done what Assange did: expose the lies and evil deeds of corrupt governments. They should be aware that with his case (as with other whistleblowers such as Edward Snowden) the very principles of freedom of speech, freedom of thought and democracy itself are at stake.

We also find here an example of a recurrent complexity in human rights: the clash between moral principles and municipal laws. Human rights as normative moral standards often clash with rules imposed by legislators, ruling politicians, corporate executives or religious leaders – and challenge us to choose between Antigone or Creon. The Greek myth tells the story of Antigone, who decides on moral grounds not to obey the laws of her king. Her brother, Polyneices, is killed in battle over the control of Thebes, and Creon, King of Thebes, forbids his burial. Creon addresses the people, saying that Polyneices is an enemy of the state and that only the state can provide salvation. Antigone ignores the ban to mourn her brother and is caught. Creon orders that she be buried alive, but Antigone hangs herself to prevent this. Antigone must die, because she must obey the rules even if she does not agree with them. Law and order must be maintained. The king's son, Haimon, tells his father that he may be wrong, that the people of Thebes do not dare to tell him, but that they whisper that Antigone actually deserves the highest praise for her deed. Haimon thinks that his father should listen to the opinion of the people, but his father insists that he is in charge of the country and that the state belongs to him.[6]

An ironic footnote to the Assange case is that on 21 December 2021, the US Department of State criticized China and the local Hong Kong authorities for silencing independent media. In response to the closing of Stand News – a critical and independent online news medium in Hong Kong – the US Secretary of State commented 'a government that does not fear the truth, should embrace a free press' (*NRC/Handelsblad*, 22 December 2021). It remains to be seen whether the Biden government will apply this rule to Julian Assange.

Censorship is flourishing in the information age. In theory, new technologies make it more difficult, and ultimately impossible, for governments to control the flow of information. Some have argued that the birth of the

Internet foreshadowed the death of censorship. Today, many governments have caught up with the tech-savvy evaders of the censoring authorities. Governments have found ways to attack journalists that bring information to the Internet that contradicts official governmental views. Among them is the wholesale purchase of newspapers through anonymous shell companies. There is also the eavesdropping on journalists' activities, taking specific tax and licensing measures against them, and ultimately in many cases their arrest. As the use of the Internet grows so does the censorship. All the moves towards restraining the freedom of information demonstrate that it is dangerous for journalists to expose what governments want to keep secret.

Reporting on the secrets of the state (the 'arcana imperii') – certainly when they reveal illegal activities by statal authorities – upsets the power relation that exists between governments and citizens. The 'powers that be' have always liked to govern without public intervention and resented free and dissident voices. As governments create a climate of uncertainty as to what is allowed to be expressed and which information will be punished, many officials in government are hesitant to speak up. This means that the sources of investigative journalism are drying up and journalism has to turn to eavesdropping and hacking to uncover what governments are up to.

The global increase in state and corporate censorship is supported by the public inclination not to want to know the truth. In the exercise of public power the capacity to keep knowledge from public diffusion is a powerful tool indeed. This is often justified with the argument of national security – which has been so widely abused that it has lost its meaning. The argument of national security in military affairs can easily provide a cover up for corrupt practices in the procurement of weapons systems and the granting of R&D budgets. An often-used argument is also that it is better for those who do not know not to know. Official public secrecy, it is argued, protects the well-being of the private person. This secrecy, however, hinders well-informed public choice and renders the political arena an unequal and unfair playing field. As Stiglitz has argued, 'Secrecy undermines democracy' (2013, 229). As citizens need access to information to hold governments accountable for their actions and their omissions to act, accountability withers away and corruption grows with the expansion of secrecy. Secrecy is also a sign of distrust. Governments do not trust their citizens and citizens do not trust their governments. One of the consequences of governmental secrecy is that it provides food for so-called conspiracy theories and the more secretive a government is the more conspiracy theories become plausible.

Citizens should have a right to know what the government keeps secret, with what justification and what monitoring mechanisms are in place to secure the legitimacy of secrecy. This means that it should be convincingly argued that the secrecy serves the public interest. We need to be aware, however, that there is in general a public disinterest in keeping or revealing state secrets. The cases of Bradley Manning and Edward Snowden have certainly not led to widespread civil mass movements of protest or support. Perhaps that is why the Obama administration and many members of Congress called for Edward Snowden's head on a spike – because the public did not appear all that concerned. The same seems to be the case with the possible extradition by the UK of Julian Assange to stand accused of violations of the Espionage Act.

Opinion polls so far have shown that while a majority of Americans may believe that Snowden and Assange should be prosecuted, a majority also believes their leaks did more good than harm. That suggests an American public that understands the need for laws to protect national secrets, but that also believes the government is abusing its power to keep secrets. The cases of Manning, Snowden and Assange have not demonstrated that grave harm was done to society by the obtaining and distributing of classified state information nor has the US government convincingly demonstrated that their actions caused such damage to society. This is possibly the reason why the public at large appears to be uninterested. It can be argued that democracy needs both transparency and secrecy and the crucial challenge is to find a balance between them.

Empowerment

Before this becomes a depressing account, it should be remembered that not all voices are muted. Many community radio stations around the world testify to this. There are inspiring examples, from Khoun Community Radio for Development in Lao PDR, to empowering community radio stations in Mozambique, or RadioToco in Trinidad. Good sources on empowerment radio are Calleja and Solis (2005), Jallov (2012) and Prendergast (2017). And there are TV stations such as Amy Goodman's Democracy Now, which celebrated its twenty-fifth anniversary in December 2021. During the celebratory broadcast, scholar and activist Angela Davis said that Democracy Now is the channel where people can tell their own stories and thus it has become a place where a better world can be imagined.

There are fortunately also many social media platforms around the world that keep the spirit of UN Resolution 59(1) alive. Among them is BlackBox Television in the Netherlands and Telegram, the cloud-based messaging service owned and operated by the Russian brothers Nikolai and Pavel Durov.

They claim to be an absolutely independent service without any censorship for more than 500 million users around the world. All these initiatives, however, will need to be up for a continuous struggle against formidable factors that stand in the way of implementing the standards of the international human rights regime.

The state-centric paradigm

Back in the 1970s, in an era of seemingly progressive governments, UN commissions and civil society organizations had high expectations that an alternative to the dominant international communication order could be reality. Much hope was invested in the creation of national communication policies. However, national policies were never about people's interests: people did not matter! The effort to democratize communication in the 1970s was never a democratic process. The international debate was an exchange between governmental and commercial actors. Ordinary people were not on the playing field at all. The whole project for cultural justice was engineered by political and intellectual elites. Little or no attention (either in politics or in research) was paid to people's interests or to the need to involve ordinary people in the project. This was largely due to the fundamental flaw of embedding the communication agenda in the realist paradigm of international relations. This paradigm conceives the world as a state-centric system and fails to take serious account of non-state actors such as nations, people's movements or individual citizens. The New International Information Order debate never reflected on the question of whether the effective protection of democratic rights could be guaranteed under the prevailing nation-state system. Aspiring towards new international orders never became a people's movement.

Epistemic coloniality

The 1970 proposals for fundamental changes in the international economic and information order were primarily motivated by the aspiration of a decolonization process. This process, however, never took place. Colonialism remained a powerful factor in international relations and in much domestic politics. One of its forms was and continues to be 'epistemic coloniality'. Many of us in the Western academic community did not see how much a part we were (and still are) of this coloniality. Our overzealous attempts to do good obscured the analysis of our biases. Our colonial minds formulated the world as we thought it should be organized. It was a formulation through the lens of a global coloniality that 'operates as an invisible power matrix that is shaping and sustaining asymmetrical power relations between the Global North and the Global South' (Ndlovu-Gatshenia, 2018, 244). Such relations continue to function in the fields of news, entertainment and scientific knowledge.

Development as an interventionist project

In the 1970s debates on the global communication divide (and later during the WSIS on the global digital divide), it was not critically questioned whether divides between rich and poor could be resolved at all within the framework of the prevailing development paradigm. In this paradigm development is conceived of as a state of affairs which exists in society A and, unfortunately, not in society B. Therefore, through some project of intervention in society B, resources have to be transferred from A to B. Development is thus a relationship between interventionists and the subjects of intervention. The interventionists transfer resources like information, ICT and knowledge as input that will lead to development as output. In this approach development is 'the delivery of resources' (Kaplan, 1999, 5–7). This delivery process is geared towards the integration of its recipients into a global marketplace. There is no space for a different conceptualization of development as a process of empowerment intended 'to enable people to participate in the governance of their own lives' (ibid., 19).

The conventional wisdom about development was based upon the colonial notion that one can develop others and that social change can be achieved through external intervention. However, development is always from within. It is an inherent process and 'In that sense, you cannot grow potatoes. Potatoes grow themselves' (Sankatsing, 2016, 34). Genuine development is a process of natural evolution, which has been largely obstructed by development projects and policies. As Sankatsing proposes, 'Development is the mobilization of inherent potentialities in iterative response to challenges posed by nature, habitat and history to realize a sustainable project with an internal locus of command' (ibid., 35). Against what has been called 'development' by international agencies and development scholars, the reality is better described as 'envelopment'.

Sankatsing defines envelopment as 'the paternalistic, disempowering control of an entity by an external locus of command at the expense of its internal life process and ongoing evolution' (ibid., 38). Contrary to a process of unfolding inherent human potentialities, development as envelopment became a 'unidirectional process of transformation by incorporating the other into an alien destiny' (ibid., 38). Envelopment is disruptive, 'since it prevents a community from responding in a natural way to contextual conditions and environmental challenges' (ibid., 39).

Many development projects – including communication projects – fell into the trap where development was really envelopment and where positive social change in the evolutionary sense was seriously obstructed. It is tempting to counter this reasoning by pointing to successful 'empowerment through communication' projects, but here also the focus is usually more on the empowerment of the other and not on their self-empowerment. Empowerment projects often take place in asymmetrical relations and hamper 'a process in which people liberate themselves from all those forces that prevent them from controlling decisions affecting their lives' (Hamelink, 1994a, 142). Development communication could have escaped the development trap if the field had been reconceptualized as an evolutionary, complex adaptive process and had accepted non-linearity in thinking about communication development.

A serious omission in the development debates of the 1970s was also the lack of a critical institutional evaluation. There was no analysis of the institutional factors that caused the continuation of colonialism. The new world order agenda would have been more realistic if it had explored the role of the extractive political and economic institutions that defined the rules of the game. Extractive institutions as the guideposts for colonial exploitation are instrumental in extracting wealth from one subset of society to benefit another subset (Acemoglu and Robinson, 2013, 76). Contrary to this, inclusive institutions encourage people's participation in economic and political activities, and guarantee the rule of law, public services and a level playing field (ibid., 74).

Facing the past failures and the 'halfway' reality of the present, it needs to be asked what went wrong with the inspiring moral ideals? And, which obstacles continue to obstruct the world community's constructive engagement with an effective implementation of human rights standards?

Limited visions on human rights

There are two prominent visions on human rights that hinder their effective implementation. The first vision perceives human rights almost exclusively as civil and political rights. The second vision focuses almost exclusively on relations between states and citizens.

The first vision

The almost exclusive perception of human rights as civil and political rights creates explosive contradictions between political conditionalities that press for good governance, democracy and respect for human rights, and economic conditions that impose such austere measures that the resulting inequalities can only be controlled by highly undemocratic policies. The policies of the International Monetary Fund (IMF) have – across the Third World – undermined the political and economic conditions for democracy, social equality and reduction of poverty. The structural adjustment programmes of the IMF in many countries weakened the capacity of governments to meet international human rights obligations. The neglect of basic social and economic rights undermines such civil and political rights as freedom of expression and freedom of association.

The second vision

This limited vision on human rights focuses on the vertical 'state to citizen' relation and provides no legal force for implementing human rights in horizontal relations such as between individuals (for example, in the family, parent–child relations) or commercial actors (for example, in business–consumer relations). This vision is increasingly contested, as human rights violations are not only perpetrated by state institutions, but also by civil institutions such as commercial corporations and families. In many countries, women's and children's rights are grossly violated within the family. Discrimination, cruelty, violence and censorship often take place within family relations. The family as the place where people should learn first about the respect for others is often the prime locus of violence against others. Human rights are often effectively threatened by ordinary people (e.g. by majorities that limit the rights of minorities). Whenever in the world innocent civilians are killed, tortured or raped, this often happens with the silent consent, if not active participation, of other civilians. Also the poor often violate the human rights of other destitute people.

The problem here is that human rights provisions tend to have little effectiveness in spheres outside the realm of the state. This goes back to the liberal origins of human rights protection. It was foreseen by the first fundamental rights drafters (in the eighteenth century) that citizens needed protection against the state, but protection against fellow citizens was not considered an issue. However, as described above, often the perpetrators of human rights abuses are private and corporate citizens.

Abstract notions and sociopolitical realities

It is a sobering thought that the post-Second World War international human rights regime was created by a strange assortment of political leaders, among which were Latin American dictators, representatives of authoritarian regimes in Eastern Europe and US politicians who had little desire to be bound by supra-national rules. Most likely the political initiators never seriously wanted a universal system of rights for their citizens that would erode their sovereign state powers. The fact that such rights acquired a prominent place on the world agenda is mainly due to the activities of non-governmental organizations and civil movements. In the late 1940s, it could not be foreseen that civil society would play such a decisive role in the defence of human rights. However, even so, governments have by and large been successful in securing that human rights remained moral standards that were not supported by robust enforcement and remedial measures.

It is harmful to the implementation of human rights that the more powerful Western states have repeatedly been hypocritical in their enforcement of human rights provisions. Usually, human rights violations in so-called client states have been generously overlooked, whereas the readiness to intervene in countries of progressive leaning if they violated human rights has been much greater. Often a double standard has been applied that served geopolitical and economic interests. Cases can be found in the different ways the international community has treated its enemies in Iraq or in former Yugoslavia.

Moreover, there is an abundance of cases to demonstrate that many states are willing to trade the defence of human rights for their business interests. The motivation to defend human rights only rarely survives the attractions of commercial contracts. Western attitudes towards the Chinese People's Republic are a case in point. A particularly serious problem in this context is caused by the stakes the five permanent members of the UN Security Council have in the world's arms trade. Almost 90 per cent of the world's weaponry is sold by these five countries. As long as these prominent UN member states facilitate a global weapons market, the chances of effective protection of human rights seem remote. The reality is that despite overwhelming lip-service paid to the respect for human rights, the desire to seriously implement human rights standards is not universally shared.[7]

Religion

In the major religious movements around the world today, there are certainly strong supporters for the implementation of the international human rights standards. There is a recognition in the different world religions (Christianity, Judaism, Islam, Hinduism and Buddhism[8]) that they share respect for human dignity and basic principles such as tolerance, integrity and equality. Yet the religious support for human rights is not universally shared. It remains in many quarters a contested issue. As a matter of fact, in countries with strong religious presence there is often a great disparity between the theory and the practice of human rights. There is also a long history of gross human rights violations by religious movements. Moreover, today there are traditional religious movements (fundamentalists of various origins) and all kinds of new religious sects that perpetrate – as part of their 'sacred mission' – human rights violations as they limit the freedom of conscience of their followers. Actually, in the history of religions, an essential human rights principle such as 'freedom of thought, conscience and expression' has always been a controversial issue because it fundamentally challenges the institutional hierarchy in religions. Even if religious movements recognize the universality of the human rights principles, their local interpretation may be influenced by religious idiosyncrasies (e.g. ideas on male–female relations) that are difficult to harmonize with these principles.

Economics: Globalization

The effects of the process of economic globalization on the defence of human rights are not homogeneous. In different societies and in different strata of the same society, these effects vary. Globalization may both promote and threaten human rights. Global network technologies strengthen free speech, but also disseminate hate speech. At the core of economic globalization stands a societal model in which economic and contractual relations determine the nature of social relations. In the modern 'contract society', human rights are subsumed under economic rationales, and its key actors are driven primarily by self-interest. This clashes with human rights standards that are inspired by compassion for the interests of others. It is a peculiar development that in current economic globalization there is a strong drive towards deregulation and a minimal role for the state, whereas in the nineteenth and twentieth centuries societies learned that deregulated free markets spell enormous social disaster. As Ghai (1999, 245) argues, 'few states, even the colonial, have found it possible or expedient to let markets unfold in the fullness of their logic, because the consequences of free markets threaten social peace and stability'.

Governments had to intervene to keep the social costs of free markets under control. Modern markets, despite all the claims to freedom, are dependent on the coercive power of national states. This power benefits some people more than others. If on the national level free markets pose serious threats to social stability, people's welfare and natural resources, it is difficult to see why anyone would expect that the project of a global free market would not lead to instability, poverty and resource depletion. A close reading of current statements and reflections on economic globalization does not reveal any serious argument to support the thesis that global autonomous markets would cause any less disaster than would national autonomous markets.

As the role of the market becomes more dominant in modern societies, the outcome is in general more access to better educational and health services for a few people and a deterioration of welfare for most. The capitalist market economy serves the surplus acquisition of a minority at the expense of the majority. Human rights teaching serves the interests of the majority. The marketization of societies also clashes fundamentally with the concept of human rights on the issue of equality. Whereas equality is a core standard in international human rights, the modern market does not foster equality. In the doctrine of a capitalist market economy people take second place. In a human rights discourse they take first place. Whereas the human rights regime aspires to democratize societies this collides with the doctrine of capitalism.

Capitalism and democracy do not go together. Their principles serve opposing interests. We could learn from the stories of the Old Testament, where the interests of kings and prophets were clear opposites. We need to once again separate empire from prophecy. The human rights teaching needs courageous, outspoken and independent prophets. I would consider it a prime task for global media to provide platforms for these teachers and loudly publicize when they are murdered, like Archbishop Óscar Arnulfo Romero y Galdámez in El Salvador (1980) by assassins who were never convicted. Max Weber wrote that capitalism is masterless slavery, and the masters are invisible (1972, 12). The constructive power of communication can render these masters very visible.

The clash between the values of a human rights culture and the realities of a capitalist market culture is summarized in table 5.1.

Table 5.1 Clash of values: Human rights culture versus market culture

Human rights culture is guided by	Market culture is guided by
Equality	Inequality
Inclusion	Exclusion
Altruism	Selfishness
Compassion	Calculation

Rights versus rights

A classical case is the situation in which the human right to the protection of privacy (Article 12 of the UDHR) conflicts with the human right to freedom of expression (Article 19 of the UDHR) or when the standard of free speech clashes with the prohibition to discriminate. This is complicated because there is no hierarchy of rights that can provide a definitive arbitration. A crucial characteristic of the human rights regime is the indivisibility of its constituent rights. In 1993, the UN World Conference on Human Rights in Vienna emphasized this by stating, 'All human rights are universal, indivisible and interdependent and interrelated.' In the conflict among human rights, one can only neglect one category of rights at the expense of other rights. In reality, however, situations that represent irresolvable dilemmas occur infrequently. In most situations, dilemmas can be resolved when the pertinent elements of a confrontation are adequately analysed. The analysis often shows that one of the claims is ill-founded. Although rights can be considered of equal significance, the grounds on which their realization is claimed may be of a different order. It may well be that the claim to the protection of privacy is grounded on a limited private interest, whereas the claim to free speech is based on a broad public interest. If the parties involved fail to resolve this conflict through social dialogue, courts of law will usually come to acceptable judgments.

Rights versus significant interests

This conflict became a global issue with the worldwide suspension of fundamental human rights under the umbrella of the war on terrorism or the protection of national security, especially after the events of September 11, 2001. In the aftermath of the attacks in the United States, human rights (such as the protection of privacy, free speech, due process of law) across the world have been severely limited on grounds of national security. After 9/11, the international agreement to cooperate against terrorism shifted to the language of 'the war on terror'. For human rights, this is problematic because the emphasis in many states was exclusively on security and order, and many national experiences have demonstrated that this tends to go hand in hand with limits to the enjoyment of basic rights. There is always the possibility that significant national or personal interests demand qualification of basic rights. However, because this qualification may undermine human rights to unacceptable levels, each conflict between rights and interests needs to be judged in the light of internationally accepted criteria.

The exercise of balancing fundamental human rights, restrictions of these rights and significant interests became very urgent during the 2020/1 Covid-19 crisis. Many countries announced and enforced measures that restricted the enjoyment of fundamental rights to physical integrity, movement, gathering, education or to privacy. Most governments around the world did not take the treaty obligation of applying the criteria of proportionality, subsidiarity, duration and effectiveness to their measures seriously. In the case of Covid-19, proportionality raises the question of whether the restriction of human rights is proportional to the protection of public health. In other words, is there a pressing social need for the restrictions? Subsidiarity raises the question of whether there is an alternative measure to protect the interest in protecting public health. Effectiveness asks, is there evidence that the proposed restriction will indeed achieve the proposed aim of effectively protecting public health? Duration asks whether the restriction is only of a temporary duration. In many cases around the world, where state authorities proposed to restrict citizens' basic civil and political rights, the proposals did not measure up to these criteria and should therefore have been rejected by national parliaments. Not seriously balancing rights, interests and criteria is a slippery road that easily leads to the erosion of human rights.

Rights versus cultural values

Under this heading, one finds conflicts between the right to physical integrity and the cultural practice of female genital mutilation, between the right to freedom of religion and culture-specific religious rulings (like fatwas), or between the right to be protected against discrimination and culture-based rejections of homosexuality. In such conflicts, it should always be questioned whose cultural values are at stake. What is presented as the cultural preferences of whole communities often only reflects the bias and interests of a social elite. Moreover, it should be realized that cultures are human constructs and, as such, are changeable and not sacrosanct. More often than not, the cultural argument is based on a selective interpretation of a culture's sources (e.g. its sacred scriptures), and a different reading of these sources might not conflict with human rights standards. Although many rights versus culture conflicts can probably be resolved in a serious dialogue among those concerned, it should not be ignored that there may indeed be situations in which the standards of international human rights law and those cherished by cultural communities clash in non-negotiable ways.

Rights versus human inclinations

Throughout history, humans have struggled with the clash between their desire to be moral and their inclination towards immorality. The moral capacity demanded by the realization of human rights is seriously handicapped by human inclinations.

Inclusion versus the tribal instinct

The moral claim to inclusivity clashes with the inclination to make exceptions. Most human beings do not always accept that the respectful treatment they are willing to give to their own circle (tribe, family, clan, race, gender, etc.) should also be granted to those who do not matter to them. The moral claim of inclusion is obstructed by the human inclination to distrust others and feel more comfortable with the members of their own community. Sentiments such as nationalism and patriotism come easily to most people. Even in times of globalization and cosmopolitanism, most people do not work, play and love in the cosmos but in a specific location that they call and experience as 'home'. Human identity is largely established in distinction from the other. We define who we are by distinguishing ourselves from others, and these others might often be seen as inferior to us. In the search for identity, we can be inclined to see ourselves as better than others.

Compassion versus hostility

The moral demand to empathize with others requires the readiness to take the other's perspective. It does not require an agreement with the other's point of view or situation. Empathy does not even require sympathetic feelings towards the other. However, if the other – the outsider, the foreigner, the migrant, the refugee – is hated or feared, putting oneself in someone else's position is not likely to be a realistic proposition. If groups have a long history of serious rivalry, their members may not be open to dialogue. Whatever peace-loving aspirations humans may have, much of their history is characterized by hostility towards others. Much of human religious and philosophical reflection begins with hostility as a basic dimension of human life. The majority of gods that humans project are hostile to the non-believers.

Actively listening versus silencing

A right to communication requires the capacity to listen to people whom one does not want to hear. But why would people listen to others if this clashes with their self-interest? Why would anyone take the risk of listening to unwanted voices when our natural inclination is to silence them? Certainly in situations where unequal power relations obtain, the temptation to silence those who challenge preferred judgements and basic assumptions is strong. Against the moral claim, the human inclination to prioritize self-interest usually prevails.

Cooperative communication versus competitive communication

The right to communication demands that people communicate in non-violent ways. This moral claim is obstructed by the human inclination to dominate others, to influence, and to change them. As a result of this inclination, human communication processes are often violent and competitive. This makes communication a battlefield in which people are hurt, wounded, traumatized and silenced. Against this competitive inclination, a right to communication demands that solipsistic, I-centred communicative practices are replaced by relational, I–thou communicative practices (Buber, 1970). This notion conflicts with the prevailing competitive spirit in modern societies where the legal system, the business world, sports and even educational programmes are all geared towards winning rather than towards cooperation.

Change versus fear

Serious engagement with the communicative modality of the dialogue, as a right to communication would demand, implies the willingness to change ideas, viewpoints and even convictions. The participants in truly interactive communication processes emerge as different persons. This notion collides, however, with a strong human natural inclination towards conservative intellectual positions. In fact, people are inclined towards the certainty of fundamentalist positions. Humans combine a sense of adventurism with a natural fear of the unknown. The adventurers have always been a minority. Most people prefer to stay at home.

The politicization of humanitarian interventions

In recent years, several international interventions in sovereign countries have been condoned as humanitarian operations with the aim to protect people's human rights. Examples are the 1991 Gulf War, the 1992 US intervention in Somalia, the 1993 intervention in Bosnia and international military action in Kosovo. Herman and Peterson have argued that human rights interventions can easily become a dehumanizing project of bombing and sanctions serving great power interests. NATO's 1998 'humanitarian war' against Yugoslavia 'was damaging to human rights, human welfare and most objectives claimed by the war-makers' (Herman and Peterson, 2002, 196). President Clinton claimed that the intervention would bring stability to the region, but in reality it created an enormous wave of refugees, ethnic hatred and post-war ethnic cleansing. It is worth noting that 'One of the most striking features of NATO's war against Yugoslavia was the support given to it by intellectuals, human rights officials, lawyers, and "advocacy journalists" . . . who accepted the official claim that NATO's main objective was humanitarian' (ibid., 198).

These so-called New Humanitarians take sides, reject neutrality and advocate state violence to end human rights abuses. Herman and Peterson provided a list of names they considered to belong to this unofficial coalition.[9] Included are many NATO affiliated individuals who did not hesitate to dehumanize Serbs and were 'minimally troubled by the wartime and postwar hardships and ethnic cleansings suffered by the Krajina Serbs, or by the Serbs, Roma, Turks, Jews and other ethnic minorities of Kosovo' (ibid., 200). The New Humanitarians promote the notion of institutions such as the North Atlantic Treaty Organization (NATO) as humanitarian instruments. Since there is a strong tendency for major powers like the United States and its allies to use force to achieve their geopolitical ends, 'there is not the slightest reason to believe that this use of force will be directed towards advancing human rights, although that will surely be part of the cover as it has been in the past' (ibid., 215). There is a strong probability that the use of human rights as cover for interventions driven by geopolitical interests does considerable harm to the credibility of the international human rights regime. Part of the New Humanitarianism is 'advocacy journalism' or 'attachment journalism' (the term was coined by BBC correspondent Daniel Bell). It rejects neutral and dispassionate reporting to influence public opinion and policy (Hammond, 2002, 176). Hammond writes, 'Rather than exercising critical independence, advocacy journalism has frequently coincided with the perspective and policies of powerful Western governments' (ibid., 180). Analysing reporting about Bosnia and Rwanda, Hammond concludes that 'Reporters who frame conflicts in terms of a good-versus-evil discourse of abusers and victims and call for ever-greater Western intervention perform a valuable service to governments which, having lost the stable framework of the Cold War, couch their foreign policy in the language of human rights and morality' (ibid., 191). A human rights discourse was abused to demonize the human rights violators and to applaud using massive violence while 'ignoring the destructive effects of Western involvement in countries such as Rwanda and the former Yugoslavia' (ibid., 194).

This is an example of how human rights as abstract notions can lead to an absolutism that sees the world only in terms of good versus evil and forgets that while human rights violators may perform gross and barbaric acts, those who hold them accountable may act in equally barbaric ways. The New Humanitarianism has lost sight of the very disagreeable observation that evil exists on all sides and that this does not go away by dumping it into the lap of just the one party in a conflict.

Enforcement

States are the major guardians and the major threats to human rights. A corrupt police force or a bribable judiciary can hardly be seen as trustworthy guardians that would protect their citizens against the abuse of power. Crucial for the protection of human rights is the notion that there can be no rights without the option of redress in the case of their violation. Rights and remedies are intrinsically related. Where human rights instruments do not provide accessible and affordable means of redress, they erode the effective protection of the rights they proclaim. An old adage of Roman law states, 'ubi ius, ibi remedium' – where there is law, there is remedy. Or to put it another way, when no remedy is available, there is no law. People should be able to seek effective remedy when state or private parties violate their human rights.

Human rights not only require mechanisms of redress. They also imply that those who rule on behalf of others are accountable. They are obliged to justify their decisions on behalf of others. It is a basic requirement of human rights standards that public policy provisions imply a mechanism for accountability. 'The requirement that every citizen has a right to take part in the conduct of public affairs is satisfied if appointed officials are in some way responsible to elected representatives' (Partsch, 1981, 239). The realization of human rights requires limitations on the power of the state as well as a defence against horizontal abuses of fundamental rights and freedoms. People should have access to effective redress when private actors interfere with their privacy, distribute misleading information, censor their access to information about matters of public interest, or threaten their cultural autonomy. On the basis of these principles (effective remedy, accountability and horizontal effect), the procedures for individuals and communities to seek redress have to contain at least the following three components.

- First, the recognition of the formal right to file complaints in the case where public or private actors do not comply with the adopted standards.
- Second, the recognition of the competence of an independent tribunal that receives complaints from both state and non-state actors, individuals and communities.
- Third, the recognition that the opinions of the tribunal are binding on those who accept its jurisdiction.

Present remedial procedures are mainly based on the Optional Protocol (OP) to the International Covenant on Civil and Political Rights (ICCPR) (1966) and Resolution 1503 adopted by the Economic and Social Council of the UN (ECOSOC) in 1970. The Protocol authorizes the UN Human Rights Committee to receive and consider communications from individuals subject to its jurisdiction who claim to be victims of a violation by a State Party of any of the rights set forth in the Covenant. Individual complaints can only come from nationals of states that are party to the OP (presently 125 states). The OP provides for communications, analysis and reporting, but not for sanctions. Resolution 1503 recognizes the possibility of individual complaints about human rights violations. It authorizes the UN Human Rights Commission to examine 'communications, together with replies of governments, if any, which appear to reveal a consistent pattern of gross violations of human rights'.

The 1503 procedure is confidential, slow and provides individuals with no redress. Other institutional mechanisms for implementation are, in addition to the UN Commission on Human Rights and the Human Rights Committee that monitors the ICCPR, the Committee on the Elimination of Racial Discrimination, the Committee on Economic, Social and Cultural Rights, the Committee on the Elimination of Discrimination Against

Women, the Committee Against Torture and the Committee on the Rights of the Child. However important the work of these bodies is, their powers to enforce human rights standards are still limited.[10]

Unwilling states

International human rights law remains a weak and largely non-enforceable arrangement. It should not be forgotten that this is a conscious political choice. Most nation-states have shown little sympathy for those interfering with their human rights record. The state-centric arrangement of world politics, in which states are unwilling to yield power over their citizens, is still dominant and stands squarely in the way of universal respect for human rights. In current world politics, states still maintain a considerable measure of sovereignty in the treatment of their citizens.

Yet the UN World Conference on Human Rights of 1993 reaffirmed that 'the promotion and protection of all human rights is a legitimate concern of the international community'. If the most important issue for the significance and validity of the human rights regime is indeed the implementation of the standards it proposes, the present worldwide lack of implementation of human rights standards poses its most serious challenge. There is abundant evidence that human rights standards around the world are almost incessantly violated and by actors with different political and ideological viewpoints. Usually in wars of liberation, for example, one finds gross violations at the hands of both the oppressors and the liberators. If one studies the annual reports from such bodies as Amnesty International, there appear to be no countries where human rights are not violated. For moral philosophers, this is actually not a very surprising problem. It represents the classic gap between the moral knowledge human beings possess and their intention to act morally.

Failure

Part of the failure of the human rights regime is found in the limits of the prevailing system of protection. It is largely a one-way process without reciprocity or common moral responsibility. The regime offers, for example, protection against the (excessive) consequences of inequality while it does not substantially address the equality issue. In the conventional human rights discourse (very much present in the UDHR) equality is – different from respect for human dignity – not an inherent feature of humanity.

Actually, human rights are based upon the inequality of power relations between the state and the citizen.

There is little the citizen can do about this inequality in power. Human rights manage this inequality by correcting its most obvious negative social effects but do not erase them. In the conventional approach human rights may contribute to minimizing the negative effects of economic inequality, for example, but do not fundamentally change this. The structural political and economic forces (state and capitalism) that are at the root of many human rights abuses are not addressed. This does not deny, though, that the prevailing international human rights regime proposes to limit the damage these forces – if left unrestrained – would impose on humanity.

When using human rights standards such as 'equality', one should note that in conventional human rights theories there is a bias towards an interpretation that assumes that all human beings are equally capable of asserting their rights. In this interpretation, the legal system is based upon the assumption of the initiative of autonomous citizens to defend their rights. These liberal foundations of human rights laws neglect the reality of widely differing capacities for such initiative. In reality, the powerful are always better at asserting their rights through litigation than the less powerful. The conventional approach to human rights provides anti-discriminatory protection in the sense of repairing the negative effects of social differentiation. Correcting social disadvantages through the equal treatment of unequals does not, however, structurally change unequal relations of power. Equal treatment can even reinforce inequality. Providing equal liberties to unequal partners often functions in the interest of the more powerful.

The United Nations

The key problem in human rights enforcement is the absence of a functioning global regulatory infrastructure to implement the universal moral aspirations human rights embody. To create such an infrastructure in the twenty-first century, we would have to begin with the transformation of the only global forum for human rights, which is the United Nations. Although the Preamble of its Charter (United Nations, 1945b) speaks on behalf of 'we the peoples of the United Nations', the organization never became an association of nations. Rather, it became an association of states, and states and nations are very different entities, even though the odd notion of the 'nation-state' suggests otherwise. A state is an administrative unit with a monopoly on the use of force, whereas a nation refers to people sharing a common heritage and a common cultural understanding. Real nations are the Inuit, the Māori, the Maasai, the Australian aboriginals or the Zapotec Indians. An association of states is inherently incapable of creating global politics 'as if people mattered'. States are by and large self-centred and practise only a limited form of altruism. They tend more towards competition than to cooperation. Their interests are primarily provincial and not global. States are often unreliable as they frequently are masters in deception and propaganda. States are minimally interested in diversity. They would like their polities to be homogeneous with one language, one culture and a single moral framework. Many states have little interest in change. There may be revolutions, but once enough people have been killed everything goes back to 'business as usual'.

From Darwinian biology we know that altruism, cooperation, diversity and change are essential conditions for the survival of a species. It seems fair to assume that the same goes for institutions. From this perspective the UN is very unfit to manage global affairs in a sustainable way. The failure of the fifteen-member UN Security Council to uphold its mandate of maintaining international peace and security when in early 2022 Russia invaded Ukraine in violation of the UN Charter demonstrated its irrelevance. The sentinel of global peace and security has outlived its usefulness when, in spite of overwhelming opposition of members of the UN General Assembly, an aggressive war cannot be avoided. The UN organization urgently needs transformation from a global association that presents statal interests towards a global people's association that defends people's interests. This institution would need to be embedded – as I will discuss in the next chapter – in a social and international order in which human rights can be fully realized.

Bureaucracies and human rights

The institutions that – like the United Nations – are the defenders of human rights are bureaucratic organizations. People may hate forms but spend much of their lives filling them out – in hospitals, universities and almost always when they want something from an institution, or when they report a robbery at the local police station, for instance. There are numerous civil servants around the globe pushing papers for no good reason. Even 'free' market economies, as they preach deregulation, present ever more rules to do with globalized trade. With a majority of societal arrangements taking the form of bureaucracies, there is little hope for human rights to be realized. Bureaucracies stand in the way of creativity, of 'thinking out of the box'. Bureaucrats want rules, protocols, standard procedures and routines. This hinders the flexibility that the realization of human rights requires in real-world settings. Bureaucratization is a mindset of 'thingification' (Kelley, in Césaire, 2000, 9) in which humans like all other sentient beings are passive objects, whereas human rights portray humans as active subjects.

Bureaucracies are, as David Graeber suggests, 'ways of organizing stupidity – of managing relationships that are already characterized by extremely unequal structures of imagination' (2015, 81). And, he continues, 'even if a bureaucracy is created for entirely benevolent reasons, it will produce absurdities' (ibid., 81). The international human rights regime is better off without such absurdities as having states that violate human rights as members of the United Nations Council on Human Rights that is supposed to promote those rights.

Conclusion

In this chapter I have argued that in spite of universal appeal and acclaim, human rights continue to be violated around the world. Effective implementation of human rights, including communication rights, is obstructed by fundamental threats to the touchstone of all human rights: the right to freedom of information. In many countries today establishment narratives have been pushed to the fore and dominate the public discourse. Often presented in a highly polarizing way, they leave limited space for those who would listen to the arguments of opposing sides and bring forward doubts about the veracity of official information. Moreover, the interests of big-tech companies tend to direct and censor information flows.

Communication rights imply the preservation of public space, which today is withering away and replaced by private platforms. At the same time the rise of authoritarian governments and hierarchical administrative structures does little to encourage the realization of the right to be heard and to participate in public debate. Moreover, with increasing numbers of journalists killed worldwide and with whistleblowers such as Snowden and Assange in exile or jail, the fragility of communication rights is all too obvious. Other factors include the state-centric paradigm, colonial thinking, limited visions on human rights, pressing political interests, religious and economic factors, the moral divide, failing enforcement and institutional bureaucratization.

In order for the connection between human rights and communication to effectively contribute to human flourishing, we need to find an equilibrium between moral claims and moral capacities. We may achieve this only temporarily. Human history is a succession of waves of morality and immorality. There is no linear progression from evil to ethics. History is circular and is locked into recurrent manifestations of gross immoral conduct and sophisticated moral reflection. Humanity and inhumanity are part of the human condition. The expectation that evil – usually represented by the others – can be eliminated is a dangerous delusion that refuses to accept that the inhuman is part of all human beings irrespective of their moral ambitions and pretences. We have to be realistic about our flaws and failures as a species and be prepared for recurrent immorality. In our uncertain walk towards the future, we may experience that failures will be followed by incredibly beautiful moments when moral claims and moral capacity are a perfect match. Like other rights, the human right to communication is a social construct that permanently collides with human inclinations and thus remains permanently vulnerable to violation.

6 Communicative Justice

Introduction

In the previous chapters I have addressed the development of an international human rights regime that incorporates a set of communication rights. This regime is widely applauded but also widely violated. The question that logically follows from this conundrum is how to get to a human rights regime that works in order for communicative justice to become a concrete reality in the practice of human communication. This practice is the sum of all the communicative actions we engage with in daily reality and in real time. Those actions are performative, i.e. ways and formats of communicating. They are also evaluative acts in which we judge the communicative behaviour of ourselves and others, including institutional others. They are also responsive acts, as our reactions to the communicative behaviour of others. In relation to human communication practice two questions have to be posed. Which rights and freedoms should be realized and what kind of social and international order can contribute to their full realization?

The building blocks

I suggest that we take the four building blocks – dignity, freedom, equality and security – of the international human rights regime as the basis for identifying fundamental communication rights and freedoms. As a preamble it needs to be stated – possibly somewhat superfluously – that these rights and freedoms are seen as human rights. I say this because in retrospective reflection I must admit that when drafting the Declaration on Communication Rights (see note 11 in chapter 3) or in the People's Communication Charter (http://www.pccharter.net) communication rights were mainly conceived of as consumer rights and not as human rights. Consumer rights are different from human rights. Consumer rights do not inhere in people because they are human, but rather because they are recipients of a transaction. In this way, consumer rights stem from principles of neoliberal economic theory and more closely resemble contractual rights. They do not have the 'inherent', 'inalienable' or 'universal' qualities of human rights. To justify an entitlement as a human right there should be a direct relation with being human. This means that the entitlement should protect the essence of being human and its restriction should be detrimental to being fully human.

Contrary to consumer rights, human rights are 'moral rights which do not depend upon circumstances' (Nino, 1991, 37), such as belonging to a certain class of moral personalities. They are 'erga omnes', which means they are always valid and for everyone. Whereas consumer rights are enforceable only against parties to a contractual relation, human rights are enforceable against everyone. Human rights represent moral principles that contribute to the development of human potential. Their violation is not a mere matter of not honouring a contractual obligation but signifies an impediment to the development of humanity's full potential. And, since the development of human potential is an infinite process, human rights are constantly actualized in a confrontation with political realities.

As human rights, communication rights extend beyond the limited sphere of civil and political interests to social, economic and cultural interests. They are actualized in widely differing realities. The potentiality of the human condition is universal, but will work out very differently in local actualities. I may share the potentiality for human fulfilment with a shoeshine under a dictatorial regime but our human actuality is deeply different. If he or she takes the human rights imagination of a more inclusive social order seriously it means to engage in a social battle, the violence of which I cannot even begin to imagine.

Moreover, human rights are not merely individual entitlements – as in consumer protection – but they address communication as the essence of community life. Human life plays out in communities, and basic to communal life is communicative behaviour in all its private and public formats and manifestations. Communities have always survived under conditions of adversity, be it from predators, climatic conditions or fellow-communities. They had and still have to sustain their existence in the reality of humiliation, exploitation and exclusion. The communities that 'made it', and that lived through centuries of foreign occupation and colonization, recognized the crucial importance of reciprocal responsibilities, and collective care for the community. This resilience was made possible when communities were based upon the art of dialogical communication. In their collective dialogue they gave all members – even small children sometimes – space to present views that were respectfully listened to. And they enjoyed the security of not being excluded or humiliated. It cannot be sufficiently stressed that human rights and freedoms are inherent to the human being.

This is important because it reveals a major flaw in the international human rights regime. Governments have ensured that they accepted human rights only under the condition that they could devise exceptions. The legal provision of abrogation collides with the inherent nature of the entitlement to human rights. It is based on the (politically convenient) misunderstanding that human rights are gifts that states grant to their citizens. And gifts can be reclaimed by the givers. Inherent rights can only be restricted by their recipients.

In the Universal Declaration of Human Rights (UDHR) four principles are essential: the respect for human dignity, the right to freedom, the right to equality and the right to security. Applying these principles to human communication – in its manifold manifestations – four basic standards emerge: communicative dignity, communicative freedom, communicative equality and communicative security.

Communicative dignity means that communicative behaviour is guided by respect for human dignity. It avoids the humiliation of people through de-individualization, discrimination, disempowerment and degradation. De-individualization means that people's personal identity is undermined, their sense of personal significance is taken away, they are reduced to numbers, cases or files, and they are treated as group members and not as individuals. Discrimination means that people are treated according to judgements about superior versus inferior social positions. The 'inferior' people are excluded from the social privileges the 'superior' people enjoy. Disempowerment of people implies denying them 'agency'. This means that people are treated as if they lack the capacity of independent choice and action. Degradation of people means forcing them into dependent positions in which they efface their own dignity and exhibit servile behaviour. This means that people are scared in ways that make them beg on their knees for approval, blessing or forgiveness.

Communicative freedom means that people are free to accept or reject each other's claims on the basis of reasons they can evaluate. The respect for the communicative freedom of others requires that we accept the other as fundamentally different from us and see their alterity as a unique feature that cannot be assimilated and reduced to similarity. Communicative freedom is the capacity 'to agree or disagree with me on the basis of reasons the validity of which you accept or reject' (Benhabib, 2011, 67).

Communicative equality means that in communicative behaviour the participants are equal to initiate communication, that speech acts are symmetrical and that communication roles are reciprocal. It requires a fundamentally egalitarian social order. As Dussel has argued, communication structures of domination and exploitation should be overcome before symmetrical communication among partners who participate as equals is possible. As he writes, 'It will be the dominated and excluded themselves who will be in charge of constructing a new symmetry; it will be a new real, historical, critical, consensual community of communication' (Dussel, 1998, 155).

Communicative security means communicating in a caring manner. Security means knowing you will be cared for. A secure society is a community of mutual care in which people are protected against forms of verbal and non-verbal harm to their physical, mental or moral integrity. Since human security can be seriously undermined by the experience of anxiety, communicative behaviour avoids practices and politics of fear-mongering. Communicative security also requires an environment in which people can trust that their interactions are not monitored by third parties.

At the core of these communication rights and freedoms I propose to place the notion of *'communicative justice'*.

DIGNITY		FREEDOM
	COMMUNICATIVE JUSTICE	
EQUALITY		SECURITY

The concept of communicative justice

'Communicative justice' refers to a not-yet-realized common standard of human communicative behaviour. This standard represents an 'erga omnes' entitlement to dignity, equality, freedom and security in all human communicative acts. It represents a mode of communication that embraces to the full the human capacity for compassion. I suggest that an important tool to realize this standard is the codification of the right to communication as a human right.

The human right to communication

It is striking that for today's local and global communities, the communication rights that have been codified so far provide protection for the freedom or the confidentiality of communication, or protection against harmful communicative acts, and protection of the intellectual contents of communication. However, there is no right to communication like there are rights to health or to education.

Earlier debates (in the 1970s and 1980s) focused on the right to communicate. I propose a shift to a human right to communication. To communicate refers to the act of communicating, which is one the most basic human acts, without which humans cannot survive. Communicating in many different ways, by signs, sounds, speech, images, and on different levels – from simple to sophisticated – is the basic feature of all human and nonhuman living beings. With or without a formally codified right, all beings will continue to communicate just like they continue to keep breathing. Communication encompasses more than the act of communicating. It refers to the totality of institutional infrastructures, technological tools and supporting resources that facilitate human communication.

A human right to communication could be constructed along the lines of the human right to health. The right to health provides not for the right to be healthy but represents the entitlement to the institutions, structures and resources that contribute to an optimal state of health. No one can have a legal right to good health and claim the parallel state obligation to provide this. States have little influence on genetic factors. The right to health is therefore seen as the entitlement to an environment that enables the attainment of the highest achievable standard of health. This means that care facilities and services must exist, including the provision of safe drinking water, good sanitation, trained medical staff and essential drugs. Health care must be affordable and accessible on a non-discriminatory basis. Information about how to obtain health care services should be freely provided. Health care facilities and services should be acceptable, which means that they should be culturally appropriate, sensitive to gender and age and respectful of ethical requirements such as doctor–patient confidentiality. Beyond these 'four As' (availability, accessibility, affordability and acceptability), health services and facilities should operate in accordance with the quality principles of professional health care and human rights standards. Health facilities and services should implement the guiding normative principles of the international human rights regime. These are:

- Respect for inherent human dignity. This means there should be no humiliating treatment.
- Recognition of equality. This means there should be no discrimination.
- Recognition of human autonomy. This means there should be no non-consensual interference with independent choice.
- Protection of security. This means there should be no non-consensual interference with physical, mental and moral integrity.

The human right to communication would be the entitlement to an environment that enables individuals and collectivities to fully participate in social communication. This means that infrastructures (such as networks, frequencies and channels) should be affordable and accessible on a non-discriminatory basis. It also implies the accessibility to and control over the resources needed for communication, such as financial resources. Also communicative capabilities, such as linguistic, dialogical skills and the know-how to retrieve and order information, should be accessible and affordable.

Codified in an international treaty, the human right to communication would be a tool to make a crucial and distinct contribution to the realization of communication rights since it would encompass the principle of 'progressive realization'. As stated in Article 2(1) of the International Covenant on Economic, Social and Cultural Rights (ICESCR), this would imply that 'Each State Party to the present Covenant undertakes to take steps, . . . especially economic and technical, to the maximum of its available resources, with a view to achieving progressively the full realization of the rights recognized in the present Covenant by all appropriate means.'[1] As part of a treaty, the human right to communication would fall under the provisions of Article 31 of the Vienna Convention on the Law of Treaties and would have to be 'interpreted in good faith in accordance with the ordinary meaning to be given to the terms of the treaty in their context and in the light of its objects and purpose'.[2] This implies that the distinctive features of the human right to communication – dignity, freedom, equality and security – would be applied 'erga omnes'. The human right to communication would form the basis of an international consensus about communication as a fundamental condition of human existence.

What kind of right?

Rights are often classified into 'generations' of rights (see chapter 2). Those generations differ concerning who holds those rights and in their degree of enforcement and recognition within the international community.

Civil and political rights (as codified in the International Covenant on Civil and Political Rights (ICCPR) 1966) are considered 'first generation' rights. Economic, social and cultural rights (as codified in the International Covenant on Economic, Social and Cultural Rights (ICESCR) 1966) are considered 'second generation' rights. A 'third generation' of rights is still much debated and has not emerged within one document that could provide an authoritative interpretation of its content. Nonetheless, a number of powerful discourses have emerged based on such rights, as. for example. those concerning development or the environment. The sequence of generations by no means indicates a moral or hierarchical ranking. As Cees Flinterman wrote:

> The concept of generations of human rights is to some extent misleading. It first of all implies that one generation is replacing the other . . . [it] also seems to imply the notion of progress and improvement. It also refers to the idea of succession and to a possible historical description of the field of human rights in neat and chronological terms. (1990, 76)

The 'first generation' of rights is clearly the least controversial and best enforced category of rights in most domestic legal regimes and in the international legal system at large. Still, one could argue that those rights are interdependent with 'second generation' rights. This was recognized in the UDHR, which did not differentiate between first and second generation rights. The human right to communication would certainly fall into both categories. The freedom of expression and the right to privacy are original 'first generation' rights, which require non-intervention by public authorities (albeit with positive obligations implied). The right to participate in cultural life, on the other hand, clearly would require state action to enable full participation. Beyond this, the characteristics of communication rights move the discussion into the realm of 'third generation' rights. McIver and Birdsall (2002) have argued that whereas communication was traditionally addressed through negative freedoms, Jean d'Arcy (1969) proposed to strengthen the positive rights concerning communication processes and following this, communication was eventually debated as a collective right. This happened especially in the context of the social and cultural impact of broadcasting in developing countries.

In a 1977 article Karel Vašák, who served as Director of the Division of Human Rights and Peace at UNESCO, credited the UNESCO Director-General Amadou-Mathar M'Bow from Senegal with creating the term 'third generation of human rights'. It was meant to capture a new emphasis on the rights to development, peace and a healthy environment. Vašák said in his inaugural lecture at the International Human Rights Institute at Strasbourg that 'human rights of the third generation are born of the obvious brotherhood of men and their indispensable solidarity; rights which would unite men [sic] in a finite world' (in Flinterman, 1990, 77). At a UNESCO experts meeting in 1978 third generation human rights were characterized as 'solidarity rights' and in his proposal for a third generation of 'solidarity' rights, it was on Vašák's agenda to include communication. There is quite a critical literature on the notion of third generation human rights (Alston, 1982, and Donnelly, 1990, among others) but I think that Flinterman is correct in writing that the debate on the third generation of human rights filled the lacuna of the non-insertion of Article 28 (UDHR) in the covenants on civil and political rights and social, economic and cultural rights. The records of the discussions on Article 28 (in the drafting group of the UN Commission on Human Rights in 1948) show that this right was not seen as a justiciable right for individuals but as an acknowledgement of the view that the enjoyment of human rights does depend upon the quality of social and international relations (Eide, 1992, 435).

The recognition of this rather abstract principle did have consequences in the practice of world politics. It inspired progressive political measures in such fields as decolonization, racial discrimination and social development. It should also inspire political measures to achieve global communicative justice. Yet, as Flinterman reminds us, 'the drafters of the Covenants of 1966 were not able to insert this far-reaching idea of article 28 of the Universal Declaration of Human Rights into these instruments' (Flinterman, 1990, 79). The social and international order referred to in Article 28, 'embodies the idea that a full promotion and protection of human rights in a particular state is dependent upon worldwide solidarity or to use the old-fashioned term "brotherhood (fraternité)"' (ibid., 79). Flinterman sees the codification of the right to development, for example, as 'a positive step toward the recognition of the implication of human rights in the development process' (ibid., 80). Obviously codification has to meet certain requirements, such as the articulation of relevant needs and aspirations and their translation into specific legal norms and an elaboration of means by which to promote the realization of these legal norms (Flinterman, referring to P. Alston, ibid., 80).

Conceived of as a solidarity right, the human right to communication could be framed as the entitlement to an environment that enables people to enjoy communication in the interactive sense of talking with others and listening to others. This communication is clearly rather different from the modality of communication that dominates most people's daily lives. Much of people's quotidian communication is interactive only in a shallow sense and is mainly tactical in nature. People ask questions, give directions, provide encouragement or mete out punishment, express praise or indignation, shout and babble. 'Tactical communication' does little to bring about mutual understanding. It often contributes to misunderstanding and misinterpretation, or to the confirmation of stereotypical images and firmly held assumptions about other people's minds. Contrary to this, human communication should be understood as 'compassionate communication'. Most people – with only few exceptions – live in communities. For these communities to flourish, people need to share language in conversations that help them to understand each other. Mutual understanding is not possible without 'compassionate communication'. This becomes even more critical as communities – through changes in global demographics – evolve into multicultural and multi-religious communities. Lest these new communities get entangled in violent and possibly lethal conflict, the freedom of their members to engage in deep dialogue is vitally important.

Compassionate communication is the essential response to the intensification of conflicts around the world between people of different origin, religious values, cultural practices and languages. It is based upon the normative principles of equal participation, symmetrical entitlement and reciprocity in communication roles. Compassionate communication refers to interactions in which others are seen as unique individuals with faces, stories and experiences through which we want to understand who this other person is. This kind of communication requires an 'enabling environment' in which people do not just talk *to* others but talk *with* others and in this interaction feel free to say what they think and thus speak up. This also implies that people listen to each other – not merely in the defensive sense in order to be prepared for rebuttal but with empathy and reflexivity in order to be able to see reality from a different perspective. The issue of listening was brought up in one of the reports that were produced by the Canadian Telecommission. Inspired by d'Arcy's work on the right to communicate, the report contains a passage on what was considered to be the essential components of the right: 'The rights to hear and be heard, to inform and to be informed' (as cited in Fisher, 1982, 15).

In 2006 the EU Commission's White Paper on a European Communication Policy considered it a matter of citizenship to have a 'right to be heard' (European Commission, 2006, 13). Clearly, the empowerment that could be effectuated by the implementation of a human right to communication directly relates to the distribution of power in political decision-making. In the end, amplifying the freedom of expression has the intention to give those a voice who would otherwise not be heard. The need for such empowerment challenges a flaw in the assumptions that underlie the ideal of freedom of speech. The ideal assumes equality of rights of the individuals taking part in communication processes, who are thus enabled to deliberate on matters of common interest and ultimately reach mutually beneficial decisions. As Alegre and Ó'Siochrú (2005) point out, we live in a society of hugely varying levels of access to power, a society in which most communication between people is heavily mediated and filtered – with mass media, governments, commercial corporations, special interest groups and many others all competing for attention, seeking to influence and control the content and flow of communications. Within such an environment, relying exclusively on the protection of the freedom of expression is inadequate to address the processes of control and prevent the abuse of power. In the last instance, this may seem to imply a right to be heard, since 'it is no good having a right to communicate if no one is listening' (Lee, 2004, 5). The claim to a right to be listened to refers to the fundamental cultural change that is inherent in a proper implementation of a human right to communication.

The key dimensions of the enabling environment for compassionate communication are trust and skills. For people to really speak up and talk with others about their thoughts they need to feel secure. This requires an environment in which people can trust that their interactions are not monitored by third parties. National measures (such as the US Patriot Act) and international instruments (such as the surveillance network ECHELON or the EU plans for digital identity cards) do not create a social climate that encourages people to speak up freely. Participation in compassionate communication is an engagement with a very difficult mode of human communication. It requires the skills to question one's own judgements and assumptions, to reflectively and actively listen, and to be silent. For the training of such skills, public resources need to be allocated to formal and informal educational institutions. In addition to the dimensions of trust and skills, other requirements would include a pluralism of information media, broad access to information sources and the inclusion of all individuals and groups that are commonly excluded from societal debate and dialogue. Compassionate communication also raises the interesting question of the right not to communicate.

In one of the first UNESCO expert meetings on the Right to Communicate (in the 1970s) one of the participants (Professor Gary Gumpert) raised the question about the right not to communicate. Should people be entitled to refuse communication? As a matter of fact, many legal systems in the world recognize the right to remain silent. This implies that the accused can refuse to speak and remain silent lest they incriminate themselves. This right is recognized in international and regional human rights instruments and in the jurisprudence of the European Court of Human Rights. The right to silence is a constitutional right in countries like the USA (in the Fifth Amendment to the Constitution), India and Ireland. In Canada it is protected under the Canadian Charter of Rights and Freedoms. France and Germany provide for it in their Criminal Codes. Should the right to silence also be accepted outside judicial proceedings?

This is a challenging proposition in societies that are increasingly communication-intensive – or even communication-saturated. In many countries one is today continuously surrounded by people incessantly talking with others via their cellphones or who communicate around the clock with text messages. Even if you are not a politician, chances are that journalists want you to communicate your ideas about the Middle East to the world at large in the ever more ubiquitous vox pops. With all this communicative pressure (some) people may want to stand to one side, away from the hubbub. People may also realize that in many situations not communicating may be much better than communicating. In disputes between people, for example, communication processes offer no guarantee that conflicts will be resolved. Communication between parties in dispute is unlikely to support de-escalation if those parties are too angry with each other, or feel too threatened.

Communication is also problematic in situations of inequality. Between unequal partners there is a strong likelihood that continued communication serves the stronger party better than the weaker party. In unequal marital relations, for example, the advice (given by professional counsellors) to continue to communicate is often fatal for the more dependent partner. He or she needs to dissociate from the relationship (maybe only temporarily), to find space for self-empowerment, and to gain a more autonomous position, which is impossible as long as the exchange continues. The stronger party is too loud and leaves no space for independent thinking. Dissociation is the deliberate withdrawal to create the silence in one's head that is essential to autonomous thought and choice. Genuine communication requires moments of silence. Just like the implementation of a right to communication would demand the proliferation of complimentary WiFi zones, the right not to communicate needs the creation of places of silence. In many urban areas such places, churches for example, have been closed down out of fear of vandalism. They need to be re-opened and preferably available 24/7. Learning the practice of non-communicative formats like silence should also be part of communication training programmes.

The core of compassionate communication is human solidarity. The notion of solidarity originates in Roman law (as 'obligatio in solidum'), where it referred to the accountability of each member of a certain community for the debts of any other. This limited view of solidarity was expanded with the French Revolution when 'solidarité' took on a meaning beyond the context of the law and came to suggest the idea of mutual responsibility between an individual and society. Solidarity began to mean a commitment of the individual to support the community and a commitment of the community to support the individual. This is primarily a moral commitment that cannot be enforced as a legal duty.

The concept, however, provides a framework of mutual obligations and responsibilities among members of communities (local, national, and even global) that binds them to the realization of standards of common achievement. This resonates with early ancient philosophers such as Socrates and Aristotle, who discussed solidarity as virtue ethics because in order to live a good life one must behave in a way that is in solidarity with the community. This conception of solidarity conflicts with notions of solidarity as they are put forward by some communitarian authors. Those notions have a tendency to emphasize the unity and coherence of the group as a way to protect it against outside threats. In the effort to maintain the unity of the group the range of individual differences and their expression in different identities tends to be restricted to 'us' versus 'them' constructions. As a result, rational behaviour ('Gesellschaftshandeln') becomes dominant at the expense of affective relations ('Gemeinschaftshandeln'). Compassion loses out to rationalization.

The proposal for a human right to communication as a solidarity right challenges us to look critically at how human rights in today's dominant political discourse are framed. The conventional human rights discourse is embedded in a liberal-humanitarian frame. This focuses on individuals as entities that – isolated from the social context – are protected against violation of their rights but without investigating the root cause of these violations. This discourse is more interested in neutrality than in taking sides, more in status quo than in transformation, more alert to 'the here and the now' than to the possibility of a new future. It provides a nominal right to freedom but not a duty to resist the abuse of power. It serves the rich and poor equally well and as a consequence disenfranchises the losers. It promotes free speech but not as speaking 'truth to power'. It represents rather a moral-legal appeal than a sociopolitical agenda, and is rooted in Enlightenment ideas that are based upon the state versus citizen relationship.

A discourse that is based upon human solidarity would start from an understanding of rights-bearers as linked to communities that accept common cosmopolitan responsibility for all of the planet, expose the root causes of oppression, poverty, inequality, power abuse and exploitation, speak truth to the institutional power-holders, stress a future-oriented view of humanity, propose a concrete political agenda that takes sides with the poor and is rooted in revolutionary views on liberation as defended by the Latin American theologians of liberation (Boff and Boff, 1987; Dussel, 1998; Gutiérrez, 1973). The conventional human rights discourse focuses on the basic entitlements that humans have, their protection and their justification. A solidarity framework prioritizes the conditions of exercising these entitlements and supports a human rights regime that is based upon people's real needs, aspirations, expectations and hopes. The conventional approach to human rights has been predominantly the expert approach with the legal and political professionals in the driver's seat. Human rights are abstractions formulated and codified for people but not by people. A bottom-up approach requires the mobilization of 'soft power' by people in their local communities. The mobilization of the power to speak out, to make claims, to demand accountability and to network with fellow-communities that have managed to achieve the respect for their basic entitlements, is a crucial tool on the road from abstractions to realities.

If the international community were to construct an International Covenant on a Solidarity Right to Communication, its preamble could read:

> *The States Parties to the present Covenant recognize the right of everyone to communication. Whereas communication is the basic requirement for human togetherness, the States Parties to the present Covenant recognize the right of everyone to the enjoyment of the highest attainable standard of the social conditions to assure access to and participation in social communication. Communication shall be directed to the full development of the human personality and the sense of its dignity, and shall strengthen the respect for human rights and fundamental freedoms. The States Parties further agree that communication shall enable all persons to participate effectively in a free society, promote understanding, tolerance and friendship among all nations and all racial, ethnic or religious groups, and further the activities of the United Nations for the maintenance of peace. Means of social communication shall be available, accessible and affordable to all. The right to communication shall be directed towards the achievement of communicative justice in the distributive and participatory sense. It will provide protection for dignity, equality, freedom, and security in human communication.*

Social order

The human right to communication as a solidarity right sounds like a promising vision of a normative standard yet-to-achieve. The immediate question this raises is whether its achievement is possible in the prevailing social order. This question relates to what arguably is the most important article of the Universal Declaration of Human Rights, Article 28, which provides that 'Everyone is entitled to a social and international order in which the rights and freedoms set forth in this Declaration can be fully realized.' From the beginning of the idea of a United Nations 'there was a concern with the need for a fundamental restructuring of national and international relations' (Eide, 1992, 438). Article 28 articulates this need and at the same time sidesteps a concrete interpretation of the concept 'social order'.

Communicative Justice

It seems to me a somewhat unfortunate choice of words. Apart from the different interpretations that social theorists have given to the meaning of social order, there is the tendency among sociologists to use the term to refer to the acceptance and maintenance of the established order in society. To plead for the importance of Article 28 I need to unpack the notion of social order so as to make it useful for the analysis of the realization of human rights. I suggest that we interpret social and international order as the combination of the way in which humans organize their societal activities and their way of thinking about these activities. Two variables thus are essential: institution and mindset. As human beings are institutionalizing animals they introduced institutions (like the law, the market, education, social communication, religion, health care, politics, family, money and arts) as abstract notions that were operationally translated into organizations such as courts, media, cultural industries, schools, hospitals, political parties, the family, the banks and trade bodies. These organizations came to be governed by hierarchical divisions of roles, by policies, codes of conduct, rules, directives, best practices and feed-back processes. Modern institutions feature hierarchization, professionalization and protocolization. The last of these is arguably the most essential feature of current institutionalization processes. Experience is replaced by protocols.

In educational institutions the competent teacher is no longer the person with a great experience in teaching, but someone who follows the teaching instructions through which his or her teaching activities are monitored and evaluated. In health care organizations, the competent physicians are the ones that rely on evidence-based practices and not on experiential knowledge. The road to reliable diagnosis is blocked by protocols designed by outside managers. The core of the protocols is the rationalization of accountability. The desire for rational justification stands in the way of creativity and innovation in organizations. In education, this leads to uninspiring and boring teachers. In health care institutions, it can kill people. The rules of the book are taking the place of the capacity for intelligent assessment based upon experience. Rules and protocols originate from decisions that are often incorrect and badly informed. The rules once laid down in protocols are no longer open to intelligent human assessment and lead to wasting time in hospitals and universities on filling out forms and ticking off boxes, whereas that time could and should have been used for teaching and caring. Obviously, personal assessment – however competent – can be abused and should be subject to some sort of check but not without a reasonable balance between freedom and control.

A key characteristic of the way in which humans have organized modern societies is bureaucratization. As I argued in chapter 5, the protection of human rights is often entrusted to bureaucracies that are inherently incapable of providing robust protection of human rights. This requires a fundamental societal transformation. This, evidently, also applies to the international level. Crucial to the present international order is that its key institutions are indeed bureaucracies, like the United Nations, the EU institutions, NATO, the Council of Europe or the Inter-American Court of Human Rights. As such they are destined to fail in the protection of human rights. They even end with absurdities such as a humanitarianism that justified slavery and genocide (Césaire, 2000, 19) and refugee policies that discriminate between those who look more like us and those who don't. Yet, however attractive proposing a wholesale transformation of social structures may sound to some, it does not solve the core problem of Article 28.

Societal institutions are nourished by ways of thinking. These are more basic than the institutional forms societies design, such as industrial or post-industrial societies, information or knowledge societies, or great re-set societies. Whether with benevolent intentions or driven by greed, I find most of today's reform plans incapable of dealing with the prevalence of what I like to see as a 'colonial mindset'. This way of thinking could and can be found in different social structures whether neoliberal, fascist or communist. That extractive politics and economics prevail in the world testifies to the continuation of colonial domination. As Kelley writes in the preface to Césaire's *Discourse on Colonialism*, 'The official apparatus might have been removed, but the political, economic, and cultural links established by colonial domination still remain with some alteration' (Kelley, in Césaire, 2000, 27). In many countries the political and economic policies of 'extractivism' never liberated the people from the relations between colonizers and colonized.

Much of the global South is still today trapped in the vicious circle of colonial rule. The prevailing predatory global economy is managed by extractive political and economic institutions, meaning 'institutions ... designed to extract incomes and wealth from one subset of society to benefit a different subset' (Acemoglu and Robinson, 2013, 76). These institutions are linked to extractive political institutions, 'which concentrate power in the hands of a few, who will then have incentives to maintain and develop extractive economic institutions for their benefit and use the resources they obtain to cement their hold on political power' (ibid., 430). The extractive society cleanses itself from everything and everyone that stands in the way of its endless accumulation of money. 'Economic cleansing', as Sassen calls it (2016), will eliminate social instruments that hinder the money-accumulating economy, such as employment guarantees, health benefits or social security support systems. This requires an ideology of growth built on violence. It is justified by a mode of thinking that stands in the way of the realization of human rights.

The realization of human rights requires the decolonization of mindsets, by everyone, everywhere, all the time. Only with a decolonized mindset will all people matter. What I mean by 'colonial mindset' is best described by the term 'thingification', which I borrow from Aimé Césaire. In this mindset the living environment is 'thingified': fellow human beings, other animals, forests and mountains are 'things' to be treated as passive objects. To transform this entrenched mindset is particularly challenging when we realize that human rights are not a 'humans only' affair but include the whole environment in which humans, animals, forests and rivers interact with one another. The mindset transformation required is particularly difficult for a species that is haunted by moral disequilibrium.

Moral imbalance

The human being is a species in disequilibrium. Unlike other animals, humans are capable of reflecting on the confrontations between their cultural constructs and their natural inclinations. Moral philosophy has always struggled with the gap between people's moral aspirations and their real actions. Solutions to this moral divide can be sought in an appeal to God to assist humanity, in the expansion of human moral capacity, in the attempt to downsize moral claims or in projects to improve humanity. Whether inspired by Enlightenment ideals, eliminationist beliefs or fundamentalist doctrines, the effort of improving humanity by breeding the superior and weeding out the inferior has always ended up with the sanctioning of extermination. It would seem that we have to search for the maximum equilibrium between moral claim and moral capacity.

There is little use in searching for a lasting, permanent solution to the moral divide. The balance we seek is temporary. The expectation that evil – usually represented by the others – can be eliminated is a dangerous delusion that refuses to accept that the inhuman is part of all human beings irrespective of their moral ambitions and pretences. We have to be realistic about our flaws and failures as a species and be prepared for recurrent immorality. The moral claims of human rights stem from human inclinations as do the violations of these claims. The human right to communication is based upon the four claims of communicative justice, to respect for dignity, freedom, equality and security. These claims stem from human inclinations to altruistic behaviour, to the desire to gain knowledge about the truth, to treat others as one would want to be treated and the longing for self-preservation. Their violations stem from equally strong human inclinations to distrust others, to the confirmation of the truth of one's convictions, the belief in hierarchy and the feverish greed for ever more. These inclinations find in modern societies their expression in the process of institutionalization of humiliation, censorship, discrimination and fear-mongering. In this process bureaucracies are in the driver's seat.

Respect for dignity and humiliation[3]

The most lethal force in the destruction of human dignity is humiliation. Today, worldwide, people's dignity is threatened by acts of humiliation, as can be seen in the treatment of women, of gay men and women, of disabled people, older people and people with darker skins. The experience of humiliation and the subsequent desire to regain lost honour often leads (as many cases of suicide bombings tell) to a level of violence that dwarfs human rights aspirations such as the right to life or the right to fair trial. The humiliation that leads to a loss of personal significance is often not the mere result of human evil but the consequence of institutional rules and procedures. This is arguably the greatest obstacle to the full realization of the respect for human dignity: acts of humiliation that are an organic part of institutional behaviour.

In many institutions (from large corporations, to hospitals, to ministries, to prisons, to the military, to churches) people are excluded, marginalized, bullied, rejected and not accepted for who they are. Against this, 'a decent society is one whose institutions do not humiliate people' (Margalit, 1996, 1). Many contemporary institutions have long traditions of hierarchical relations and have difficulty in giving up the privileges of their vertical prerogatives. In humiliating institutions victims are seen to have so little dignity that they can be treated in abusive ways. Institutionalized humiliation occurs when people are reduced to numbers, cases or files. This humiliation is experienced as an essential loss of personal significance.

Right to freedom and institutionalized censorship

A grave threat to the freedom of thought and expression is the bureaucratic capacity for censorship as institutionalized policy. Bureaucratic institutions curtail people's right to freedom with humanitarian arguments such as public health or national security. During the Covid-19 pandemic many governments intervened in people's freedoms (e.g. of movement) or rights (to physical integrity) by arguing that lockdowns and vaccinations would be good for such humanitarian purposes as public health. At the same time there was worldwide a measure of censorship in the mainstream media (bureaucratic institutions, although they will not happily admit to that status) that limited – disproportionately – the freedom to speak and the freedom to receive information. Embedded in an unequal set of power relations, corporate media – worldwide – robbed many people of their fundamental communication rights. They managed to create a culture of denial and silence about abuses of power.

A characteristic of bureaucratic institutions (both political and commercial) is also the hiding of information from those affected by their strategies. This usually happens under the cover of institutional transparency that the institutions claim was always there. And, as David Graeber writes, 'when we complain that we were not informed of a new policy or responsibility, the bureaucrats triumphantly produce the date (usually months in the past) and details of the document where the new rules were listed' (2015, 185).

Right to equality and institutionalized discrimination

There is a very obvious, persistent and dangerous worldwide fracture between the rich who continue to profit from economic growth and the poor who are facing economic stagnation. The world has different sets of rules for the winners and losers. Governments bail big banks out, whereas ordinary citizens lose their houses when they cannot foot their bills. Globally, austerity policies have mainly exacerbated social polarization. These policies have made 'women, ethnic minorities, the young, the old, the disabled ... the losers and the international super-rich and national elite classes have been the winners, and the beneficiaries of other people's suffering' (Bradley, 2016, 268). The international bureaucracies have not been able to solve the problem that for around 1 billion people there is no access to safe drinking water. Three decades of global summits on climate issues have not diminished the CO_2 emissions in any significant way.

According to John Holmes, the United Nations Under-Secretary-General for Humanitarian Affairs, the world is losing 10,000 children to hunger each day (*UN Chronicle*, 45(3), December 2009) and the website of The World Counts informs us that 'A child dies from hunger every 10 seconds. Poor nutrition and hunger is responsible for the death of 3.1 million children a year. That's nearly half of all deaths in children under the age of 5. The children die because their bodies lack basic nutrients.'[4] All the meetings, committees, experts, high-level task forces and comprehensive frameworks for action have not been able to change this. A special problem of bureaucratic institutions is that the bureaucratic elites are often privileged social groups that tend to favour their own people over others. In my country, the Netherlands, for example, it is at present being slowly recognized that there is institutional racism in such entities as the tax office and the police force.

Right to security and the institutionalization of fear

The international human rights regime provides protection against violations of people's physical, mental and moral integrity. The right to the protection of privacy as provided in Article 12 of the UDHR and in Article 17 of the ICCPR protects people against arbitrary interference with their private sphere and against unlawful attacks on their honour and reputation. The meaning of human security, however, goes far beyond the privacy issue. It relates obviously to living in a peaceful and non-violent world, but it also refers to a basic dimension of the human condition: the human biological weakness. As Fromm formulates it, the human being is 'the most helpless of all animals at birth' (Fromm, 1942, 26). In the process of human development, we become individuals and as the biblical myth tells: we lose paradise and our intimate connection with nature. We become free but also 'powerless and afraid' (ibid., 28).

Our mental capacity and mastery over nature increase, but at the same time our growing individuation 'means growing isolation, insecurity, and thereby growing doubt concerning one's role in the universe, the meaning of one's life, and with that a growing feeling of one's own powerlessness and insignificance as an individual' (ibid., 29). The price we pay for becoming free individuals is fear. In the UDHR the 'freedom from fear' is proclaimed as one of the highest aspirations of the common people. This moral declaration sounds very inspiring, but it is insufficient to provide humanity with a deep sense of security. In today's surveillance society (with all kinds of sophisticated algorithmic 'big brothers' watching us) it certainly does not free us from the fear of permanently being spied upon. On a more basic level, the freedom from fear does not address the ontological anxiety of human beings.

Humans are the only species that is ontologically fearful. We know we are mortal and that life is finite but are uncertain about the time and manner of our death. We know about the basic ambiguities of life and try throughout our life to avoid them. We spend a life hoping to learn how we should live and then by the time we have an idea, we have to learn how to die. As if our ontological fear was not enough, we are surrounded by a culture of fear (Furedi, 1997) in which politicians and media invest energies in peddling fear about nature, fellow human beings, nuclear or climatic Armageddons and pandemics. As Richard Louv argues, many institutions – among them schools – associate nature with doom and children are not being allowed or encouraged to have a relationship with or appreciation of their natural environment (Louv, 2008).

Imagining alternatives

I conclude that the institutionalization of humiliation, censorship, discrimination and fear-mongering poses serious threats to the building blocks of communicative justice. But what does that mean? What would be the alternative to a social order that institutionalizes these threats? If the alternative social order were to honour concretely the key principles of communicative justice, this would mean the creation of a caring, convivial, egalitarian and secure social and international order.

A caring social order

As I have mentioned before, the revolutionary core of the international human rights regime is that 'all people matter'. The most powerful motive for the protection of human rights is 'compassion'. Respecting human rights needs a culture of compassion. Samuel and Pearl Oliner investigated the motives of people who rescued Jews during the Holocaust (Oliner and Oliner, 1988). The rescuers are characterized by feelings and experiences of compassion, care and solidarity. These are not hereditary personality traits. They are not fixed parts of our genetic constitution. They can be learnt however, and should therefore be taught.

In a caring social order, education focuses on experiential learning of caring togetherness. All people are students in the 'music of life' (Noble, 2006). As Denis Noble has proposed, there is a concert played by genes, proteins, cells, tissues and organs and their environments. And this music is performed largely without a conductor. The ensemble most resembles that of the jazz band, because it manifests the crucial variables for human survival: collaboration and improvisation. The conductor-less performance of music also liberates us from creationist inclinations towards an external force domineering over the musicians. The 'music of life' is a serenade to love for life, to prosocial behaviour that stands for cooperation, altruism, generosity, trust and trustworthiness, and thus to human survival. A caring social order also accepts that life is not a humans only affair. It includes the whole of our living environment.

A convivial social order

The notion of conviviality was introduced by Ivan Illich (1973) as the ability of individuals to interact creatively and autonomously with others and their environment to satisfy their own needs. He contrasted the convivial society with the industrial society, where individuals are reduced to 'mere consumers', unable to choose what is produced or how things are made in a world governed by a 'radical monopoly' that divides the population into experts that can use the tools and laypeople that cannot. As the title of Illich's book, *Tools for Conviviality*, suggests, his initial focus was on how industrial tools and the expertise required to operate them constrain individuals' autonomy. He proposed that convivial tools were those that promoted and extended people's autonomy. In modern industrial society people become increasingly dependent upon tools that steer their lives in pre-programmed ways and undermine their liberties.

Convivial ways of life are threatened such as to enhance people's feelings of loneliness and insignificance. The concept 'convivial' denotes the combination of cheerfulness with cooperative helpfulness. The link is important as we know from a range of experiments in social psychology that people who are cheerful tend to be more helpful and cooperative, they evaluate themselves and others more positively and think more creatively. Alain Caillé, a French sociologist who published in 2020 *The Second Convivialist Manifesto: Towards a Post-Neoliberal World* (signed by 300 intellectuals from thirty-three countries), defines convivialism as a broad-based humanist, civic and political philosophy that spells out the normative principles that sustain the art of living together at the beginning of the twenty-first century (Adloff and Caillé, 2022). This is precisely what distinguishes the convivial social order from the abusive social order.

Convivial organizations are non-hierarchical places where humans learn, develop and produce through creative storytelling. People are not seen as resources or as raw processable materials in the convivial organization, but as creative artists. In the convivial organization transformation is fun. It is known that when we want people to change their behaviour or mindsets, then we should be able to demonstrate to them that the alternatives are fun. People are willing to do all kinds of (new) things if they are pleasurable. Pleasure is an underrated motivating force in processes of change.

An egalitarian social order

We cannot achieve global agreement on the common destiny of humanity without the premise of equal dignity of all. An egalitarian society would be based upon distributive justice, i.e. upon the idea that it is unjust 'for some to be worse off than others through no fault of their own' (Temkin, 1993, 7). Among the essential conditions for people's self-empowerment are access to and use of the resources that enable them to express themselves, to communicate these expressions to others, to exchange ideas with others, to inform themselves about events in the world, to create and control the production of knowledge and to share the world's sources of knowledge. These resources include technical infrastructures, knowledge and skills, financial means and natural systems. Their unequal distribution among the world's people obstructs the equal entitlement to the conditions of self-empowerment. The perspective of an egalitarian social order has important implications for processes of public choice.

Benjamin Barber (1984) has convincingly suggested that most current liberal-democratic arrangements are 'thin democracies' as they are based upon the outsourcing of citizens' power to representatives that steal 'from individuals the ultimate responsibility for their values, beliefs, and actions' (ibid., 145). Democratic representation is also, as Robert Michels (1915) argued, a logical impossibility as the rule by the people cannot be transferred. In the liberal-representative democracies citizens are subjected to laws in the making of which they do not participate. In liberal-representative democracies, social relations are eroded and individual citizens are left cut off, 'not only from the abuses of power but from one another' (Barber, 1984, 101). They become 'very easy targets for authoritarian collectivism' (ibid., 101). As Gould (1988) has argued, conventional conceptions of democracy propose a system of governance that provides a maximum degree of 'negative' freedom for the governed, while largely ignoring that full human freedom necessitates 'positive' freedom. The latter implies that people should be free to exercise their capacity for self-empowerment (Hamelink, 1994a, 142).

A democracy that involved most citizens in the decisions that affect their lives would be 'a decisive shift of power into the hands of ordinary citizens' (Baker et al., 2004, 98) Against the very common objection that ordinary people would not be able to make wise decisions, President Theodore Roosevelt observed that 'the majority of the plain people will day in and day out make fewer mistakes in governing themselves than any smaller body of men will make in trying to govern them' (quoted in Barber, 1984, 151). In a strong democracy citizens would think and act together without the intervention of professionals that pursue their own political and financial interests. In a strong democracy the standard of political equality would be extended to mean the broadest possible participation of all people in processes of public decision-making. This would move the democratic process beyond the political sphere and extend the requirement of participatory institutional arrangements to other social domains. The principles of maximum participation and extended equality call for the participation of people in decision-making in former elitist fields such as information, technology and culture.

A secure social order

In a fearful social order there are too many environments in which women, gay men and women, people of non-white ethnic origin, disabled persons, dissident activists or elderly do not feel safe. Most human anxiety is related to perceived dangers of future conditions, and such perceptions are socially mediated. In social mediation processes, media – both entertainment and news media as well as both conventional and new media – have become central institutions. Day after day, they offer a discourse of anxiety. Every single day, the media warn us of some impending danger. Thus they amplify our already existing ontological anxiety, and in doing so create a particular perspective on the world and on people's place within it.

There is a growing cottage industry of 'anxiety marketeers', offering their services to help with concerns people might not even have realized they harboured. These concerns are about health, lifestyles, funeral fashion, appearance, ageing, financial status, home security, kids with attention deficit hyperactivity disorder (ADHD), marital stress, sexual performance, the size and appearance of their genitals, culinary expertise, vinological knowledge, the psychopathology of their pets, or garden architecture (even if they have no garden). In this industry, the news and entertainment media are key vehicles for promoting worry and an anxious perspective on the world. Most of the popular perceptions on the dangers of crime and terrorism are mediated to people via news reports and entertainment programmes. People become anxious when the media tell them there is something wrong with them (like advertising or medical TV programmes do), when they suggest uncertain and probably very troubled futures (like in daily newscasts about issues such as the credit crisis) or by making them fearful (with discourses on terror, evil and war).

Media render anxiety a shared perspective on life. For the first time in history, millions of people across the globe can watch simultaneously stories of fear and crisis. For these global audiences, the media construct a world that is replete with warnings that the world is a dangerous place and that things may get worse. According to Furedi (1997), the media amplify people's sense of risk and danger but do not cause it. They exacerbate people's disposition to expect that things will not work out well by constantly warning of one or another danger. As David Altheide observed,

> Fear has become a staple of popular culture, ranging from fun to dread. Americans trade on fear. News agencies report it, produce entertainment messages (other than news) about it, and promote it, police and other agencies of social control market it. And audiences watch it, read it, and, according to numerous mass entertainment spokespersons, demand it. (2002, 64)

Altheide's research also leads him to conclude that 'Fear is more prevalent in news today than it was several years ago, and it appears in more sections of the newspaper' (ibid., 99). Contrary to this, in a secure society people are protected against the harm that fear-mongering engenders among them. Since fear is an ontological given of human existence, the safe society also equips people to deal with fundamental anxiety. The human condition, as Simone de Beauvoir (1947) proposed, is fundamentally ambiguous and many philosophers have tried to obscure this ambiguity.

In moral philosophy particularly, often the attempt was made to eliminate ambiguity. But the truth of living cannot be hidden: we have to live with life and death, in loneliness and connectedness, in nothingness and uniqueness, in freedom and slavery. De Beauvoir's question is how can we consciously accept the fundamental ambiguity of the human state? This cannot be done in isolation. Accepting the finitude of life without drowning in uncertainty and fear needs collective reflection. The questions surrounding the theme of death – in modern cultures often a taboo – need to be faced as a community, however small. And, the great questions about the existential risk of extinction of the human species can only be dealt with in communal togetherness. The secure society is a community of solidarity because its members know that the full realization of freedoms and rights requires a communal effort in which communication (in the sense of 'deep dialogue' (Hamelink, 2019, 67–86)) is the key.

A tall order

The proposed liberation from bureaucratic institutions is indeed a tall order because, as Graeber (2015) suggests, humans love bureaucracies for their impersonal efficiency, neutrality, value-freeness and rationality, even if they know that these implied qualities are convenient smokescreens to cover indifference, irrational decision-making and incompetence. Even when people suspect that the organizational rules, procedures and protocols were designed in a lunatic asylum they most likely prefer them over a free-wheeling, playful, improvised handling of their taxes, passports, driver licences and banking affairs.

Moreover, since the social order is based on the colonial mindset, the liberation from bureaucracy also requires the mental transformation to a decolonized mindset. I will get back to this in the final chapter.

Transformation and communication

Here we encounter a Catch-22. It may be that communication rights can only be genuinely implemented in a transformed society, but that transformation may need communicative acts inspired by such human rights as the freedom of speech. The challenge is of course that the current infrastructures, resources, contents and capabilities of human communication are exactly the mechanisms we need to transform in order to realize communicative justice. The sobering reality is that the prevalent modes of human communicative behaviour (on both the personal and institutional level) are impediments rather than facilitators for the transformations described above.

The caring social order and communication practice

The communication practice of a caring society is a communal effort in storytelling. All members of a community actively participate rather than being mere spectators. All can express their perceptions and all are listened to. The most adequate metaphor for this communication practice is the jazz big band. The band is a cooperative exercise in which the skill of listening is highly developed and the improvised solos are not competitive performances to outdo the others but contributions to achieving togetherness. There is unlimited space for individual expressions that contribute to the communal and dialogical enjoyment. The leadership rotates between the soloists and the accompanists. The institutions of social communication are – like the band – sanctuaries for a freedom of thought and speech that is open for critical, respectful exchanges. This communication practice is not achieved through mandatory codes of decent behaviour. Codes of ethics have seldom inspired people to a higher level of morality in their behaviour.

A caring communication practice can only be achieved through communal reflection.

The egalitarian social order and communication practice

Globally, human communication functions in a deeply hierarchical and unequal set of power relations. Crucial in an egalitarian society is the communication of citizens with one another. Democratic communication should include the whole repertoire of human communicative behaviour, from song to poetry, passionate proclamation, testimony and analysis. This requires protective rules for freedom of thought and expression. The communicative behaviour in abusive societies usually means that those who represent citizens speak on their behalf, but do not listen to them. In a strong democratic and egalitarian society, citizens would speak to one another and listen to one another. They can do that very well without the intervention of professionals. A strong democracy has strong citizens and does not need strong leaders.

The convivial social order and communication practice

Processes of social communication have become institutionalized and leave little space for creative, critical thinking. In the convivial society conventional and new media are sanctuaries of free thought and speech. They function as conduits for the views of the social losers and operate as tools for conviviality. A major obstacle in the road is the increasing oligopolization of the global information market. Multi-billion-dollar actors such as Alphabet (owner of YouTube), Amazon and Facebook direct and censor through their editorial interventions information about public matters. They typically claim to operate as private actors that act within their entrepreneurial freedom. Yet, the scope and scale of these corporations make them too big to be private actors. Moreover, they are unaccountable to the public. However, they are players on the public grounds, using infrastructures such as airwaves that are the common heritage of humanity – and with more financial and resource power than most governments. They transform public goods into private goods and create an increasing dependency by lock-ins to these products and the restriction of choice. In the convivial society, citizens have political control over these entities.

The secure social order and communication practice

It is obvious that news media should report the awful events that happen in the world and portray the evil that is part of human behaviour. As Rebecca Solnit reminds us, 'This is Earth. It will never be heaven' (Solnit, 2016, 77). However, Jorge Luis Borges tells us, 'There is no day without its moments of paradise' (ibid., 82). In the communication practice of the secure society there is a generous space for the moments of paradise. Astonishingly large volumes of encouraging and inspiring events take place. New forms of community life emerge, projects for food sovereignty develop, support and cooperation among ordinary people in times of disasters are common phenomena, young people demonstrate for ecological sanity, the search for a holistic cure is on its way and new models of circular, sustainable small-scale economies are explored. The many solutions to humanity's common problems that constitute 'small victories' are often neglected by the mainstream media and political leaders. The communication mode of the secure society (both in mediated and personal communication) is de-escalatory. Its main features are reflexivity (it prefers questions over all-knowing pedantry), non-violence (it prefers listening over judgemental statements), dialogical (it prefers interactive conversation over monologues) and diachronicity (it prefers to accept the fluidity of the other's identity above entrenchment in monolithic identities). The beauty of this communication mode is that it is educable. We can learn communicative security without losing sight of the dark side of our realities.

In summary, the communication practice of a human rights-based social order – both in its organization and mindset – is a practice of compassionate communication. Compassion means caring for the dignity, freedom, equality and security of all sentient beings. Compassionate communication is an act of constructive power against the destructive power of communication. This mode of communication presents alternative solutions, includes all in an open and critical dialogue, explores the multiplicity of knowledge and exposes deliberate acts of harm to the living environment.

Imagination

Human rights tell inspirational stories through which people can become agents of their own destiny. They are roadmaps for liberation and analytical tools to understand the root causes of domination. The international human rights regime proposes a compassionate world in which we communicate with respect, freedom, equality and security. This is an imagination of a possible future. Aristotle told us that 'imagination is the process by which we say that an image is presented to us' (*De Anima*, 428a, 1–4). The human rights regime presents us with an image of a compassionate world. It challenges us to go from imagining a human rights-based society to realizing a human rights-based society. Against the imagination of a world that accepts human rights as a 'common standard of achievement' (Preamble to UDHR) there are formidable forces that are hostile to the imagination of autonomy, equality and human security. The communicative justice that I have described requires a process of institutional and mental transformation to a caring, egalitarian, convivial and secure social order.

Conclusion

In this chapter I have suggested that the four building blocks of the international human rights regime constitute the basis for identifying fundamental communication rights and freedoms. Applying these principles to human communication – in its manifold manifestations – communicative dignity, communicative freedom, communicative equality and communicative security emerge. At the core of these four standards is the key principle: communicative justice. I furthermore suggested that an essential tool to realize this standard is the codification of the human right to communication as a solidarity right. This right cannot be realized within the prevailing social and international order. It requires an institutional and mental transformation to a caring, convivial, egalitarian and secure living environment. The question that remains is, why should we go through all this trouble of imagining human rights friendly societies and committing ourselves to their realization? What could inspire us to strive towards 'communicative justice'? To paraphrase the words of Kai Nielsen (1989) with those of Reinhold Niebuhr (1932) – 'why be moral in an immoral society?' I intend to discuss this question in the final chapter.

7 The Practice of Communicative Justice

Introduction

The quest for communicative justice leads to the conclusion that to live and flourish together, we need compassionate communication. This is a communication practice in which people communicate with respect for human dignity, in freedom, in symmetrical exchanges and without fear. The full realization of communicative justice is not possible within the prevailing social and international order. It requires a fundamental transformation to a caring, convivial, egalitarian and secure social order. Intrinsic to this transformation is also the transformation of the prevailing colonial mindset. This means that communicative justice represents not merely a set of moral and/or legal prescriptions. As an image of a possible future it provides – beyond the human right to communication – a political frame of institutional arrangements and a decolonized mindset for the exercise of this right. The realization of human rights should go beyond social actions for change and engage with political transformation.

Political ethics

However important social actions such as Amnesty International's 'naming and shaming' campaigns may be, they have decided limits. They inspire victims and irritate perpetrators. They do not address the systemic political structure under which the perpetrators can often act too long with impunity. Fortunately, the international community now has an International Criminal Court that addresses the most serious crimes against human rights and freedoms and that occasionally puts perpetrators behind bars. Although this promises a progressive realization of human rights, it does not change the institutional conditions and the ways of thinking under which the perpetrators flourish(ed) and commit(ted) their crimes. An illustration comes from the so-called 'war on drugs'. Every once in a while a drug capo like Joaquín 'El Chapo' Guzmán may be arrested and imprisoned. However, locking up a leading actor in drug trafficking does not address the real problem: a culture of addiction, a mental proclivity towards growth and dominion, an expanding global buyers' market, a powerful circle of beneficiaries, a corrupt political system and an enforcement bureaucracy that was set to fail.

The realization of communicative justice is more than anything else a political project that needs permanent critical reflection on the practice of human communication. Politics as the management of organized society is political ethics in the sense of a material ethics that sets standards for common behaviour. I propose to conceive this political ethics as an ethics of 'liberating togetherness'. This political ethics means the debut of those who were always absent from history. They should participate as equals. They should not be included as an act of charity but take the place that was always theirs. This requires a conceptualization of justice as the liberation of everyone from the enemies of life: the forces of humiliation, exploitation and exclusion that stand in the way of human fulfilment.

The starting point of an ethics of 'liberating togetherness' is the liberation from oppressive political and economic structures, but it also means spiritual liberation, and especially the liberation from fear. But human beings cannot liberate others or themselves alone, 'because liberation is a communal process, which can only be achieved by experiencing together the reality which they must transform' (Freire, in Torres, 2014, 43). Liberation implies communal solidarity as togetherness. As there are no solid moral prescriptions for living together, the human community is invited to join in a long and difficult journey that needs permanent reflection. This reflection is a continuous, reiterative process that is firmly grounded in the imperative of responsibility (Jonas, 1984), the human eccentric positionality (Plessner, 1928/1975) and the ethics of liberation (Dussel, 2013), and is inspired by moral intuitionism (Haidt, 2001).

The bioethical imperative

Ethical reflection goes beyond a 'humans only' project. Pastor and philosopher Fritz Jahr (in his 1927 article 'Bio-ethics: A review of the ethical connections of humans to animals and plants') refined Kant's original Categorical Imperative discourse by propounding the notion of the Bioethical Imperative. This means respect for every living being as an end in itself, as the guiding principle for our actions. It acknowledges the relationships not only between conscious human beings, but also human solidarity with plants and other animal species. Jahr believed that beyond solidarity among humans, one must be in solidarity with all forms of life.

The biological basis of Enrique Dussel's material ethical principle also leads to the obligation of responsibility to all life on the planet. According to Dussel, moral acting 'ought to produce, reproduce, and increase responsibly the concrete life of every singular human being . . . having as an ultimate reference all of humanity and all life on the planet Earth' (2016, 69). The existence of the living human subject side by side with nature makes ethical behaviour possible (ibid., 78). In Dussel's ethics, life and nature cannot be circumvented and therefore to undermine life and nature is to undermine the possibility of existence in the future. For Dussel the material ethical principle is that all development of human life has to be 'in community and in harmony with Mother Earth' (in Mills, 2018, 81). Following Hans Jonas, life predestines us to responsibility for life. Life cares about life. The human condition implies responsibility for life. Parents with conscious minds take responsibility for their offspring. They have the obligation of transgenerational justice. According to Hans Jonas (1984) this responsibility is grounded in the reverence for all life on Earth.

The eccentric positionality

Critical reflection is a moral imperative. This thesis can be defended by turning to the philosophical anthropology of Helmut Plessner and his concept of the human eccentric positionality (1928/1975). For Plessner the core question of philosophical anthropology has to do with the conditions under which human acts (writing poems, composing music, torturing fellow human beings) are possible. What is the a priori of human acting? There is the fact of human life, but what are the conditions that make this fact possible? Intrinsic to human life, as for animal and plant life, is that it ends. The dialectic structure that binds all living beings to their environment is called 'positionality' by Plessner. And the nature of this positionality distinguishes living beings from one another. The animal coincides with itself. It is its body but it also steers its body. Animals have feelings and moods but do not reflect on them. The animal is conscious but not self-conscious. The human being, on the other hand, knows reflexivity and thinks about himself or herself. The a priori of human life is the 'eccentric positionality'. Unlike the animal coinciding with itself, human beings live eccentrically, which means that they can say no, resist, change the world and themselves. The implication is that humans are constantly at odds with themselves. They search for a safe place ('Heimat') that they will never find. They are part of nature and estranged from nature (the felicitous formulation of Plessner is 'naturbedingte Un-natur'). As constitutively homeless, humans will forever unsuccessfully try to escape from their positionality. As the only reflective animal, the human being cannot escape from the imperative to think about life and its relation to other lives.

The ethics of liberation

Enrique Dussel's ethics of liberation sees

> the transformation of the prevailing system as necessary for bringing about a more just order of things. A communication community that assumes the prevailing capitalist system with its structural inequality as an inevitable state of affairs, cannot claim, in good faith, to be promoting maximal symmetrical participation of all who may be impacted by the policy decisions of such bodies. (in Mills, 2018, 82)

This ethics starts from those who are excluded. It locates itself from the perspective of the 'exceptional situation of the excluded' (Dussel, 2013, 295). At the core of this ethics are the poor, oppressed, exploited people of our world. Contrary to the discursive ethics of Apel (1980) and Habermas (1991), which begins with the community of communication, 'the ethics of liberation departs from the excluded-affected from such a community. These are the victims of noncommunication' (Dussel, 2013, 294).

Moral intuitionism

Ethics as proposed here is different from a discursive ethics in which moral judgement is reached by rational reasoning and consensual argumentation (as per Apel and Habermas). The ethics of liberating togetherness is a practical-philosophical reflection that takes our intuitive judgements very seriously. Different from laws that tell us how we should behave, morality stems from moral intuitions that may tell us not to obey the law. I would argue that the law/morality dilemma is theoretically best expounded in the intuitionist model of Jonathan Haidt (2001). The basic claims about moral positions in this model are that intuitions come first and that they are justified or explained after the fact in order to convince others of the legitimacy of our moral decision. The model de-emphasizes the role of reasoning in reaching moral conclusions. Haidt asserts that moral judgement is primarily moved by intuition, with reasoning playing a smaller role in most of our moral decision-making. Conscious thought processes serve as a kind of post-hoc justification of our decisions. Haidt's model also states that moral reasoning is more likely to be interpersonal than private, reflecting on social motives (such as reputation or alliance-building) rather than on abstract principles. The model proposes that social and cultural factors are more important in moral decision-making than individual rational reasoning. In the context of philosophical reflection on human communicative praxis it is apposite that Haidt's social intuitionist model stresses the role of social interaction in moral judgements.

Towards an ethics of 'liberating togetherness'

Liberating togetherness poses the crucial question of how we can flourish together in the paradoxical ambiguity of loving and hating the world. Togetherness means sharing the limited space of one planet with a concrete, pluralist collective of others who differ from us and with whom we share existential meanings and future perspectives. It is the collective responsibility for shaping human relations – which are always communicative relations – in ways that make human survival possible. Sheer human togetherness aspires to the inclusion of the stranger, the 'other'. However, this should not be driven by the colonial imperialist position that invites the others to be together with us on our conditions. A good descriptor for the human togetherness I have in mind is the word 'cosmopolitan'. This implies the feeling that you are part of humanity and have obligations towards others who may be different from you. As Appiah formulates it, 'People are different, the cosmopolitan knows, and there is much to learn from our differences' (Appiah, 2006, xv).

The cosmopolitan takes local concerns about these differences seriously. It is intellectual laziness to simply categorize people's anxieties about changes they observe in their environs as xenophobia or populist fascism. We should not underestimate the importance of our local habitat in the definition of our identity. The localities we live in are where we find the joy and comfort of sociocultural proximity, as expressed in our mother tongue, customs, jokes and culinary preferences. We embrace the stranger but from an embeddedness in our localities.

Hannah Arendt's articulation of politics as 'sheer human togetherness' (1993, 180) is particularly helpful here. It reflects a real-life aspiration towards communal belonging, towards being incorporated in a community and experiencing an 'inclusive togetherness'. Furthermore, Arendt claims that the content of political life is 'the joy and the gratification that arise out of being in company with our peers, out of acting together' (ibid., 263).

This reflects a longing for the 'collective joy' of synchronous group activities that is so characteristic of human life.

Communication

An obvious question that now emerges is where to position communicative practice in the process of the structural political transformations that are required to realize communicative justice. What is the role of human communication? Over the past years there has emerged a growing literature on social actions (including means of communication) to promote human rights. Most of such contributions, like Robert Hornik's 'Why can't we sell human rights like we sell soap?' (2013), focus on questions related to behavioural or attitudinal change. In my analysis the crucial theme is whether media – commercial or public, mainstream or alternative platform – can seriously address the structural-political problems that obstruct the realization of human rights. The prospect is not very encouraging. Already in the 1970s and 1980s critical communication scholars were analysing the deep embeddedness of the media in the system of extractive capitalism supported by 'liberal' political interests. Back in 1973 Herbert Schiller, for example, described the emerging network of American economics and finance and how it utilizes the mass media for 'mind management' (Schiller, 1973).

In 1977 I edited (with Armand Mattelart) *The Corporate Village*, in which we analysed the control of capital, technology and marketing by the communication-industrial complex. Then in 1988, Noam Chomsky and Edward S. Herman described how the corporate mass media were structured to 'manufacture' consent for economic, social and political policies. This is the problem: how to change a social order with tools that are an essential part of that social order? Most of the world's public communication is owned and managed by giant transnational corporations. Most of the world's private communication is enabled and surveilled by giant transnational corporations. Most of the corporations that 'rule the world' (Korten, 1995) are not particularly inspired by the idea of communicative justice and the transformation of the social and international order it requires. They prefer the 'establishment' mood music.

Cooperative spirit

The longing for relation is an innate characteristic of the human being and constitutes the basis of human communication. Conversation is the most basic process in human life. Throughout human history conversation in myriad forms and constellations has been the central element in the organization of life. Humans are uniquely well wired for conversation because their communicative processes (different from all other species on the planet) are fundamentally cooperative as they are based on seeking common conceptual ground and shared intentionality. Human communication – as summarized by Tomasello (2008) – is grounded in shared understanding of the context of social interaction and is performed for fundamentally prosocial motives: informing others and sharing emotions.

We are able to communicate in cooperative ways because humans have the cognitive skills to create common ground. This cooperative spirit is characteristic of human communication. Human communication is motivated by mutualism and reciprocity. We request from others information that is helpful to us and offer others information that is useful to them. In the way we interact there needs to be recognition of the different assumptions that should be freely expressed but also freely questioned as a means to understand why we have different beliefs. The dialogical social conversation ('deep dialogue') does not resolve disagreement but it will seek to understand why we disagree and how we might live together in fundamental disagreement. This requires an extraordinarily strong moral commitment to the dignity of human agency as this conversation is liberated from all domineering intentions.

This dialogue, as an exercise in moral reasoning, is a reiterative and dynamic process in which participants' choices are rendered visible and justifiable. As there are multiple interpretations of what people hold to be right versus wrong, there are no last words in morality since moral positions are forever contestable propositions. There is no single morality. The deep dialogue assists in finding minimal agreements on procedures that optimally accommodate the interests and principles of various parties. The basic principle is communicative freedom. As argued before, this means that people should be free to accept or reject each other's claims on the basis of reasons they can evaluate. The respect for the communicative freedom of others is a basic recognition of their human agency (Benhabib, 2011, 68). It requires that we accept the other as fundamentally different from us and see their alterity as a unique feature that cannot be assimilated and reduced to similarity.

Communicative freedom is the capacity 'to agree or disagree with me on the basis of reasons the validity of which you accept or reject' (ibid., 67). The dialogue opens the possibility of recognizing that a different position is justified and that there can be real differences and genuine otherness. In the deep dialogue participants do not hold on to only one position as the absolute truth. They accept the willingness to cope with real and deep differences. This is a tall order, however. In many conversations participants take positions that for them are no longer negotiable because they hold their assumptions to be truths and defend them even against overwhelming evidence of their absurdity. Caught up in our own prejudices, fears and feelings we often listen to ourselves and not to the others. We often accuse the other of not listening, of being prejudiced, and prefer not to see those same flaws in our own thinking.

We seldom ask real questions and more often than not produce opinionated statements to which we add a question mark. In many encounters that are termed dialogue the participants do not question their own assumptions and take positions that they see as non-negotiable. We all bring assumptions about ourselves, others, the world, our societies, relationships and ways of life to the encounter. In today's world people will encounter others that come from different cultures with different cultural assumptions. And here, as Bohm noted, the problem is that 'they may not realize it, but they have some tendency to defend their assumptions and opinions reactively against evidence that they are not right, or simply a similar tendency to defend them against somebody who has another opinion' (1996, 11). Many conversations are in fact negotiating processes in which ideas are traded off against each other seeking accommodations that will satisfy all participants.

Against communication as tactical negotiation stands the genuine mode of compassionate communication. Its features (respect for the agency of the other, recognition of the equality of communication partners to initiate communication, acceptance of communicative freedom and the reciprocity of communication roles) constitute *communicative justice*. This is the essence of the human rights-based communication that I have sought in this book.

Amor mundi

On its long journey, humanity has developed, applauded and ignored fundamental moral principles. It took until 1948 for these principles to get universal recognition and in 1966 their codification in international law took an important step forward. In this moral evolution, normative standards for communicative behaviour also emerged. They had to be realized, though, in an environment that is largely inimical to their basic principles: respect, freedom, equality and security. This is a global challenge that cannot be resolved through global strategies. The imagination of a social order that realizes rights and freedoms begins at the local level, with the utopia of local participatory democracy. A crucial and powerful tool in local communities is – against all the political and corporate odds – the unique capacity for critical reflection.

In the communal reflective dialogue people will discover how their basic human rights intuitions collide with systemic impediments, and they will begin to draft plans for concrete action. The essence of the communal dialogue – about information, health, education or food – is human togetherness. I use this in the sense of Hannah Arendt's articulation of politics as 'sheer human togetherness' (1993, 180). Politics implies taking multiple perspectives into account and bringing them in dialogue. Totalitarian regimes have always understood the enormous transformative power of people acting and speaking together and have tried through coercive and discursive measures to break down human togetherness. As Arendt formulates it, 'Plurality is the condition of human action because we are all the same, that is, human, in such a way that nobody is ever the same as anyone else who ever lived, lives or will live' (1958, 8).

Following Hannah Arendt, we must develop the capacity for (politics as) togetherness and I think that basic to this capacity is the uniquely human moral intuition that our flourishing in plurality is possible through communicating with respect, in freedom, equality and security. We can realistically assume that few of our fellow human beings would prefer to communicate in humiliating, censorial, abusive and fearsome ways. Yet, that is how we communicate much of the time. As is common in behavioural choice we aspire to follow our moral intuitions but there are formidable impediments that drive us towards less benign acts. I have described some of these institutional and psychological obstacles in chapters 5 and 6, and want to suggest that – against all the odds – we may overcome them. In their study on the altruistic personality Samuel and Pearl Oliner concluded, 'we need to cultivate varied forms of moral sensibilities' (Oliner and Oliner, 1988, 258). They focused on the importance of the parental home, but also stated that 'it is a community responsibility . . . the school can play a particularly important role. . . . Schools need to become caring institutions' (ibid., 258). In the same way, it could be argued that communicative institutions, such as the news media, should become 'caring institutions'. In the transformation of societies characterized by totalitarian, abusive, predatory and fearmongering features to compassionate communities, 'caring communicative institutions' will play a crucial role. To quote the Oliners again, 'caring media will acknowledge diversity on the road to moral concern. They will involve emotion and intellect in the service of responsibility and caring' (ibid., 259). Human rights imagine a world without degradation, abuse, inequality and insecurity. With reference to the famous Thomas theorem,[1] we could state that if we believe that the human rights imagination is real, it will be real in its consequences.

The transformation that is essential to the realization of communicative justice requires the courage to love the world. The book about political theories that Hannah Arendt wanted to entitle 'Amor Mundi' was never written. We will never know how she would have interpreted – against the background of her writings about totalitarianism, anti-Semitism and evil – love for the world. It is possible that her pessimism about the state of the world stood in the way of loving the world. Yet, the first biography written of her has as its subtitle 'For Love of the World' (Young-Bruehl, 1982). Maybe Arendt realized that in the middle of the world's gross evil, we must relate lovingly to the world, to Mother Gaia, lest we leave her and ourselves to perish. And it is precisely communicative justice that could help us to recognize the dignity of Mother Earth and thus discursively find possible solutions to life-threatening developments.

Without the recognition and implementation of communicative justice human communication is impossible or is an exercise in futility. If indeed conversation is critical to human survival, then communication based on communicative justice makes the difference in people's lives between life and death. As I have argued in this book, communicative justice can only be found in a fundamentally transformed social order. This transformation requires the moral strength to love the world. The ancient Roman poet Horace coined the phrase 'Aude sapere', meaning dare to know. This phrase was embraced by the philosopher Kant and it ultimately became the motto for the intellectual revolution of the Enlightenment period. A motto for our time could be 'dare to love the world'. This means having the moral courage to commit to active participation in the public cause, to revolt against situations that we experience as unjust and immoral, to accept that our moral universe extends to future generations but also to new arrivals in our societies such as refugees and migrants. Realizing that living always means living with others, we have to take responsibility for a world in which we and others can live with dignity, freedom, equality and security. We have to decide how we will relate to this moral challenge.

Max Weber wrote in 1917 that the fate of our times 'is characterized by rationalization and intellectualization and, above all, by the "disenchantment" of the world' (in Gerth and Wright Mills, 1946, 155). I believe that the major forces in the process of disenchantment are bureaucratic institutions. They colonize dreams and imaginations about possible futures by turning them into prospective evaluations, technology assessment and risk analyses. The colonizers of modern times are the rational experts on committees and sub-committees. There may be a gradual decline of mystery but modern science has also opened our eyes to the magic of reality (Dawkins, 2012). There is secular enchantment in discovering how magic the reality of our living environment is. As Dawkins writes, the truth is more magical than made-up mysteries. Science has the power to excite our imagination as we see the wonders of a rainbow (ibid., 158).

It is not the rational rigour of scientific method that disenchanted the world but the increasing embeddedness of science in bureaucratic institutions where academics spend more time ticking off questions on application forms for funds they will never receive than in adventuring into all the questions we have no explanations for. What hinders the feeling of the enchantment that science can bring is the conception of science as a tool to master the natural world. This conception, with its long history, separated the body from the mind, subjects from objects, values from facts and humans from nonhumans. It continues to have deep consequences for the relationship between humans and their natural environment. Contrary to this 'colonial mindset' amor mundi means feeling at home in the world and interacting without trepidation with nature and learning from it. The world can only be our home when we are once more receptive to the magical wonders of our living environment. The greatest, most beautiful and complex wonder seems to me the capacity of all members of this environment to communicate. Amor mundi means an intense, passionate relationship with this enchanting wonder.

Hannah Arendt concluded her study on the origins of totalitarianism with words that are a perfect fit with my conviction that the end of the international human rights regime as we have known it since 1948 is at the same time the beginning of a human rights culture inspired by our courage to love the world. She wrote, 'there remains the truth that every end in history necessarily contains a new beginning; this beginning is the promise, the only "message" which the end can ever produce. Beginning, before it becomes a historical event, is the supreme capacity of man [sic]; politically it is identical with man's freedom' (Arendt, 1968, 478).

Conclusion

To live and flourish together we need to communicate with one another. And throughout history we have asked: how should we do this? What normative rules should guide our communicative behaviour? Since 1948 the international community has had a shared catalogue of such rules. These are the standards offered by the Universal Declaration of Human Rights: the basis of the international human rights regime. Abdul Aziz Said (1998, xi) writes, 'Human rights may be difficult to define but impossible to ignore.' It is indeed true that in the early twenty-first century human rights have become a reality, but so too have their worldwide violations.

In this book, I have explored how the rights and freedoms of the international human rights regime became essential guides for human communicative behaviour. I concluded that these moral and legal abstractions could only become a human rights-based communication practice if the international community endorsed and codified the human right to communication. The cornerstones of this solidarity right would be communicative freedom, communicative equality, communicative respect and communicative security. These four normative dimensions constitute what I searched for: 'communicative justice'.

For this justice to become reality I turned to the often overlooked Article 28 of the UDHR, which links human rights to an international and social order in which these rights could be realized. Analysing the main features of prevailing worldwide societal arrangements as humiliating, predatory, exploitative and fearful, this international and social order seemed poorly equipped to provide effective protection for the solidarity right to communication. The society that offers better conditions for communicative justice would have to be caring, convivial, egalitarian and secure. This is a society in which people dare to love the world.

This 'amor mundi' often seems like an insurmountable challenge. However, against all the odds of humiliation, censorship, surveillance, abuse, deception and biological extermination, humanity can find common ground in an ethics of liberating togetherness and design concrete strategies to re-enchant the world. This is the very practical commitment to a shared responsibility that goes beyond 'humans only' and includes those who are not yet there. Like all sentient beings we can learn. We've done it before. We can live in harmony with one another and all the others. We did it before. We can love the world even when we have hated it.

No one has the perfect recipe for amor mundi. But we should realize that we have all the tools and resources for a cosmopolitan and transgenerational togetherness. As Graeber and Wengrow (2021) demonstrate, with much archaeological evidence, there is nothing inevitable in history. There are few if any fixed points in history. Humanity has also experimented with many different social arrangements and there are no inevitable correlations between scale of communities and complexity, hierarchy or violence. The flexibility of human history suggests that 'the possibilities for human intervention are far greater than we're inclined to think' (ibid., 524). Therefore the 'grand récit' about a social order that facilitates the realization of human rights is more than a utopian imagination. It is a historical possibility and it is part of human freedom to create that new social reality. We have unique talents for compassionate communication. The courage to love the world empowers us to not waste our capacity for communicative justice.

Notes

Chapter 1: Human Rights Before Human Rights

1 Olympe de Gouges (who lived from 7 May 1748 to 3 November 1793) was a French playwright and political activist. In her feminist writings she demanded that French women be given the same rights as French men. In her Declaration of the Rights of Woman and the Female Citizen (1791), she challenged the practice of male authority and the notion of male–female inequality. As a precursor to the right to communicate, she declared: 'Women have the right to mount the scaffold, they must also have the right to mount the speaker's rostrum.'
2 For overviews of African, Asian and Latin American/Caribbean histories of human rights I recommend Lakatos, István. *Comparative Human Rights Diplomacy*. London: Palgrave Macmillan, 2022.
3 Excellent sources are Cardenas, Sonia. *Human Rights in Latin America: A Politics of Terror and Hope*. Philadelphia: University of Pennsylvania Press, 2010. Ishay, Micheline R. *The History of Human Rights: From Ancient Times to the Globalization Era*. Berkeley: University of California Press, 2007. Serrano, M. and V. Popovski (eds). *Human Rights Regimes in the Americas*. Tokyo: United Nations University Press, 2010.
4 A well-documented, readable and fascinating history of dignity from classical Greece, to Stoic thought, Confucian, Buddhist and Islamic conceptions, to Kant and Marx, is Debes, R. *Dignity: A History*. New York: Oxford University Press, 2017.
5 Sources are surviving oral history and written accounts by, inter alia, J. Teit, in Cooper (1998, 113).
6 A point of caution here is that the *Times of Israel* reported on 4 September 2021 that Ariely's field study on honesty might be based on false data and might be retracted: 'Israeli-American celebrity academic Dan Ariely has said he "undoubtedly made a mistake" in a famous study of his that has been revealed as based on falsified data. In an interview with Channel 12 Friday, Ariely denied responsibility for the forgery and expressed belief that his reputation would recover from a recent slew of problematic revelations.' Whatever may be the case I do not think this negates his conclusions in the 2012 book.
7 An interesting source is the historian J.B. Bury (1913) in a little book entitled *A History of Freedom of Thought*.
8 Most of the official positions on tolerance as expressed in various edicts were of a limited nature and suited political convenience. The Edict of Nantes

Notes to pages 31–68

(1598), for example, tolerated the Huguenots but with restrictions (Bury, 1913, 35). Locke, who pleaded for a broad scope of toleration, did not include the Catholics. Also the Edict of Toleration in 1781 by Emperor Joseph II was of a limited kind. Voltaire's (1694–1778) tolerance was limited: he was against persecution but confined access to public functions to officials who belonged to the state religion, Catholicism. Mirabeau (1749–91) protested against the use of toleration, 'since the authority which tolerates might also not tolerate' (ibid., 36). Thomas Paine (1791/1984) wrote in his *Rights of Man* 'that toleration is not the opposite of intoleration, but is the counterfeit of it'. In his view both are despotisms. One despot assumes to himself the right of withholding liberty of conscience, and the other assumes the right of granting it.

Chapter 2: Human Rights and Communication
1 The text of the UDHR can be found at https://www.un.org/en/about-us/universal-declaration-of-human-rights
2 The text of the ICCPR can be found at https://www.ohchr.org/en/instruments-mechanisms/instruments/international-covenant-civil-and-political-rights
3 The text of the CPPCG can be found at https://www.ohchr.org/en/instruments-mechanisms/instruments/convention-prevention-and-punishment-crime-genocide

Chapter 3: Communication Rights
1 The text for the Convention can be found at https://www.ohchr.org/en/instruments-mechanisms/instruments/convention-elimination-all-forms-discrimination-against-women
2 Text for Fourth World Conference on Women can be found at https://www.un.org/en/conferences/women/beijing1995
3 Text for the UNCRC can be found at https://www.ohchr.org/en/instruments-mechanisms/instruments/convention-rights-child
4 https://resourcecentre.savethechildren.net
5 The text for the UDHR can be found at https://www.un.org/en/about-us/universal-declaration-of-human-rights
6 Text for the Declaration on Race and Racial Prejudice can be found at https://en.unesco.org/about-us/legal-affairs/declaration-race-and-racial-prejudice
7 https://unesdoc.unesco.org
8 Ibid.
9 Source: cns.miis.edu nam
10 This section was written in cooperation with Maria Hagan, PhD candidate at Oxford University.
11 For the list of proposed rights, see the Draft Declaration on Communication Rights (UN WSIS, Geneva 2003: https://www.itu.int). For a critical commentary by Article XIX see: https://www.article19.org › files › pdfs › analysis.
12 https://www.itu.int
13 Ibid.

14 Human rights provisions to be found at: https://www.un.org/en/about-us/universal-declaration-of-human-rights; https://www.un.org/en/genocideprevention/genocide-convention.shtml; https://www.ohchr.org/en/instruments-mechanisms/instruments/international-covenant-civil-and-political-rights

Chapter 4: Challenges and Communication Rights
1 https://opennet.net
2 https://youtu.be/1j7TpoLmR60

Chapter 5: The Trouble with Human Rights
1 Source: GMMP Results: Glacial progress towards media gender equality 25 years on. WACC, https://waccglobal.org/
2 Ibid.
3 U.S. Supreme Court *Gertz* v. *Robert Welch, Inc.*, 418 U.S. 323 (1974), No. 72-617, Argued November 14, 1973.
4 The European Court of Human Rights has extended the standards of the European Convention on Human Rights to corporations, using as legal basis Article 1 of the Convention that provides to 'secure to everyone within its jurisdiction the rights and freedoms defined . . . in the Convention'. For Article 10 of the European Convention see https://www.echr.coe.int
5 In 2022, these eighteen journalists were murdered in the line of duty. Source: Committee to Protect Journalists' report: https://www.cpj.org
6 Sophocles (translation of 1947) *Antigone* in *The Theban Plays*. Harmondsworth: Penguin Classics.
7 It is difficult to expect worldwide respect for human rights if the Secretary General of the United Nations is not forthright in blaming and shaming the perpetrators of serious violations such as in the killing of children in Yemen, Syria and Myanmar. Jo Becker (Director Children's Rights Advocacy with Human Rights Watch) commented: 'We continue to be disappointed that the Secretary General is not using the "list of shame" to hold all parties accountable for their grave violations against children' (source: Thalif Deen, Inter Press Service, June 2021). Whereas the humanitarian organization Save the Children reported that in 2020 194 Yemeni children were killed or maimed, the UN Report on Children and Armed Conflict failed to hold the perpetrators to account.
8 In the strict sense of the word Buddhism is not a religion.
9 Herman and Peterson name as 'New Humanitarians', inter alia, Vaclav Havel, Bernard Kouchner, Michael Ignatieff, Susan Sontag, Jüurgen Habermas, Richard Falk, David Held, Louis Henkin, Steven Ratner, Brian Urquhart and Ian Willlams.
10 Please note that the United Nations Commission on Human Rights was on 15 March 2006 replaced by the Human Rights Council.

Chapter 6: Communicative Justice

1. The text can for the Covenant be found at https://www.ohchr.org/en/instruments-mechanisms/instruments/international-covenant-economic-social-and-cultural-rights
2. https://legal.un.org
3. For those interested in the topic of human dignity and humiliation: https://www.humiliationstudies.org
4. https://www.theworldcounts.com

Chapter 7: The Practice of Communicative Justice

1. William Isaac Thomas and Dorothy Swaine Thomas (1928, 571–2): 'If men define situations as real, they are real in their consequences.'

References

Acemoglu, A. and J.A. Robinson (2013). *Why Nations Fail: The Origins of Power, Prosperity and Poverty*. London: Profile Books.
Adloff, F. and A. Caillé (2022). *Convivial Futures*. [Open Access]. Bielefeld: Bielefeld Verlag.
Ahmad ibn Naqib al-Misri (1997). *The Reliance of the Traveller*. Beltsfield, MD: Amana Publications.
Alegre, A. and S. Ó'Siochrú (2005). Communication rights. vecam.org/2002–2014/article670.html
Alston, P. (1982). A third generation of solidarity rights: Progressive development or obfuscation of international human rights law? *Netherlands International Law Review*, 29(3), 307–22.
Altheide, D.L. (2002). *Creating Fear: News and the Construction of Crisis*. New York: Aldine de Gruyter.
An-Na'im, A.A., J.D. Gort, H. Jansen and H.M. Vroom (eds) (1995). *Human Rights and Religious Values: An Uneasy Relationship?* Grand Rapids, MI: William B. Eerdmans Publishing Company.
Andrejevic, M. (2007). *iSpy: Surveillance and Power in the Interactive Era*. Lawrence, KS: University of Kansas Press.
Annan, K. (1997). Statement at the Fiftieth Anniversary of the Universal Declaration of Human Rights, 10 December, at the University of Tehran, Iran.
Apel, K.O. (1980). *Towards a Transformation of Philosophy*. London: Routledge.
Appiah, K. (2006). *Cosmopolitanism*. New York: W.W. Norton.
Arendt, H. (1958). *The Human Condition*. Chicago: The University of Chicago Press.
Arendt, H. (1968). *The Origins of Totalitarianism*. New York: Harcourt Inc.
Arendt, H. (1993). *Between Past and Future*. New York: Penguin Books.
Ariely, D. (2012). *The (Honest) Truth about Dishonesty: How We Lie to Everyone – Especially Ourselves*. New York: Harper Collins.
Aristotle (1907). *De Anima* [On the Soul]. Translated by R.D. Hicks. Cambridge: Cambridge University Press.
Baehr, P.R. (1999). *Human Rights: Universality in Practice*. Basingstoke: Macmillan.
Baker, J., K. Lynch, S. Cantillon and J. Walsh (2004). *Equality: From Theory to Action*. New York: Palgrave Macmillan.
Barber, B. (1984). *Strong Democracy*. Berkeley: University of California Press.
Barnet, R.J. and J. Cavanagh (1994). *Global Dreams: Imperial Corporations and the New World Order*. New York: Simon & Schuster.

References

Beck, U. (1992). *Risk Society: Towards a New Modernity*. London: Sage.
Benhabib, S. (2011). *Dignity in Adversity: Human Rights in Troubled Times*. Cambridge: Polity Press.
Bennett, S., J. Ter Wal, A. Lipiński, M. Fabiszak and M. Krzyżanowski (2013). The representation of third-country nationals in European news discourse: Journalistic perceptions and practices. *Journalism Practice*, 7(3), 248–65.
Berlin, J. (1969). *Four Essays on Liberty*. Oxford: Oxford University Press.
Birdsall, W.F. (2006). A right to communicate as an open work. *Media and Development*, 53(1), 41–6.
Boff, L. and C. Boff (1987). *Introducing Liberation Theology*. New York: Orbis Books.
Bohm, D. (1996). *On Dialogue*. New York: Routledge.
Bok, S. (1978). *Lying: Moral Choice in Public and Private Life*. New York: Pantheon Books.
Bostrom, N. (2002). Existential risks: Analyzing human extinction scenarios and related hazards. *Journal of Evolution and Technology*, 9(1), 1–30.
Boulding, K. (1959). National images and international systems. *Journal of Conflict Resolution*, 3(2), 120–31.
Bradley, H. (2016). *Fractured Identities*. Cambridge: Polity Press.
Brecht, B. (1932). Essay 'Radio as a communication device', *Der Rundfunk als Kommunikationsapparat* [Radio as a communication apparatus]. Berlin.
Brynjolfsson, E. and A. McAfee (2015). *The Second Machine Age*. New York: W.W. Norton.
Buber, M. (1970). *I and Thou*. New York: Simon & Schuster.
Bury, J.B. (1913). *A History of Freedom of Thought*. London: Williams and Norgate.
Calleja, A. and B. Solis (2005). *Con permiso. La radio comunitaria en México* [Excuse me. Community radio in Mexico]. México: Friedrich Ebert Foundation.
Cardenas, S. (2010). *Human Rights in Latin America: A Politics of Terror and Hope*. Philadelphia: University of Pennsylvania Press.
Castells, M. (2001). *The Internet Galaxy: Reflections on the Internet, Business and Society*. Oxford: Oxford University Press.
Césaire, A. (2000). *Discourse on Colonialism*. New York: Monthly Review Press.
Chan, J. (1999). A Confucian perspective on human rights for contemporary China. In J.R. Bauer and D.A. Bell (eds), *The East Asian Challenge for Human Rights*. Cambridge: Cambridge University Press, pp. 212–37.
Chomsky, N. and E.S. Herman (1988). *Manufacturing Consent: The Political Economy of the Mass Media*. New York: Pantheon Books.
Cooper, T. (1998). *A Time before Deception: Truth in Communication, Culture, and Ethics*. Santa Fe: Clear Light Publishers.
Dahl, R.A. (1956). *A Preface to Democratic Theory*. Chicago: The University of Chicago Press.
D'Arcy, J. (1969). Direct broadcast satellites and the right to communicate. *EBU Review*, 118, 14–18.
Darwin, C. (1891/2010). *The Descent of Man*. New York: Dover Publications.

Dawkins, R. (1989). *The Selfish Gene*. Oxford: Oxford University Press.
Dawkins, R. (2012). *The Magic of Reality*. London: Transworld Publishers.
De Beauvoir, S. (1947). *Pour une morale de l'ambiguïté* [The ethics of ambiguity]. Paris: Gallimard.
De Dijn, A. (2020). *Freedom: An Unruly History*. Cambridge, MA: Harvard University Press.
De Wulf, M. (1904). *Les Quatre premiers Quodlibets de Godefroid de Fontaines* [The four first 'any whatevers' of Godefroid de Fontaines]. Louvain: n.p.
Debes, R. (2017). *Dignity: A History*. New York: Oxford University Press.
Delimatsis, P. (2007). *International Trade in Service*. Oxford: Oxford University Press.
Dembour, M.-B. and T. Kelly (2011). Introduction. In M.-B. Dembour and T. Kelly (eds), *Are Human Rights for Migrants?* Abingdon: Routledge, pp. 1–22.
Diamond, J. (2013). *The World until Yesterday*. London: Allen Lane, Penguin Books.
Donnelly, J. (1990). Human rights, individual rights and collective rights. In J. Berting, P. Baehr and J. Burgers (eds), *Human Rights in a Pluralist World: Individuals and Collectivities*. London: Mecker, pp. 39–62.
Duchrow, U. (1995). *Alternatives to Global Capitalism*. Heidelberg: Kairos Europe.
Dunbar, R. (1996). *Grooming, Gossip and the Evolution of Language*. Cambridge, MA: Harvard University Press.
Dussel, E. (1998). *Ethics and Community*. New York: Orbis Books.
Dussel, E. (2013). *Ethics of Liberation*. Durham, NC: Duke University Press.
Dussel, E. (2016). *14 Tesis de etica: hacia la esencia del pensamiento critico* [14 theses on ethics: towards the essence of critical thinking]. Madrid: Editorial Trotta.
Dworkin, R. (1985). *A Matter of Principle*. Cambridge, MA: Harvard University Press.
Eide, A. (1992). Article 28. In A. Eide and G. Alfredson (eds), *The Universal Declaration of Human Rights: A Commentary*. Oslo: Scandinavian University Press, pp. 433–48.
European Commission (2006). Communication of 1 February 2006. White Paper on a European Communication Policy. Brussels.
Finegan, J. (2019). *Archaeological History of the Ancient Middle East*. Abingdon: Routledge.
Fisher, D. (1982). *The Right to Communicate: A Status Report*. Paris: UNESCO.
Flinterman, C. (1990). Three generations of human rights. In J. Berting, P. Baehr and J. Burgers (eds), *Human Rights in a Pluralist World: Individuals and Collectivities*. London: Mecker, pp. 75–82.
Fowers, B.J. (2015). *The Evolution of Ethics*. New York: Palgrave Macmillan.
Fox, J. (2007). The uncertain relationship between transparency and accountability. *Development in Practice*, 17(4 5), 663–71.
Freire, P. (1970). *Pedagogy of the Oppressed*. Harmondsworth: Penguin.
French, M. (2008). *From Eve to Dawn, a History of Women in the World*. New York: The Feminist Press at CUNY.
Friedman, T.L. (2003). The humiliation factor. *The New York Times*, 9 November.

References

Fromm, E. (1942). *The Fear of Freedom*. London: Routledge.
Fuller, L.K. (ed.) (2007). *Community Media: International Perspectives*. London: Palgrave Macmillan.
Furedi, F. (1997). *Culture of Fear*. London: Cassell.
Gallagher, M. (2001). *Gender Setting: New Media Agendas for Monitoring and Advocacy*. London: Zed Books.
Gandhi, M. (1947). Letter to the Director of UNESCO, in UNESCO archives.
Gerth, H.H. and C. Wright Mills (eds) (1946). Science as a vocation. *From Max Weber: Essays in Sociology*. Oxford: Oxford University Press, pp. 129–56.
Gertz, E. (1974). *Gertz v. Robert Welch Inc. The Story of a Landmark Libel Case*. Carbondale, IL: Southern Illinois University Press.
Ghai, Y. (1999). Rights, social justice and globalization in East Asia. In J.R. Bauer and D.A. Bell (eds), *The East Asian Challenge for Human Rights*. Cambridge: Cambridge University Press, pp. 241–63.
Gould, C.C. (1988). *Rethinking Democracy: Freedom and Cooperation in Politics, Economy and Society*. Cambridge: Cambridge University Press.
Graeber, D. (2015). *The Utopia of Rules*. New York: Melville House Publishing.
Graeber, D. and D. Wengrow (2021). *The Dawn of Everything: A New History of Humanity*. London: Allen Lane.
Grande, F., J.J. De Ruiter and M. Spotti (eds) (2012). *Mother Tongue and Intercultural Valorization: Europe and its Migrant Youth*. Milan: FrancoAngeli.
Gruson, L. (2017). Comment mettre la culture au service de l'accueil des migrants? [How could culture be used to welcome migrants?]. *Hommes & Migrations*, 1, 170–9.
Gumpert, G. and S. Drucker (1998). The demise of privacy in a private world: from front porches to chat rooms. *Communication Theory*, 8(4), 408–25.
Gutiérrez, G. (1973). *A Theology of Liberation*. New York: Maryknoll.
Habermas, J. (1991). *Justification and Application*. Cambridge, MA: MIT Press.
Habermas, J. (1993). *Moral Consciousness and Communicative Action*. Cambridge, MA: MIT Press.
Haidt, J. (2001). The emotional dog and its rational tail: A social intuitionist approach to moral judgment. *Psychological Review*, 108(4), 814–34.
Hamelink, C.J. (1994a). *Trends in World Communication: On Disempowerment and Self-Empowerment*. Penang: Southbound.
Hamelink, C.J. (1994b). *The Politics of World Communication*. London: Sage.
Hamelink, C.J. (2001). Introduction: Human rights and the media. *Critical Arts*, 15(1–2), 3–11.
Hamelink, C.J. (2003). Human rights for the information society. In S. Ó'Siochrú and B. Girard (eds), *Communicating in an Information Society*. Geneva: UNRISD, pp. 121–63.
Hamelink, C.J. (2004a). Did WSIS achieve anything at all? *Gazette: The International Journal for Communication Studies*, 66(3–4), 281–90.
Hamelink, C.J. (2004b). The 2003 Graham Spry Memorial Lecture: Toward a human right to communicate? *Canadian Journal of Communication*, 29, 205–12.

Hamelink, C.J. (2006). *Regeert de leugen?* [Is the lie in charge?] Amsterdam: Boom.
Hamelink, C.J. (2011). *Media and Conflict*. Abingdon: Routledge.
Hamelink, C.J. (2019). *Communication and Peace*. London: Palgrave Macmillan.
Hamelink, C.J. and A. Mattelart (eds) (1977). *The Corporate Village*. Rome: IDOC.
Hamilton, C. (2017). *Defiant Earth*. Cambridge: Polity Press.
Hammond, P. (2002). Moral combat: The new humanitarianism and advocacy journalism. In D. Chandler (ed.), *Rethinking Human Rights*. New York: Palgrave Macmillan, pp. 176–95.
Henderson, H. (1978). *Creating Alternative Futures*. New York: Putnam & Sons.
Herman, E.S. and D. Peterson (2002). Morality's avenging angels: The new humanitarian crusaders. In D. Chandler (ed.), *Rethinking Human Rights*. New York: Palgrave Macmillan, pp. 196–215.
Hickel, J. (2020). *Less is More: How Degrowth Will Save the World*. London: Windmill.
Holl, W. (1985). Geschichtsbewusstsein und Oral History. Geschichtsdidaktische Uerberlegungen [Historical consciousness and oral history]. In L. Niethammer and W. Trapp (eds), *Lebenserfahrung und Kollektives Gedaechtnis* [Life, Experience and Collective Memory]. Frankfurt: Suhrkamp, pp. 63–82.
Hoogendijk, W. (1991). *The Economic Revolution: Towards a Sustainable Future by Freeing the Economy from Moneymaking*. London: Green Print.
Hornik, R.C. (2013). Why can't we sell human rights like we sell soap? In R. Goodman, D. Jinks and A.K. Woods (eds), *Understanding Social Action, Promoting Human Rights*. Oxford: Oxford University Press, pp. 47–69.
Illich, I. (1973). *Tools for Conviviality*. London: Marion Boyars.
Inagaki, R. (1986). Some aspects of human rights in Japan. In UNESCO, *Philosophical Foundations of Human Rights*. Paris: UNESCO, pp. 179–92.
Innis, H. (1972). *Empire and Communications*. Toronto: University of Toronto Press.
International Commission of Jurists (1982). Report of a seminar on Human Rights in Islam.
Isaacson, W. (2011). *Steve Jobs: The Biography*. New York: Simon & Schuster.
Ishay, M.R. (2007). *The History of Human Rights: From Ancient Times to the Globalization Era*. Berkeley: University of California Press.
Jahr, F. (1927). Bio-Ethik. Eine Umschau über die ethischen Beziehungen des Menschen zu Tier und Pflanze [Bio-ethics. A review of the ethical connections of humans to animals and plants]. *Kosmos. Handweiser für Naturfreunde*, 24(1), 2–4.
Jallov, B. (2012). *Empowerment Radio: Voices Building a Community*. London: Panos Institute.
Jansen, S.C. (1991). *Censorship*. Oxford: Oxford University Press.
Jonas, H. (1984). *The Imperative of Responsibility: In Search of an Ethics for the Technological Age*. Chicago: The University of Chicago Press.
Jongman, J.J. and A.P. Schmidt (1994). *Monitoring Human Rights*. Leiden: PIOOM.

References

Jordan, J., A. Peysakhovich and D.G. Rand (2015). Why we cooperate. In J. Decety and T. Wheatley (eds), *The Moral Brain*. Cambridge, MA: MIT Press, pp. 87–101.

Kant, I. (1785/1957). *Grundlegung zur Metaphysik der Sitten* [Foundations of the Metaphysics of Morals]. Hamburg: Felix Meiner Verlag.

Kaplan, A. (1980). Human relations and human rights in Judaism. In A.S. Rosenbaum (ed.), *The Philosophy of Human Rights*. Westport, CT: Greenwood Press, pp. 53–86.

Kaplan, A. (1999). *The Development Capacity*. Geneva: Non-Governmental Liaison Service.

Korten, D.C. (1995). *When Corporations Rule the World*. West Hartford, CT: Kumarian Press.

Kuhlen, R. (2003). Why are communication rights so controversial? In O. Drossou and H. Jensen (eds), *Visions in Process: WSIS, Geneva 2003 – Tunis 2005*. Berlin: Heinrich Böll Foundation.

Kurzweil, R. (2005). *The Singularity is Near: When Humans Transcend Biology*. New York: Viking Books.

Lakatos, I. (2022). *Comparative Human Rights Diplomacy*. London, Palgrave Macmillan.

Lane, P., L. Brown, J. Bobb and M. Bobb (1984/2020). *The Sacred Tree*. Twin Lakes, WI: Lotus Press.

Lee, P. (2004). The right to communicate affirms and restores human dignity. In P. Lee (ed.), *Many Voices, One Vision: The Right to Communicate in Practice*. London: WACC.

López Obrador, A.M. (2021). *A la mitad del camino* [The middle of the road]. Ciudad de México: Editorial Planeta Mexicana

Louv, R. (2008). *Last Child in the Woods*. Chapel Hill, NC: Algonquin Publishers.

Lukes, S. (1993). Five fables about human rights. In S. Shure and S. Hurley (eds), *On Human Rights*. New York: Basic Books, pp. 19–40.

MacBride Commission (1980). *Many Voices, One World: Report of the International Commission for the Study of Communication Problems*. Paris: UNESCO.

Marcus, K.L. (2012). Accusation in a mirror. *Loyola University Chicago Law Journal*, 43(2), 357–93. https://lawecommons.luc.edu/luclj/vol43/iss2/5

Marcuse, H. (1968). *Psychoanalyse en politiek* [Psychoanalysis and politics]. Amsterdam: Van Gennep.

Margalit, A. (1996). *The Decent Society*. Cambridge, MA: Harvard University Press.

McIver, W.J. Jr and W.F. Birdsall (2002). Technological evolution and the right to communicate: The implications for electronic democracy. Paper presented at EURICOM conference, Nijmegen, October 2002.

McIver, W.J. Jr, W.F. Birdsall and M. Rasmussen (2003). The internet and the right to communicate. *First Monday*, 8(12). https://doi.org/10.5210/fm.v8i12.1102

Michels, R. (1915). *Political Parties: A Sociological Study of the Oligarchical Tendencies of Modern Democracy*. Glencoe, IL: Free Press.

References

Mill, J.S. (1859). *On Liberty* (3rd edn). London: Longman, Green, Longman Roberts & Green.

Mills, F.B. (2018). *Enrique Dussel's Ethics of Liberation*. New York: Palgrave Macmillan.

Milton, J. (1644/2017). *Areopagitica: a Speech for the Liberty of Unlicensed Printing*. Oxford: Clarendon Press.

Morozov, E. (2011). *The Net Delusion: How Not to Liberate the World*. London: Penguin Books.

Mosco, V. (2014). *To the Cloud*. Boulder, CO: Paradigm.

Moyer, B. (1987). *The Movement Action Plan*. Cambridge, MA: Dandelion.

Nail, T. (2016). A tale of two crises: Migration and terrorism after the Paris attacks. *Studies in Ethnicity and Nationalism*, 16(1), 158–67.

Ndlovu-Gatshenia, S.J. (2018). *Epistemic Freedom in Africa: Deprovincialization and Decolonization*. New York: Routledge.

Niebuhr, R. (1932). *Moral Man and Immoral Society*. Louisville, KY: Westminster John Knox Press.

Nielsen, K. (1989). *Why Be Moral?* New York: Prometheus Books.

Nino, C.S. (1991). *The Ethics of Human Rights*. Oxford: Clarendon Press.

Noble, D. (2006). *The Music of Life*. Oxford: Oxford University Press.

Noel, N.A. (2020). *Critical Analysis of Christianity and Human Rights*. Google Books.

Oliner, S.P. and P.M. Oliner (1988). *The Altruistic Personality*. New York: The Free Press.

Paine, T. (1791/1984). *Rights of Man*. London: Penguin Books.

Partsch, K.J. (1981). Freedom of conscience and expression, and political freedoms. In L. Henkin (ed.), *The International Bill of Rights*. Creskill, NJ: Hampton Press, pp. 209–45.

Pateman, C. (1970). *Participation and Democratic Theory*. Cambridge: Cambridge University Press.

Piketty, T. (2013). *Le Capital au XXIe siècle* [Capital in the 21st century]. Paris: Éditions du Seuil.

Pinker, S. (2011). *The Better Angels of Our Nature*. London: Penguin Books.

Plessner, H. (1928/1975). *Die Stufen des Organischen und der Mensch. Einleitung in die philosophische Anthropologie* [The stages of the organic and the human being]. Berlin: Walter de Gruyter.

Prendergast, P. (2017). *Voice to action: Community radio empowering rural communities*. PhD Dissertation at the University of Amsterdam.

Preston, R. (1991). The provision of education to refugees in places of temporary asylum: Some implications for development. *Comparative Education Review*, 27(1), 61–81.

Rehof, L.A. (1992). Article 12. In A. Eide and G. Alfredson (eds), *The Universal Declaration of Human Rights: A Commentary*. Oslo: Scandinavian University Press, pp. 187–202.

References

Rich, A. (1995). *On Lies, Secrets, and Silence: Selected Prose 1966–1978*. New York: W.W. Norton.

Ritzer, G. (1993). *The McDonaldization of Society*. London: Pine Forge Press.

Robertson, A. (2010). *Mediated Cosmopolitanism: The World of Television News*. Cambridge: Polity Press.

Robson, J.M. (ed.) (1966). *Mill, On Liberty*. New York: The Odyssey Press.

Roht-Arriaza, N. (1995). *Impunity and Human Rights in International Law and Practice*. Oxford: Oxford University Press.

Rundle, H. (2019). Knowledge can help solve the biodiversity crisis. Scientific American blog.

Said, A.A. (ed.) (1998). *Human Rights in World Order*. New York: Praeger.

Sankatsing, G. (2016). *Quest to Rescue Our Future*. Amsterdam: Rescue Our Future Foundation.

Sassen, S. (2016). Economic cleansing: Failure dressed in fine clothes. *Social Research*, 83(3), 673–87.

Sayad, A. (2004). *The Suffering of the Immigrant*. Translated by D. Macey. Cambridge: Polity Press.

Scheinin, M. (1992). Article 18. In A. Eide and G. Alfredson (eds), *The Universal Declaration of Human Rights: A Commentary*. Oslo: Scandinavian University Press, pp. 261–74.

Schiller, H.I. (1973). *The Mind Managers*. Boston: Beacon Press.

Schumacher, E.F. (1973). *Small is Beautiful*. London: Blond & Briggs.

Schumpeter, J.A. (1942). *Capitalism, Socialism and Democracy*. London: Allen & Unwin.

Schwab, K. (2016). *The Fourth Industrial Revolution*. Geneva: World Economic Forum.

Schwab, K. with T. Malleret (2020). *COVID-19: The Great Reset*. Geneva: Forum Publishing.

Senghaas, D. (1977). *Weltwirtschaftsordnung und Entwicklungspolitik* [World economic order and development policy]. Frankfurt: Suhrkamp.

Serrano, M. and V. Popovski (eds.) (2010). *Human Rights Regimes in the Americas*. Tokyo: United Nations University Press.

Shannon C.E. and W. Weaver (1949). *The Mathematical Theory of Communication*. Chicago: University of Illinois Press.

Shiva, V. (2000). North–south conflicts in intellectual property rights. *Peace Review*, 12(4), 501–8.

Silvey, R.J.E. (1961). Broadcasting and the consumer's rights. Lecture held at the General Assembly of the International Association of Mass Communication Research, Vevey, 19 June.

Sinaceur, M.A. (1986). Islamic tradition and human rights. In UNESCO, *Philosophical Foundations of Human Rights*. Paris: UNESCO, pp. 193–226.

Skogly, S. (1992). Article 2. In A. Eide and G. Alfredson (eds), *The Universal Declaration of Human Rights: A Commentary*. Oslo: Scandinavian University Press, pp. 57–72.

Smolla, R. (1992). *Free Speech in an Open Society*. New York: Knopf Doubleday.
Solnit, R. (2016). *Hope in the Dark*. Edinburgh: Canongate.
Stearns, P.N. (2006). *American Fear: The Causes and Consequences of High Anxiety*. Abingdon: Routledge.
Stiglitz, J.E. (2013). *The Price of Inequality*. New York: W.W. Norton.
Stone, I.F. (1989). *The Trial of Socrates*. New York: Doubleday.
Temkin, L. (1993). *Inequality*. Oxford: Oxford University Press.
Thomas, P.N. (2011). *Negotiating Communication Rights: Case Studies from India*. New Delhi: Sage.
Thomas, W.I. and D.S. Thomas (1928). *The Child in America: Behaviour Problems and Programmes*. New York: Knopf.
Tomasello, M. (2008). *Origins of Human Communication*. Cambridge, MA: MIT Press.
Tönnies, F. (1887/2002). *Community and Society [Gemeinschaft und Gesellschaft]*. New York: Dover Publications.
Torres, C.A. (2014). *First Freire*. New York: Teachers College Press.
Traer, R. (1991). *Faith in Human Rights*. Washington, DC: Georgetown University Press.
Turkle, S. (2015). *Reclaiming Conversation*. New York: Penguin Press.
United Nations (1945a). *Documents of the Conference of the United Nations on International Organization, San Francisco*, volume 7.
United Nations (1945b). *Charter of the United Nations*. New York: United Nations.
United Nations (1993). *Declaration and Action Programme of the Vienna UN Conference on Human Rights*. New York: United Nations.
Vacanti, C. (1998). Bio-tech bodies. *Business Week*, 27 July.
Van Dijk, J.A.G.M. (2012). *The Network Society*. London: Sage.
Vašák, K. (1977). Human rights: A thirty-year struggle: The sustained efforts to give force of law to the Universal Declaration of Human Rights. *UNESCO Courier*, 11, 29–32.
WACC (2021). *Who Makes the News?* https://whomakesthenews.org/
Warren, S.D. and L.D. Brandeis (1890). The right to privacy. *Harvard Law Review*, 4(5), 193–220.
Waters, T. and K. Leblanc (2005). Refugees and education: Mass public schooling without a nation-state. *Comparative Education Review*, 49(2), 129–47.
Weber, M. (1972). *Wirtschaft und Gesellschaft* [Economy and Society]. Tubingen: J.C.B. Mohr.
Winner, L. (1993). Citizen virtues in a technological order. In E.R. Winkler and J.R. Coombs (eds), *Applied Ethics*. Oxford: Basil Blackwell, pp. 46–68.
Young-Bruehl, E. (1982). *Hannah Arendt: For the Love of the World*. New Haven, CT: Yale University Press.

Index

Abrahamic religions 73
abrogation 124
active listening 113, 130
Adam and Eve 12, 14
advertising 90
advocacy journalism 115
Aeschylus 19
affective relations 133
Africa 3
African Charter on Human and
    Peoples' Rights (1981) 28
Albigeois 16
Alegre, A. and S. Ó'Siochrú 130
Alphabet 72, 98, 147
Altheide, David 145
Amazon 71, 72, 79, 147
American Convention on Human
    Rights (1969) 28, 37
American Declaration of Independence
    (1776) 2
American Federation of Labor 31
Amnesty International 26, 150
amor mundi 160, 161
Anabaptists 23, 24
Anaxagoras 16, 23
ancient Middle East 2–3
Ando Shoeki 4
Annan, General Kofi 1
Anthropocene era 88, 89
Antigone 100
anxiety 144
    media-generated 144–5
anxiety marketeers 144
Appiah, K. 154
Apple 71, 72
Arendt, Hannah 154, 158, 159, 160

Ariely, D. 13, 163n6
Aristotle 14, 23, 133, 149
arms trade 107
Artificial Intelligence (AI) 80–2
    thinking machines 83
Asia 4
Assange, Julian 99–100, 102
Athenian democracy 18, 19
attachment journalism 115
Augustus, Emperor 23
austerity policies 139
Australian aboriginals 54, 119
autonomous agency 8

Bacon, Sir Francis 17
Baehr, P. R. 33
Barber, Benjamin 143
Basil of Caesarea 7
Beauvoir, Simone de 145
Bennett et al. 62
Berne, Treaty of (1874) 15
Bhagavad Gita 4
big data 79
Bill of Rights (1689, English) 2, 20
Bill of Rights of the State of Virginia
    (1776) 2, 20
biodiversity, declining 88–91
    growth and 89–90
bioethical imperative 151–2
BlackBox Television 102
Bohm, D. 157
Bok, Sissela 13
Book of Ecclesiastes 73
books, burning of 17, 22, 23
Borges, Jorge Luis 148
brain, the 83

Brandeis, Louis D. 14
Brecht, Bertolt 65–6
Bronze Age 10
Bruno, Giordano 17
Brynjolfsson, E. and A. McAfee 83
Buber, Martin 5
Buddhist tradition 4
bureaucracies 119–20, 135–6, 138–9, 140, 159–60
  liberation from 145–6
Burgos, Law of 4–5
Bury, J. B. 16
Bush, George W. 78

Caillé, Alain 142
Cain and Abel 12
Calvin, John 17, 23, 24
Campaign for Communication Rights 66, 67
Canada 131
Canadian Charter of Rights and Freedoms 131
Canadian Telecommission report 130
capitalism 78, 80
  culture clash with human rights 109–10
  democracy and 109
  marketization of societies 109
  masterless slavery 109
  see also growth
Caribbean 4–5
caring society 141–2, 146–7
  communication practice and 146–7
Castells, M. 74
Catholic Church 16–17, 21
  prohibited texts 23
censorship 22, 23, 79
  Athenian 22–3
  by big info monopolists 98
  in the information age 100–1
  institutionalized 138–9
  of journalists 101
  of newspapers 101
  by the state 101

certainty/uncertainty 86
Cesaire, A. 136, 137
Chamarik, Sanek 4
Chan, Joseph 4
change 113–14
Chanukah 6
Charles II, King 17
Charter of the United Nations 27
children, communication rights 52–4
China 96, 107
Chomsky, Noam 155
Christianity 7, 16
  privacy 14
citizenship 96–7
civil and political rights 5, 6, 29, 106, 123
  'first generation' rights 33, 127, 128
  UDHR 31
  see also International Covenant on Civil and Political Rights (ICCPR)
classic human rights *see* civil and political rights
Clinton, President Bill 114
cloud computing 79
Code of Hammurabi 14
Cohn, Haim 6
colonial mindset 136–7, 160
colonialism 103–4, 105
Committee Against Torture 117
Committee of Ministers of the Council of Europe 52
Committee on Economic, Social and Cultural Rights 116
Committee on the Elimination of Discrimination Against Women (CEDAW) 50–1, 116–17
Committee on the Elimination of Racial Discrimination 116
Committee on the Rights of the Child 117
Committee to Protect Journalists (CPJ) 99
common good 96

Index

communal dialogue 158
communication 155
  confidentiality 13–15, 40–2
  contested ideas 22
  control versus freedom 22
  conversation 155–6
  cooperative versus competitive 113
  ethics of 10
  human right to 125–7
  importance of 126
  informational transformation 84
  interactive process of 65
  mathematical theory of 64
  national policies 103
  pressure to communicate 131–2
  right to remain silent 131
  situation of inequality 132
  understanding and 84
communication practice 146–8
communication rights 69–70
  of children 52–4
  as cultural rights 69
  enforcement 67
  fragility of 69
  of indigenous peoples 54–60
  of migrants 60–4
  population growth 90
  provisions and violations 70
  right to be heard 68
  right to communicate 64–9
  of women 50–2
  World Summit on the Information Society (WSIS, UN) 66–9, 70
Communication Rights in the Information Society (CRIS) 66
communicative dignity 124
communicative equality 124
communicative freedom 124, 156
communicative justice 122–5, 149, 150, 157, 159
  building blocks 122–5
  concept of 125
  realization of 150–1

communicative security 125
communities 123, 129–30
compassion 112–13, 141
compassionate communication 129–30, 131–2, 148, 150
competitive communication 113
confidentiality 15
  of communication 13–15, 40–2
Confucian tradition 4
Constantine the Great, Emperor 23
consumer rights 122–3
contractor society 108
Convention and Protocol Relating to the Status of Refugees (1951) 97
Convention on the Elimination of All Forms of Discrimination Against Women (1979) 43, 50
Convention on the Prevention and Punishment of the Crime of Genocide (CPPCG)
  Article 3 45, 70
  Article 4 45
Convention on the Rights of the Child (UNCRC) 52–3
Convention Relating to the Status of Stateless Persons (1954) 97
conventions 28–9
conversation 155–6
conviviality 142
  communication practice and 147
cooperative communication 113
cooperative spirit 155–7
Copernicus 23
cosmopolitan 154
Covenant of the League of Nations (1919) 42
Covid-19 pandemic 69, 111, 138–9
Creon 100
crimes against humanity 45–6
critical reflection 152
cultural domination 57
cultural identity, protection of 57–8

cultural imperialism 57, 58
cultural life 55, 56
cultural rights 55–6, 69
cultural values 111–12
culture 55–8
    cultural interpretations 95–6
cyberspace *see* Internet

d'Arcy, Jean 64, 65, 66, 127
Davis, Angela 102
Dawkins, R. 160
De Dijn, A. 19–20
de-individualization 124
deception 84
deceptive behaviour 12
Declaration of the Rights of Man and of the Citizen (1789) 2, 5, 17, 20
Declaration of the Rights of Woman and the Female Citizen (1791) 2
deep dialogue 156–7
defamation 38
degradation 124
democracy 18, 143–4
Democracy Now 102
Democritus 16
Demosthenes 19
Der Stürmer 46
deregulation 108–9
development, interventionist project 104–5
dialogue 156–7
digital trace 77–8
digitization *see* Internet
dignity *see* human dignity
discrimination 124
    institutionalized 139–40
    prevention of 35
    prohibition of 42–3
disempowerment 124
Disney 72
Donnelly, Jack 3
Dr Frankenstein 88

Draft Declaration on Communication Rights (Hamelink Declaration) 67, 122
Durov, Nikolai and Pavel 102
Dussel, Enrique 124–5, 152, 153

eccentric positionality 152–3
Ecclesiastical Courts 17
ECHELON 131
economic, social and cultural rights 29, 31, 55, 123, 129
    second generation rights 33, 127
    see also International Covenant on Economic, Social and Cultural Rights (ICESCR)
Economic and Social Council (ECOSOC) 28
    Resolution 1503 116
economic cleansing 136
economics 108–10
education 60–1
egalitarianism 4, 143–4
    communication practice and 147
Egypt 22
electronic surveillance 76, 78, 80
elimination beliefs 46, 47, 48
Elizabeth I, Queen 17
email 76, 78
Emir of Kuwait 6
empowerment 102–3, 105, 130
enabling environment 130
encryption techniques 77
enforcement 115–17
Enlightenment, European 8–9
envelopment 104–5
Epicureans 19
epistemic coloniality 103–4
equality 42, 43, 109, 117
    principle of 35
    right to 139–40
Espionage Act (US) 99
Ethical Guide for the Transformation of Mexico 36
ethics of liberation 153

Index

ethnic conflicts 45
Euripides 19, 23
European Communication Policy (EC White Paper) 130
European Convention for the Protection of Human Rights and Fundamental Freedoms (1950) 28, 37, 97
　Article 10 98, 99
European Court of Human Rights 27, 40, 44, 98, 99
expert system 80
expression, freedom of *see* freedom of expression
extractivism 136

Facebook 71, 72, 78, 98, 147
fake news 69
fear 113–14
　institutionalization of 140–1, 144–5
Ferrer, Francisco 18
Finegan, Jack 2
first generation rights 33, 127, 128
Flinterman, Cees 34, 128, 129
Fox, J. 61
France 96, 131
Francis, Pope 89
Frederick II, Emperor 24
free markets 109
free thinking 16
freedom
　Africa 3
　earliest recording of 2–3
　principle of 16–24, 35
　right to 138–9
　women, exclusion of 2–3
freedom of expression 19, 20, 36, 37, 39–40, 48, 65, 99, 130–1
freedom of information 19, 20, 65, 97–8
　Article 19 (UDHR) 36–8
　conference (1948, UN) 36
　threat to 98
freedom of reception 36–7

freedom of speech 18–24, 37, 97–102
　limitations 37, 38
　standards 37
　threats to 22–4
freedom of thought 16–18, 19, 38–40
　Article 18 (UDHR) 39
freedom to gather information 36
freedom to hold opinions 36
freedom to impart information and ideas 37
freedom versus responsibility 37–8
French, Marilyn 2
French Revolution (1789) 34
Fromm, E. 140
Furedi, F. 145

Galdamez, Archbishop Oscar Arnulfo Romero y 109
Galileo 23
Gallagher, M. 51
Gandhi, Mahatma 4, 30
General Artificial Intelligence (GAI) 83
General Assembly (UN) 27–8, 31, 33
　Resolution 59 (1) 36, 97
Geneva Convention (Third) 49
genocide, prohibition of incitement to 45–8
Germany 131
Gertz v. Robert Welch, Inc. (1974) 98
Ghai, Y. 109
Ghazali, Imam Abu Hammid 12
Global Media Monitoring Project (GMMP) 93
globalization 108–10
Gnostic texts 23
Godfrey of Fontaines, Doctor Venerandus 7
Goodman, Amy 102
Google 71, 72
Gouges, Olympe de 2, 163n1
Gould, C.C. 143
Graeber, D. and D. Wengrow 8, 161
Graeber, David 120, 139, 145
Great Council of Lateran (1215) 14

Index

Greeks 16
  democracy 18
Gregory IX, Pope 23
Gregory of Nyssa 7
growth 89–90, 92
  continued pursuit of 90
  damage caused by 89–90
  declining biodiversity 89–90
  exploitation 92
  technology and 87
Gruson, L. 61, 63
Gulf War (1991) 45
Gumpert, G. and S. Drucker 76
Guzmán, Joaquin 'El Chapo' 150

Haidt, Jonathan 153–4
Haimon 100
Hamilton, Clive 89
Hammond, P. 115
hate speech 38, 47, 48
health, right to 126
health care 126
Henry II, King 24
Henry VIII, King 17
Heraclitus 16
heresy/heretics 16–17, 23
Herman, E.S. and D. Peterson 114
Herman, Edward S. 155
Herodotus 19, 20
High Commissioner for Human Rights 86
Hindu tradition 4
Hippocratic Oath 15
Hobbes, Thomas 17, 24
Holmes, John 139
Horace 159
horizontal effect 116
hostility 112–13
Human and Peoples' Rights (1981) 37
human autonomy 30, 35
human dignity 1, 4, 15–24
  Christianity 7
  humanistic liberalism 8
  Islam 6–7
  notion of, difficulties 32
  principle of 36
  respect for 9–11, 138
  truth 11–13
  UDHR 32
human intelligence 83
human rights
  as abstract notions 107, 115, 134
  accountability 115–16
  balancing of 110–11
  bottom-up approach 134
  bureaucracies and 119–20
  business interests and 107
  challenges 30
  as civil and political rights 106
  core rights 34–5
  versus cultural value 111–12
  culture clash with capitalism 109–10
  dilemmas 110
  documents (instruments) 28–9
  emergence of 1
  failure 117–18
  generations of 33–4, 127–8
  as gifts 124
  halfway to equality 93–4
  versus human inclination 112–15
  hypocrisy of Western states 107
  inclusive nature of 49, 52, 56
  individual rights 30
  indivisibility of 110
  liberal-humanitarian framework 133
  moral principles 35, 100, 123
  municipal laws 100
  new set of 86–8
  origins of 106–7
  participatory democracy 87
  proportionality 111
  reciprocity of 48, 99
  redress/remedy 115, 116
  as relations between states and citizens 106–7
  in robotic times 85–6
  versus significant interests 110–12
  solidarity framework 133–4

Index

human rights (*cont.*)
  standards 30
  universality of 29–30, 123
  violations 106–7, 108, 117, 123
  world politics 29
  see also international human rights law
Human Rights Committee (UN) 116
Human Rights Day (1948) 31
Human Rights Watch 26–7
humanitarian interventions, politicization of 114–15
humanitarian law 48–9
humanity
  ambiguity of human condition 145
  cooperation with other species 81
  cyclical conception 73
  existential questions 85
  extinction, threat of 88–90
  linearity 72–3
  moral evolution 157
  rich and poor, fracture between 139
humanoid robots *see* robots
humiliation 138
Humphrey, John 31
hunger, deaths from 139–40
hunter-gatherer societies 14

identity 57–8
  establishing 112
  migrants 63–4
Illich, Ivan 142
imagination 148–9
incitement 47–8
inclusive togetherness 154
inclusivity 112
India 131
Indian literature 12
indigenous peoples/societies 8–9
  colonial imperialist forces 54
  communication rights 54–60
  cultural rights 55–6
  importance of 54–5
  knowledge 58–60
  protection of cultural identity 57–8
  future of 54
individual freedom 7
individual rights 30, 96
industrial society 142
inequality 132
information, freedom of *see* freedom of information
information and communication technologies (ICTs) 73–4
information revolution 72
Innocent III, Pope 16
Inquisitions 23
institutionalization of fear 140–1
institutionalized censorship 138–9
institutionalized discrimination 139–40
institutions 136, 140
  humiliation of victims 138
instruments 38
intellectual property rights (IPR) regimes 69
  global 59
  innovation and 59
  WTO rules 59
Inter-American conference (1938) 5
Inter-American Court of Human Rights 27
interference 41
Intergovernmental Conference on the Institutional, Administrative and Financial Aspects of Cultural Policies 56
International Association for Media and Communication Research conference (2021) 53
International Bill of Rights 28, 31, 34, 55
International Commission of Jurists on Human Rights in Islam (1980) 6

Index

International Convention on the Elimination of All Forms of Racial Discrimination (1965) 39, 42
International Convention on the Protection of the Rights of All Migrant Workers and Members of Their Families (1990) 97
International Covenant on a Solidarity Right to Communication 134
International Covenant on Civil and Political Rights (ICCPR) 28, 34, 35, 37, 39, 42–3, 127
  Article 4 (freedom of thought) 40
  Article 14 (presumption of innocence) 44
  Article 17 (protection against arbitrary interference) 41, 140
  Article 18 (freedom of religion or belief) 39
  Article 19 (freedom of expression) 65
  Article 20.1/20.2 (prohibition of war propaganda) 44
  Optional Protocol (OP) 116
International Covenant on Economic, Social and Cultural Rights (ICESCR) 28, 34, 39
  Article 2(1) 127
International Criminal Court (ICC) 47, 150
international declarations 29
International Federation of Human Rights 26
international human rights law 25, 41, 60, 65, 70, 112
  weak and non-enforceable arrangement 117
international human rights regime 91, 92
  flaw 124
  key aspirations 94
  normative principles 126

International Law Commission (UN) 46
International Military Tribunal (IMT, Nuremberg) 46, 47
International Monetary Fund (IMF) 106
International Telecommunication Union (ITU) 66
International Year of the Child (1979) 52
Internet
  algorithms 77
  challenges of 73–4
    accountability 75
    democratic arrangements 75
    governance challenge 74–6
    human rights 79–80
    surveillance challenge 76–7
  cookies 77
  dark side of 74
  deceptive behaviour 73
  moral distance 73
  net neutrality 75
  worldwide access 74
  see also technology
interventions 114–15
Inuit 54, 119
Ireland 131
Islam 6–7
  truth 12
Islamic Council 28
Islamic Declaration of Human Rights 28
iWorld 78

Jahr, Fritz 151
Jansen, Sue 22
Japan 4, 96
Jewish law 6
Jonas, Hans 152
journalists
  censorship against 101
  eavesdropping on 101
  imprisonment of 99

183

Index

journalists (*cont.*)
  murder of 99
  reporting on government activities 101
Judaism 5–6
Justinianus, Emperor 19

Kant, Immanuel 8
Kaplan, A. 5
Khoun Community Radio for Development 102
Khushalani, Yougindra 3
knowledge 58–60
  commercialization of 69
  hierarchy 59
  human right to 59–60
knowledge societies 59–60
Kurzweil, Ray 82

Lakatos, I. 3–4
Landa, Diego de 22
Lane et al. 10
language 63–4
Latin America 4–5
League of Nations 24, 29, 52
  Covenant of (1919) 42
libel law 38
liberal-representative democracies 143
liberating togetherness 151
  ethics of 154–5
lies/lying 11–13
Louv, Richard 92, 141
Luther, Martin 17, 23–4

Maasai 54, 119
MacBride Commission 57, 66
Macharia, Sarah 93
Magna Carta (1215) 2
Malik, Charles 28
Manning, Bradley 102
Māori 54, 119
material ethical principle 152
mathematical theory of communication 64

Mayan books 22
McIver, W.J. Jr, and W.F. Birdsall 128
media
  censorship 139
  confidentiality 40
  fostering anxiety 144–5
  new 72
  war propaganda 45
  women and 51–2
  see also social media
media performance 43
Melanchthon, Philip 24
Mexican Revolution 34
Mexico City conference (1945) 5
Michels, Robert 143
Microsoft 71, 72
migrants 60–4
  identity and language 63–4
  migrant issue 62–3
Mi'kmaq 9
Mill, John Stuart 20–1
Milton, John 20
mindset 136–7, 160
moral imbalance 137–8
moral intuitionism 153–4
moral philosophy 8, 81, 137, 145
Morozov, Evgeny 74
Mosco, Vincent 79
music of life 141–2

Nail, T. 62–3
nation, definition 118–19
national security 101, 110–11
National Security Agency (NSA) 27, 78, 79
NATO (North Atlantic Treaty Organization) 114
nature 89–91
Navajo Indians 10, 11
NBIC technologies 82
Netflix 72
Netherlands 140
  eavesdropping by intelligence services 87

new digital age 71–2
New Humanitarians 114–15
New International Information Order 58, 67, 103
new media 72
New Testament 11–12
New World Order 31
The New York Times v. *Sullivan* (1964) 38
Niebuhr, Reinhold 149
Nielsen, Kai 149
Noble, Denis 141
Non-Aligned Summit (1973) 57
non-citizens 96–7
normative principles 1, 9–24
 confidentiality of communication 13–15
 freedom 16–24
 human dignity 9–13

Oge, Vincent 2
Old Oligarch 18
Old Testament 5–6, 11–12, 109
Oliner, Samuel and Pearl 141, 158
On Liberty (Mill) 20–1
On the Revolution of the Celestial Spheres (Copernicus) 23
ontological fear 140–1, 144
Optional Protocol (OP) 116
Order on the Freedom of the Printing Press (1766, Sweden) 20
Organization of American States 31
Oslo Challenge 53

Paine, Thomas 17–18
Panama 27
parrhesia 19
Partsch, Karel 39, 116
Patriot Act (US) 131
Pen-Chung Chang 28
People's Communication Charter 67–8, 75, 122
Pericles 16
personal data 77

Pinker, Steven 94
Plato 15, 18, 22, 23
Plessner, Helmut 152–3
Plutarch 20
political ethics 150–1
politics 154, 158
Polybius 19
Polyneices 100
power, inequality of 118
power elites 22
press freedom 20
Press Licensing Act 17
presumption of innocence 44, 70
printing press 20
prisoners of war 48–9
privacy
 limits to 40
 protection of 13–15, 41, 69
 right to 14, 41
 as seclusion 14
 surveillance technology 76–7
private sphere 14, 15
progressive realization 127
propaganda 44–5
 Nazi politics 46
property rights 98
Protagoras 23
Protestant Church 16–17
protocols 135
Ptahhotep, Vizier 9–10
public sphere 14

Quran 6, 7, 12

racial discrimination 42
RadioToco 102
Ramayana Epos 12
rational behaviour 133
Recommendation on Equality between Women and Men in the Media (1984) 52
Reformation 17, 23
Regulation of Printing Act (1695) 20, 24

Index

religion 108
religious beliefs 39
resolutions 29
responsibility to protect doctrine 94
revolutions 34
Rich, Adrienne 13
Right to Communicate 75
rights *see* human rights
Robespierre 18
robots 81, 83
   communication with 84–5
   human rights and 85–6
   robotic environment 85
Roman Catholic Church *see* Catholic Church
Romans 16, 19–20
Roosevelt, Eleanor 26, 28, 31
Roosevelt, Franklin D. 31
Roosevelt, Theodore 143
Ross, Karen 93
Rousseau, Jean-Jacques 17
rules 135
Russian Revolution 34

Sacred Tree, The (Lane et al.) 10
Said, Abdul Aziz 161
Sankatsing, G. 104
Sassen, S. 136
Sayad, A. 62
Sceptics 19
Scheinin, Martin 40
Schiller, Herbert 155
scribe, the 22
second generation rights 33, 127, 128–9
secrecy 101
   of governments 101–2
   legitimacy of 102
secure society 144–5
   communication practice and 148
security 125
   principle of 35
   right to 140–1
self-determination 35

self-empowerment 35, 143
self-learning neural networks 76, 82
Shannon, C.E. and W. Weaver 64
Shiva, Vandana 59
Shuswap community 10, 11
significant interests 110–11
silence
   disassociation 132
   right to 131
   time for 132
silencing 113
Snowden, Edward 27, 79, 100, 102
social, economic and cultural rights *see* economic, social and cultural rights
social media 74, 102, 144
social order 134–7
   caring 141–2, 146
   communication practice 146–8
   convivial 142, 147
   egalitarian 143–4, 147
   secure 144–5, 148
Social Summit (UN, 1995) 51
Socrates 16, 19, 22–3, 133
solidarity 34, 132–4
solidarity rights 33–4, 128, 129
Solnit, Rebecca 148
Sophists 16, 18
Spain 5
speech, freedom of *see* freedom of speech
Spence, Doreen 55, 60
St Augustine 17
Stand News 100
state, the
   censorship 100–1
   communication rights 15
   definition 118
   human rights record 117
   nature of 119
   power over citizens 117, 118
   secrecy 101, 102
   surveillance by 77
state-centric paradigm 103

Index

Stiglitz, J.E. 101
Stoics 19
Stone, I.F. 19, 20
storytelling 5
Streicher, Julius 46
surveillance society 140
surveillance technology 76–8, 80

Tacitus 19, 20
tactical communication 129
Talmud 6
technological culture 88
technological progress 88
technology
  challenges of 71–3
  human rights assessment 87
  policies on 87
technology fix 88
technology opportunity 88
Telegram 102
Ten Commandments 11
The World Counts 139
Thiam, Iba Der 3
thingification 137
thinking machines 83
third generation rights 33–4, 127, 128
Thomas, Pradip 63–4
Thomas theorem 159
thought, freedom of *see* freedom of thought
Thucydides 18
Tiberius, Emperor 23
togetherness 154, 158
tolerance 16, 19, 20–1, 163–4n8
Torah 6
Trade-Related Intellectual Property Rights (TRIPS) Agreement 59
Traer, R. 4, 7
treaties 28–9
tribal instincts 112
Trobriand Islands 14
truth 11–13

Ubangi 10
UDHR (Universal Declaration of Human Rights) *see* Universal Declaration of Human Rights (UDHR)
Ukraine/Russia war 69
UN Charter 28, 29, 42
  Preamble 118
UN Commission on Human Rights (UNCHR) 26, 28, 31, 39, 96
UN Security Council 107, 119
UNESCO
  Constitution (1945) 36
  Declaration on Race and Racial Prejudice (1978) 56
  Mass Media Declaration (1978) 37
  Right to Communicate 66, 131
UNICEF 53
United Kingdom (UK) 96
United Nations (UN) 26, 118–19
  Charter 28, 29, 42, 118
  Freedom of Information conference (1948) 36
United Nations Conference on International Organization (1945) 27
United States of America (USA) 96, 131
  Constitution (1787) 5
Universal Declaration of Human Rights (UDHR)
  Article 2 (protection against discrimination) 42, 70
  Article 11 (presumption of innocence) 44, 70
  Article 12 (confidentiality of communications) 40–1, 70, 110, 140
  Article 18 (freedom of thought) 39, 70
  Article 19 (freedom of expression) 26, 36–8, 64, 65, 68, 70, 110
  Article 21 (language) 64
  Article 22 (cultural rights) 55

Index

Universal Declaration of Human
    Rights (UDHR) (*cont.*)
  Article 26 (education) 60
  Article 27 (cultural life) 55, 63, 70
  Article 28 (social and international
    order) 33, 34, 129, 134–5,
    136, 161
  Article 29 (duties to the community)
    33, 68
  Article 30 (destruction of rights and
    freedoms) 33
  composition 28
  drafting of 31
  emergence of 31
  essential principles 124
  freedom from fear 140
  human dignity 1
  humanistic universalism of 1
  importance of 49
  key aspirations 94
  legal weight 29
  nature of 33–5
  normative rules 160–1
  political agreements and
    disagreements 27
  Preamble 32
  universal acceptance 94–6
universality 94–6
Urukagina, King 2

value judgements 98
value system 96
Vašák, Karel 33–4, 128
Vienna Convention on the Law of
    Treaties (1969)
  Article 31 127
virtual people 81
Voltaire 17

war on drugs 150
war on terror 111
war propaganda, prohibition of 44–5
Warren, Samuel D. 14
Weber, Max 109, 159
Welch Jr, Claude E. 3
Western identity 96
whistleblowing 99–100
Wolof societies 3
women
  communication rights 50–2
  exclusion from freedom 2–3
  see also Committee on the
    Elimination of Discrimination
    Against Women (CEDAW);
    Convention on the Elimination
    of All Forms of Discrimination
    Against Women (1979)
World Association for Christian
    Communication (WACC) 93
World Conference on Human Rights
    (UN, 1993) 50–1, 95, 110,
    117
World Conference on Women (Fourth,
    1995) 51
World Press Freedom Committee 66–7
World Summit on the Information
    Society (WSIS, UN) 64, 66–8,
    70, 75
  final declaration of 68–9
World Trade Organization (WTO) 59

Yom Kippur 6
YouTube 72, 98
Yugoslavia 114

Zapotec Indians 119
Zwingli, Huldrych 24